Industrial Celts

Making the modern Cornish identity, 1750-1870

by Bernard Deacon

Published by CoSERG, Redruth, Cornwall
https://bernarddeacon.wordpress.com/

© Bernard Deacon, 2018

Bernard Deacon has asserted his right to be identified as the author of this work in accordance with the Copyright, Designs and Patents Act 1988.

All rights reserved. No part of this publication may be reproduced in any form, stored in or re-introduced into a retrieval system, or transmitted in any form or by any means, electronic, mechanical, photocopying, recording or otherwise without the prior consent of the author.

ISBN: 978-0-9513918-4-6

Printed by Create Space

Contents

Introduction	iii
1. Identity and territory	1
2. Cornwall, Cornishness and the academy	27
3. Images of Cornwall and its people	41
4. Cornish consciousness	71
5. Social institutions and elites	88
6. Mines and mining: capital formation	108
7. People on the move	144
8. A society of dispersed paternalism	167
9. Cultural formation: Methodism	196
10. From proto-region to proto-nation?	228
Index	247

Introduction

In Cornwall it always seems time to remember our roots. None more so than at present as we watch familiar landscapes torn up and towns and villages transformed in an unsustainable rush to profit from the demand to enjoy a fast-disappearing 'Cornwall lifestyle'. Cornwall and Cornishness as we have known them can seem threatened, even doomed, in the face of an unstoppable process backed by powerful economic and political interests and legitimated daily by the media.

However, turn the clock back 200 years or more and we find Cornwall living through an equally torrid time of social and economic change, although one where insiders played a far greater role. That transformation resulted from its precociously early industrialisation. It also created the foundations of what has been called the 'classic' Cornish identity, one that endured decades of de-industrialisation to survive through to the 1960s. The heartland of this identity lay among Cornish working-class communities in the towns and villages of Cornwall. It was the Cornishness that most Cornish folk turned to when thinking of Cornwall in those decades, a domestic, almost private identity unappreciated and misunderstood by many outsiders who increasingly read Cornwall only through the hype of tourist imagery.

In an article in 2001 in *Tourist Studies* (1, 185-196), Amy Hale coined the phrase 'industrial Celts' to describe the addition of industrial artefacts to a Celtic past in order to represent the Cornish and their heritage. This echoed what some of us had claimed to detect in the 1990s. We argued that Cornwall's classic working-class industrial identity was converging with Cornish Revivalist culture. Symbols of Celticity were being stitched onto traditional icons of popular Cornishness, such as support for Cornwall's rugby team. At the same time the consensus was that the Cornishness rooted in the Cornish experience of industrialisation was becoming increasingly residual and a focus for nostalgia. That process in turn reflected the withering of its material base in mining and Methodism. However, the term 'industrial Celts' should not be restricted to (post)-modern Cornwall. There were voices in the mid-nineteenth century and as early as the eighteenth century that appended the term 'Celtic' to the Cornish even when their primary identity was industrial. The 'industrial Celt' of the far south west of the British Isles has a longer genealogy that predates the conscious Celtic revivalism that began in the 1870s.

In recent decades there has been a conscious attempt to revalorise classic Cornishness. Alan Kent's work in the Cornu-English dialect, Neil Kennedy's search for usable cultures, the Institute of Cornish Studies' community memories projects are all more than nostalgia; they are the latest version of Robert Morton Nance's project of the 1920s to build a new Cornwall from the ashes of the old, while respecting rather than rejecting the traditions of our forebears. As commercialisation and the rise of 'Lifestyle Cornwall' tighten their strangleholds on Cornish communities it is therefore the perfect time to revisit what was the principal identity of Cornishness into the late twentieth century and ask how it was produced and sustained.

The contention of this book is that to understand traditional classic Cornishness, we must understand the Cornish experience of industrialisation in the late eighteenth and early nineteenth centuries. This was the period when modern Cornwall was born. Less fashionable perhaps than modern imageries of Celtic Cornwall, the contours of traditional Cornishness were being blurred as the twentieth century came to its close. This book restores this formative period of our past by supplying an analysis of Cornwall's period as an industrial region. These years, I argue, were critical for producing a Cornish sense of difference, without which the modern Cornish Revival would not have emerged.

This is not a new book. The bulk of it was first written as a doctoral dissertation eighteen years ago. For this version I have toned down the theory (a little), improved the flow (a bit), added one or two more recent references and an index, while getting rid of the extensive bibliography that accompanied the thesis. I toyed with the idea of removing the theory entirely but soon realised that that would have entailed considerable re-writing and an alternative structure, so eventually left it in. Impatient readers can easily skip the first two chapters to get straight to the nub of the historical argument in Chapter 3. Nonetheless, the central elements of the original work have weathered well and still appear to be valid. As Cornwall's industrial past recedes further into memory, becoming the haunt of industrial archaeologists and technological historians and a fit subject for the 'heritage industry', it is time for social historians to reclaim it and add it to that corpus of work re-stating the distinctiveness of Cornwall. By making this work more accessible, this publication – a work of historical geography or sociology as much as history – can hopefully stimulate a new generation to look again at our industrial past. It provides the basis for renewed and updated work on what some of us insist was Cornwall's second (or was it third) 'golden age'.

In the original thesis I acknowledged my debt to my two supervisors, Rees Pryce of the OU and Philip Payton, my colleague at the University of Exeter. I also listed others whose work had particularly influenced my thinking at the time. These were Allen Buckley, Roger Burt, Treve Crago, Amy Hale, Fred Harris, Alan Kent, Ronald Perry, John Probert, John Rowe, John Rule, Tim Saunders, Sharron Schwartz and Garry Tregidga. For this book version I should add Neil Kennedy to that list. Furthermore, although the original research for this book took place (too) many years ago I must again record my thanks to the Cornish Studies Library (now Kresen Kernow) at Redruth and to all those students who attended Cornish history classes organised by the WEA and Exeter University's former Department of Continuing and Adult Education in the 1980s and 1990s. I was indeed fortunate to be able to benefit from their criticisms and input before liberal adult education was brutally cut down by a succession of philistine governments.

Bernard Deacon
Redruth, February 2018

Chapter One
Identity and territory

What do we mean when we talk about the Cornish identity? Who shaped it and when? These are the questions I pursue in these pages. But only in one particular period - its 'classic phase'. The modern Cornish identity, I argue, was born in the cauldron of Cornwall's precociously early industrialisation. This occurred from the mid-eighteenth century to the early nineteenth century. It was then re-shaped in the middle third of that century when aspects familiar from other British industrial regions were stitched onto it. But Cornwall's equally early de-industrialisation, from the early 1870s onwards, meant that a gradual convergence after mid-century was again overlain by divergence as its sons and daughters fled a disintegrating industrial society at home to take up new opportunities on mining and farming frontiers across the globe.

Before setting out on this quest I have a more boring, yet essential, task. This is to define some terms and establish some theory, in order to tackle the idea of identity. To do this, I employ three conceptual tools. First, I note that a broad inter-disciplinary spectrum of writers on identity home in on five core elements, common to all identities. Geographers provide us with a sixth to add to these, that of scale. After reviewing some key historical and geographical literature on identity formation in the past we will meet the second key idea used in this book, the dynamic model of regional identity formation proposed by the Finnish geographer, Anssi Paasi.[1] In chapter 2 I review how social scientists and historians have written about Cornwall and add the third and final aid to understanding identity formation in eighteenth and nineteenth century Cornwall. This is the interdisciplinary field of enquiry termed here 'new Cornish Studies'. Once armed with a clear definition, a dynamic model and a disciplinary perspective, we can embark on the historical and geographical terrain.

---

[1] Anssi Paasi, 'The institutionalization of regions: a theoretical framework for understanding the emergence of regions and the constitution of regional identity', *Fennia* 164 (1986), 105-146; 'Deconstructing regions: notes on the scale of social life', *Environment and Planning A* 23 (1991), 239-256; *Territory, boundaries and consciousness*, Chichester, 1996.

The elements of identity

At the core of identity is a personal identification with a group or a community. Identity thus has both an individual and a collective aspect, referring to the identity of the individual or the identity of the group. Although the topic under study here is a collective identity, there are, nevertheless, consistencies across the multi-disciplinary work on identity. Certain elements regularly appear, whether the writer is concerned with the individual's moment of identifying or the formation of group identities such as ethnicity. We can usefully categorize these aspects of identity as distinction, integration, process, narrative, and context.

The idea that identities involve a search for individuality, for what makes people 'different or worthwhile, or, at least, peculiar', is common to most writings on the subject.[2] But difference can only be claimed in relation to something else. Distinction necessarily entails a comparison with that which has been excluded. Each cultural identity presupposes a relationship with what is often termed 'the Other', those identities that are not one's own. In turn, the concept of the Other contains two implications. First, it suggests that identities are never formed or lived in isolation. The external helps to structure the internal. Thus, identities are mutually constitutive. Mutual constitution does not occur however in a context of equality. Dominant identities impose definitions on subaltern identities. Thus, Edward Said insists that Orientalism tells us much more about the dominant West than it does the subaltern East.[3] However, in practice the focus of study has been on either subaltern or dominant identities and rarely the two together, despite the mutual and interdependent ways identities are reproduced.

'Integration', as a feature of identities, is less prominent than distinction in the literature. Yet identities involve a search for sameness as well as difference. The boundaries that symbolise distinction from others are also 'means of securing sociospatial and ethnic homogeneity'.[4] All collective identities involve some common origins or shared characteristics. Integration and distinction, while separated here to aid analysis, are thus in practice linked. Indeed, it may be expected that the two are correlated.

On the other hand, distinction and integration are never fully secure. Identities, despite vigorous bolstering of borders and assertions of

---

[2] The quote is from Tom Nairn, *Faces of Nationalism: Janus Revisited*, London, 1997, 183.

[3] Edward Said, *Orientalism: Western Concepts of the Orient*, London, 1985

[4] David Newman and Anssi Paasi, 'Fences and neighbours in the postmodern world: Boundary narratives in political geography', *Progress in Human Geography* 22 (1998), 19

homogeneity, remain tentative, never achieved but always prone to dissolution, on a 'terrain of uneasy collectivity'.[5] This is to be explained by their relational character. Located in 'connections between individuals and groups rather than in the minds of particular persons or of whole populations', identity is not fixed.[6] As relationships shift, then identity itself shifts. In consequence, many observers have seen identity as a construction, 'in process', a 'project' or 'variable'.[7] Despite the apparent fixity of binary oppositions and codes of distinction that mark specific identities off from each other, the construction of distinction is itself part of an open process and must be seen as contingent. If identity is a 'process' or a 'project', then it is constantly being reproduced over time. Moreover, its malleability implies two distinct ways of looking at the history of identities. First, we can study the history of identity creation, how the identity takes shape, how it amplifies and proliferates, how it is reproduced over time. Second, we must be alert to the way in which identity projects themselves transform the past by creating histories of their own to reflect and justify the present.

This issue reminds us of the role of language in the making of identity. 'Identity is not fixed, it has no essence, it does not reside in any given body of texts or symbols or sacred sites. It is carried in language and made and remade in routine social practice'.[8] Symbols of identity are given meaning within narratives. Narrative reintroduces concepts of 'time and space and analytical relationality' to more categorical or essentialist approaches to identity.[9] Actors are embedded in shifting stories and relationships. Struggles over narratives become struggles over identity. Such a view emphasises the importance of studying the linguistic representation of identities. For instance, work on national and regional identities reminds us of the active role of elites in reproducing, re-inventing and manipulating narratives of identity.[10]

---

[5] Nairn, 1997, 183.
[6] Charles Tilly, 'Citizenship, identity and social history', *International Review of Social History* 40 (1995), 5.
[7] Stuart Hall, 'Who needs identity?' in Stuart Hall and Paul Du Gay (eds), *Questions of Cultural Identity*, London, 1996, 2; Craig Calhoun (ed.), *Social Theory and the Politics of Identity*, Oxford, 1994, 1; Richard Jenkins, *Rethinking Ethnicity: Arguments and Explorations*, London, 1997, 40.
[8] P.W.Preston, *Political/Cultural Identity: Citizens and Nations in a Global Era*, London, 1997, 49.
[9] Margaret Somers, 'The narrative constitution of identity: a relational and network approach', *Theory and Society* 23 (1994), 620.
[10] For the relevance of this to Cornwall see Bernard Deacon, 'Under construction: culture and regional formation in south-west England',

Yet memories and narratives are not created in a vacuum. Stories are told and re-told within a social context. Stuart Hall notes that identities are reproduced within narratives but also 'in specific historical and institutional sites'.[11] A growing emphasis was placed a few years ago on the role of administrative and political institutions in the formation and reproduction of group identity. For example, Rhys Jones argued that 'maturing territorial institutions' were linked to the growing coherence of 'ethnies' in thirteenth century Wales.[12] At the same time, we must not forget the role of local contexts and local social relations in lending shape to a sense of belonging.

Finally, the issue of identity is of interest precisely because it lies across some crucial borders. It is located between the present and the past: 'identity marks the conjuncture of our past with the social, cultural and economic relations we live within'.[13] It also inhabits critical borderlands between structure and agency and between materialist and idealist approaches. For people do not adopt identities passively. Even 'a dominant or hegemonic culture is rarely passively internalised; commonly it is negotiated, resisted or selectively appropriated by people in everyday life'.[14] Perhaps the most sophisticated rendering of this is via Hall's concept of 'suturing'. People are summoned to take up positions through ideology. But the subject actively takes up and invests in those positions in a manner which involves the unconscious, plus discursive formations and practices and language as well as social context.[15] This can be seen in one common lived form of identity – nationalism.

European Urban and Regional Studies 11 (2004), 213-225; David Harvey, Harriet Hawkins, Nicola Thomas, 'Regional imageries of governance agencies: practising the region of south west Britain, *Environment and Planning A* 43 (2011), 470-486; Joanie Willett, 'The production of place: perception, reality and the politics of becoming', *Political Studies* (2014), 1-16.

[11] Hall, 1996, 4.

[12] Rhys Jones, 'Changing geographies of governance and group identities in the Middle Ages: the role of societal interaction and conflict', *Political Geography* 19 (2000), 917

[13] Jonathan Rutherford, 'A place called home: identity and the cultural politics of difference', in Jonathan Rutherford (ed.), *Identity: Community, Culture, Difference*, London, 19.

[14] James Duncan and David Ley (eds), *Place/Culture/Representation*, London, 1993, 11.

[15] Hall, 1996, 5-6.

Territory and identity: nation and ethnicity
National and ethnic identities are the most frequently written about forms of territorial identity. Most accounts of nationalism agree that it was a product of modernity. Materialist writers stress the role of communications, print media or the growth of fiscal-military states. On the other hand, idealist writers are more likely to look to the influence of the French Revolution, the counter-Enlightenment or eighteenth and nineteenth century German philosophers.[16] But while there is scholarly consensus about the link between nationalism and modernity there is less consensus about ethnicity. Anthony Smith makes the case that nationalism could only be constructed on the basis of pre-existing ethnic groups, or 'ethnies', a position finding some favour amongst historians of the early-modern and mediaeval periods.[17] However, it is not clear how far such groups were 'ethnic categories', groups whose members shared some objective features, or 'ethnic communities', groups with a self-consciousness.

Empirical work by Colin Kidd on British identities before modernity suggests that ethnic consciousness played a minor role before the eighteenth century. It was only with the rise of Romanticism and a racialist ethnology that more clearly distinguishable ethnic categorizations took shape. Ethnic identities, he concludes, were only of 'second order' importance in the early modern period: indeed, the 'very notion of "identity" … might itself be anachronistic' when applied to the period before 1700.[18] What Kidd's conclusions reinforce is the critical watershed of the eighteenth and early nineteenth centuries, that period bridging a world with few nationalisms and a world dominated by nationalist imaginings. It is exactly this critical period of change that I focus on here.

How, exactly, do places and territory relate to identity? Erica Carter et.al. define place as 'space to which meaning has been ascribed', spaces that are named.[19] This naming is important as it provides the nominal aspect crucial to all group identities. We might identify three other ways in which places relate to identity. First, places provide contexts in which

---

[16] For an overview of theories of nationalism see Umut Ozkirimli, *Theories of Nationalism; A Critical Introduction*, Basinsgtoke, 2017.
[17] Anthony Smith, *National Identity*, London, 1991.
[18] Colin Kidd, *British Identities before Nationalism: Ethnicity and Nationhood in the Atlantic World, 1600-1800*, Cambridge, 1999. For an alternative view see the work of Mark Stoyle, especially *Soldiers and Strangers: An Ethnic History of the English Civil War*, London, 2005.
[19] Erica Carter, James Donald and Judith Squires, *Space and Place: Theories of Identity and Location*, London, 1993, xii.

identities are played out and in which they have meaning. For David Kaplan territory provides the terrain that defines a group and its locational context viz-a-viz other groups.[20] Second, places provide representations of identity. The historic legacy of a specific area becomes part of the cultural resources of the group inhabiting that area. Territory thus adds an 'additional layer of meaning' to ethnic and cultural identities.[21] Rob Shields points to the empirically specifiable discourses, stories about space and places that are central to everyday understanding.[22] Smith writes of the 'poetic spaces' of the nationalist, imagining certain parts of the national territory as sacred territory, symbols of collective salvation or redemption.[23] In this way territorial identities 'are inextricably bound up with particular townscapes and landscapes', one type of Cornish identity with Tintagel for example, another with Carn Brea. Place is thus intimately connected to two of the elements in our earlier definition of identity above: context and narrative. But places are more than merely passive and inert containers in which things happen and about which stories are told. They are connected to identity formation in a third form, linked to process.

The humanistic geographer Edward Relph made the fundamental distinction between the identity of a place and identity with a place.[24] One reading of the identity of a place could approach older 'residualist' views of place identities as remnants of traditional society, remnants that may disappear as modernisation proceeds and places get homogenised. In this view identities are linked to 'the motivational power of tradition'.[25] However, others have convincingly contested this position. Territorial identities are actively constructed and reconstructed and evolve over time, interacting with changing material circumstances. Territorial identities are, in consequence, 'multilayered' and 'complex', 'embedded in their particular historical contexts and material circumstances'.[26] Identities of

---

[20] David Kaplan, 'Conflict and compromise among borderland identities in northern Italy', *Tijdschrift voor Economische en Sociale Geografie* 91 (2000), 44-60.
[21] Guntram Herb and David Kaplan (eds), *Nested Identities: Nationalism, Territory and Scale*, Lanham: MD, 1999, 2.
[22] Rob Shields, *Places on the Margin: Alternative Geographies of Modernity*, London, 1991, 6.
[23] Smith, 1991.
[24] Edward Relph, *Places and Placelessness*, London, 1976, 195.
[25] David Harvey, *The Condition of Postmodernity*, Oxford, 1989, 303.
[26] Kaplan, 2000; Jouni Hakli, 'Cultures of demarcation: Territory and national identity in Finland', in Herb and Kaplan (eds), 1999, 123. See also Doreen Massey, 'Places and their pasts', *History Workshop Journal* 39 (1995), 182-

places are therefore marked by process. In the course of this process there is a transformation: 'instead of the group defining the territory, the territory comes to define the group'.[27] Identities are embedded in specific places, but places help to re-affirm and shape the construction of identity.

A further point may be made. It should not be inferred from this that a transparent relationship exists between changing places and changing identity. Such transparency falters in practice because place identity is bound up with memory. Jon May, in a study of place identity in Stoke Newington, London, notes that different memories of the same place co-exist, with conflict between the nostalgia of the 'old' white population of the area and the imaginings of a 'new' white gentrifying population.[28] Different groups thus possess different mental pictures of the same place and these multiple place identities intersect with other class and race-based group identities. While memories are constantly being re-worked they also have a stability and an inertia that makes the remembering of a place to some degree autonomous of that place.

Moreover, the discussion of territorial identities adds another element to our five-point definition – that of scale. Scale gives rise to qualitatively different kinds of identity. Shared activities in places help to produce small-scale territorial identities, identification with the locality. But territorial identities are by no means restricted to the locality. As we move to a larger scale, the role of narrative and imagination arguably becomes more important than integration via shared attributes. Therefore, territorial identities can co-exist at widely varying scales and have different bases. Such co-existing identities have been viewed as 'nested' identities, providing a choice of identity constructs depending on the context.[29] In Cornwall therefore we might identify with our town, when upcountry with Cornwall, when in France with Britain and even, when in the States, with Europe.

At a macro-level of identity Anthony Richmond argues that all nationalisms depend on a territorial base; for nationalisms 'an historical association with a certain place is a *sine qua non*'.[30] Underlying national identity there is an intrinsic notion of territory. 'Whatever else it may be, nationalism is always a struggle for control of land' and 'a mode of

---

192.

[27] Kaplan, 2000, 45.

[28] Jon May, 'Globalization and the politics of place: place and identity in an inner London neighbourhood', *Transactions of the Institute of British Geographers* NS21 (1996), 194-215.

[29] Herb and Kaplan (eds), 1999.

[30] Anthony Richmond, 'Ethnic nationalism: social science paradigms', *International Social Science Journal* (1987), 4.

constructing and interpreting social space'.[31] Michael Billig points out that the national organisation of space is continually flagged. Nationalism, for Billig, is deeply embedded in the 'embodied habits of social life' especially in the West. It thus becomes 'banal', in that it is the taken for granted way to divide up space. Yet there is also a potential disjunction here. As Billig points out, the ideological project of nationalism 'entails the binding of the name of the nation-state to the collective name of the people'. This binding then appears natural, an example, according to Billig, of 'semantic cleansing'.[32] For nation-states rarely coincide with homogenous cultural groupings.

Sub-state cultural groupings, with notions of shared ancestry produced and sustained by characteristics such as language, religion or more subjective imagined factors, are often described as ethnic groups. Moreover, there can be a perceived continuum from the ethnic group to the nation. Smith proposes that ethnies of the pre-modern period were transformed, or had the opportunity to transform themselves, into nations during modernity.[33] Smith's ethnies, tied together by the concept of descent, underwent a territorialization in their demand for bounded space associated with their transition to nations. As part, therefore, of this proposed continuum from ethnic group to nation, we might note an associated spatialization of group identity.

But is this the case? Pierre Bourdieu, in contrast, argues that all ethnicities are already territorial.[34] This is also the position of Richard Jenkins.[35] He suggests that the sheer ubiquity of nationalism in the modern world has led observers to prioritise this level of territorial identity. However, nationalism is a historically specific ideology. Indeed, he turns the notion that there is a continuum from a (pre-modern) ethnicity to a (modern) nationalism on its head. It is ethnic affiliation and classification which is ubiquitous, whereas nationalism (and racism) are 'historically specific allotropes' of ethnic identity, a second order cultural notion, as opposed to the 'first order dimension of human experience' that is ethnicity. Jenkin's model has the advantage of incorporating territorial ideologies that are not nationalist. In demonstrating this he shows that different bases of identity are associated with different territorial ideologies as in Figure 1.1 below.

---

[31] Colin Williams and Anthony Smith, 'The national construction of social space', *Progress in Human Geography* 7 (1983), 502.
[32] Michael Billig, *Banal Nationalism*, London, 1995, 78.
[33] Smith, 1991
[34] Pierre Bourdieu, *Language and Symbolic Power*, Cambridge, 1991, 220-229.
[35] Jenkins, 1997.

Figure 1.1 Territorial bases and ideology

Basis of identity	Ideology
Co-residence	Localism Regionalism
Ethnicity	Regionalism Ethnicism
Ethnic/nationalist	Nationalism
Ethnic/racist	Racism

Adapted from Jenkins, 1997, 85.

Jenkins proposes that concepts of ethnic nationalism and ethno-regionalism are thus redundant, as all nationalism and regionalism is ethnic.[36] However, while this may be the case for nationalism, it may not be the case for regionalism, which, according to his own model, can be generated by co-residence as well as ethnicity. For empirical validation of this we need look no further than Europe, where older ethnically based regions co-exist with a regionalism generated by co-residence and the contingency of administrative boundaries.[37] Nevertheless, Jenkins' model reminds us that ideologies are linked to territorial bases and that these bases differ in terms of scale.

Sub-state identities and the region
The subject of this book is a specific territorial identity, situated between locality and nation-state. The term 'region' is one of a number, along with 'county', 'district', even 'nation', that might be applied in everyday discourse in the UK to this intermediate spatial level. In its more common usage as a description of a block of territory between locality and state, 'region' can be defined in two ways. First, it refers functionally to blocks of territory carved out of a state for the purposes of administration or tracts of territory influenced by and looking towards a central place. Second, 'region' can be used in the sense of cultural regions, based on the sense of identity and interactions of their inhabitants. Peter Wagstaffe makes this distinction either as a 'territory given the status of a region for administrative purposes', or a 'territory having a claim to a cultural and political individuality of its own, marked out by ethnic, historic, linguistic features, moulded by shared myths and traditions'.[38] In practice, of course, these are not binary categorisations,

---

[36] Jenkins, 1997, 85.
[37] See Christopher Harvie, *The Rise of Regional Europe*, London, 1994.

but best seen as overlapping. For example, Wagstaffe goes on to suggest regions may be both administrative and cultural; Michael Keating also argues that regions are 'strong' when 'economic cohesion, cultural identity, administrative apparatus, popular identity and territorial mobilisation coincide in space'.[39]

The consensus however is that regional identities remain generally weak. Keating, while noting that territorial identities are a widespread and malleable part of the world-view of individuals, concludes that 'popular identification with regional units of government and administration is rather weak except in historic nationalities like Scotland, Wales, Catalonia or the Basque Country'. Such a generalised European conclusion is mirrored in the UK. Here, devolution of (differing) levels of meso-government to Scotland and Wales in 1999 reflected a historic sense of sub-state/national identity in those territories. In contrast, English regionalism 'appears to lack political salience. On the surface at least, there are no strong regional cultures which would provide the political demand and support for new democratic institutions'.[40]

Perhaps the consensual view on the absence of English regional identities is over-determined by a dominant elite political culture that idealizes parliamentary sovereignty. Peter Taylor, in arguing the case for a northern (or rather a north-eastern) English political identity, cited Robert Key, Parliamentary Under-Secretary of State for the Environment, as replying in 1991 to the call for English devolution with the statement that 'regional government is un-English'.[41] Yet, despite the disdain of the political classes, there may exist territorial regional identities not stitched into the top-down planning regional paradigm that dominates English governance. The suspicion remains that regional identities in England have a nostalgic dimension that cannot easily be linked to pro-active contemporary economic and social projects. Nonetheless, the appearance of the Yorkshire Party and North East Party in 2014-15, calling for devolution of power, is an interesting development that might imply the dog of English regionalism has finally woken up and begun to bark, or at least whimper.

---

[38] Peter Wagstaffe, 'Region, nation, identity', in Peter Wagstaffe (ed.), *Regionalism in Europe*, Oxford, 1994, 4.

[39] Michael Keating, *The New Regionalism in Western Europe: Territorial Restructuring and Political Change*, Cheltenham, 1998, 10.

[40] Peter John and Alan Whitehead, 'The renaissance of English regionalism', *Policy and Politics* 25 (1997), 7.

[41] Peter Taylor, 'The meaning of the North: England's "foreign country" within?', *Political Geography,* 1993, 144.

Ambiguous regional identities in England partly explain the lack of empirical work on contemporary sub-state regional identities. It also serves to obscure the cases of regions that do have a relatively more pronounced regional consciousness. Cornwall is one of these. Although Montserrat Guibernau cites Cornwall (along with Brittany) as a region which has a 'rather weak sense of identity',[42] this 'weak' identity can still give rise to exactly those contemporary economic and social projects rarely fuelled by English regionalism. As an example, the 50,000 signatures raised in 2000-01 for a petition calling for the establishment of a regional assembly for Cornwall suggests a certain level of contemporary regional identity. But this is the identity of a 'historic' region. Cornwall 'remains the one part of England where not all indigenous inhabitants automatically describe themselves as "English"'.[43] Such an observation suggests that Cornwall is also an exceptional region, a point to which I will return.

Let's at this stage summarise what the literature on territorial identities tells us. First, nationalism provides an integrating story but co-exists with diverse territorial identities at differing scales. These identities may or may not be in competition with the nationalist meta-narrative. Second, sub-state identities, like all identities, are contested. Top-down administrative and functional versions of regions compete with more vernacular, culturally based notions of regions. Bourdieu reminds us that struggles over regional and ethnic identities are struggles to establish meaning.[44] In these struggles groups and classes may use territory for different purposes, attempting to establish their hegemonic definition over the social construction that constitutes the region. Such a contestation again implies that regional identities, like all identities, are neither fixed nor static. In contrast, they are open to change.

Colin Williams points out how a regional identity might be recognised prior to its active promotion through nationalism.[45] In contrast, Keating notes that the new regionalisms do 'not so much hark back to pre-modern forms of territorial identity, as reinvent the notion of territory in ways consistent with contemporary experience'.[46] Regional identities,

---

[42] Montserrat Guibernau (ed.), *Governing European Diversity*, London, 2001, 17.

[43] Bryan Ward-Perkins, 'Why did the anglo-saxons not become more British?', *English Historical Review* 115.462 (2000), 521.

[44] Bourdieu, 1991.

[45] Colin Williams, 'Territory, identity and language', in Michael Keating and John Loughlin (eds), *The Political Economy of Regionalism*, London, 1997, 117.

[46] Michael Keating, *Nations Against the State: The New Politics of Nationalism in Quebec, Catalonia and Scotland*, London, 1996, 47.

therefore, like state nationalisms, to some extent write their own histories and create their own pasts. But how have historians written the past of regions and regional identities?

Historians and past territorial identities
The focus of historical work on past identities in the British Isles has been on national identities. However, as Sarah Radcliffe finds in her study of identity on the Ecuador-Peru frontier, there is a 'multifaceted and complex affiliation to places within and beyond the nation ... the nation is only one space onto which senses of belonging are mapped'.[47] And it may not be the main place. Linda Colley suggests that an 'intense localism and regionalism' was more powerful in eighteenth-century England, Scotland and Wales than allegiance to nation.[48] Similarly, Patrick Joyce argues that industrialism was more likely to forge a regional than an English sense of identity.[49] Returning to Jenkins' schema, ethnicity could give rise, in the British context, to national ideologies of identity, but either ethnicity or co-residence could also give rise to regional or local identities. In addition, these identities 'nested' at different scales. As Smith suggests in relation to Spain, 'most members of the minority ethnic communities also share an overarching Spanish political loyalty, in addition to their often intense ethnic sentiments. But, then, this is the norm in most Western states today'.[50]

Wagstaffe rather romantically claims that 'in England ... [there exist] ... age-old local identities rooted in administrative and socio-cultural traditions which can be traced back for a thousand years'.[51] The study of localities and regions over vast periods of time is the province of the local historian as well as the historical geographer. Local historians have always been interested in the particular, and place is central to their work. Herbert Finberg and W.G. Hoskins' preferred theme of the local historian, the development of a community through time, enthused a generation of local historians.[52] In practice, this usually meant the study

---

[47] Sarah Radcliffe, 'Frontiers and popular nationhood: geographies of identity in the 1995 Ecuador-Peru border dispute', *Political Geography* 17 (1997), 289-290.
[48] Linda Colley, *Britons: Forging the Nation 1707-1837*, London, 1992, 373.
[49] Patrick Joyce, *Visions of the People: Industrial England and the Question of Class 1840-1914*, Cambridge, 1991, 279-292.
[50] Smith, 1991, 59. More recent events in Catalonia might prompt us to question this.
[51] Wagstaffe, 1994, 11.
[52] Herbert Finberg, *The Local Historian and his Theme*, Leicester, 1952; W.G.Hoskins, *The Making of the English Landscape*, London, 1955.

of a single, normally rural, parish. However, after the 1970s some local historians turned their attention to the regional level.

Local historians adopt two broad approaches to the history of regions. The first stresses elements of continuity over very long time-periods. Charles Phythian-Adams has drawn a framework of 'cultural provinces' based on river drainage systems. These provincial settings provide a 'meaningful context for its inhabitants and with which may be associated a set of distinguishable cultural traits'.[53] For Phythian-Adams, industrialisation intensified sentiments of regional identity that were already very deeply based. The second approach, in contrast, emphasises change rather than continuity. Alan Everitt had previously noted that different types of region – for example 'pays', 'county communities', craft regions', 'industrial regions' - co-existed alongside each other, 'each with its own independent life span, each at any one time at a different phase in its evolution'.[54] To some extent these contrasting views can be reconciled. For Phythian-Adams, continuity focuses on continuing local differentiation and uniqueness whereas Everitt's regions identify the local response to changing economic and political contexts.

But local history suffers from several drawbacks if we are studying regional identities. The first is the lingering geographical determinism that hovers over Phythian-Adams' 'cultural provinces', defined as they are ultimately by physical features of river basins and watersheds. While medieval and early modern farming regions may be linked to discernible cultural differences, this physical basis becomes more questionable as we move into the modern period. Second, regions are not, for most local historians, the preferred scale: they are seen as secondary, while the primary scales remain locality and nation-state. Thus, in this approach, the region becomes the 'critical cultural intermediary between its constituent local societies and the level of the nation'.[55] Such an approach tends towards a conservatism that produces an uncritical acceptance of the nation-state, a functional approach to the region and a failure to appreciate the group-specific and contingent dynamics of either regional or state formation.

---

[53] Charles Phythian-Adams, 'Local history and national history: the quest for the peoples of England, *Rural History* 2 (1991), 1-23; 'An agenda for English local history', in Phythian-Adams (ed.), *Societies, Cultures and Kinship 1580-1850: Cultural Provinces and English Local History*, Leicester, 1993, 9.

[54] Alan Everitt, 'Country, county and town: patterns of regional evolution in England', *Transactions of the Royal Historical Society* 29 (1979), 79-108

[55] Phythian-Adams, 1993, 18.

An alternative method prioritises regional history as synthesis, combining levels of analysis in one territory. John Marshall was the most persistent in calling for a synthesised regional history, a project that might avoid the over-specialisation of much academic history but, at the same time, not replicate the 'effete and disorientated' nature of much local history. Instead, he called for 'empiricists of imagination' to write the new regional history.[56] Sadly, the actual output of the 'new' regional historians has been more limited. Studies of regional history still too often result in an over-focus on an empirical description of changing patterns of life, failing to link these to the more discursive invention and re-invention of tradition.[57] In addition, unfortunately, the virtual elimination of university-level extra-mural education has adversely affected the output of local and regional historians since the millennium.

It may be significant that in Marshall's own writings on regional history there was a detectable shift away from identifying empirical patterns towards issues of regional identity. In 1986 he was arguing a pragmatic approach: regions would 'take shape as a consequence of the developing investigation', although 'however broadly and vaguely [they would] carry the hallmark of tradition and even self-awareness and identity'.[58] His own work on the Lake District had pre-disposed him to accept that a 'deep local and regional patriotism' could exist, at least in the modern period.[59] In later writings Marshall expanded on this. In a study of the 'habitual territory' of the inhabitants of Furness, he called on local historians to 'attempt to find out how contemporaries formed their allegiance to particular districts'.[60] Later, he asserted that attitude to place should be the 'first and most basic theme of the local historian', a considerable modification of the traditional local historian's concern with the observable and material traces of the past.[61]

---

[56] John Marshall, 'The study of local and regional "communities": some problems and possibilities', *Northern History* 17 (1981), 228-229.

[57] For an example see Philip Swan and David Foster (eds), *Essays in Regional and Local History*, Beverley, 1992. For an exception see Luis Castells and John Walton, 'Contrasting identities: north-west England and the Basque Country, 1840-1936', in Edward Royle (ed.), *Issues of Regional Identity*, Manchester, 1998, 44-81.

[58] John Marshall, 'Why study regions? (2): Some historical considerations', *Journal of Regional and Local Studies* 6 (1986), 2.

[59] John Marshall and John Walton, *The Lake Counties from 1830 to the mid-twentieth century*, Manchester, 1981, x.

[60] John Marshall, 'Communities, societies, regions and local history. Perceptions of locality in High and Low Furness', *The Local Historian* (1996), 39.

[61] John Marshall, *The Tyranny of the Discrete. A Discussion of the problems of Local History in England*, Aldershot, 1997, 98.

The strength of the regional history approach lies in its emphasis that regions are 'historically ... not a fixed concept, but a feeling, a sentimental attachment to territory shared by like-minded people' and that the meaning of a region resides in 'the view from the bottom'.[62] In drawing attention to the lived experience of regions the regional historian sympathises with the view that social science accounts of nationalism and regionalism have been too top-down, too concerned with notions of 'homogeneity at the expense of recognising difference'.[63] Regional historians, in their focus on difference and their sensitivity to scale, have been able to deconstruct regional identities. Thus, in a study of northern identities in the nineteenth century, Neville Kirk concluded that detailed historical investigation indicates that intra-regional identities were much more important at this time than a sense of either northern or north-eastern identity.[64] His conclusions are reinforced by Adrian Green and A.J.Pollard, who state that the North East has not 'been a coherent and self-conscious region over the *longue durée*'.[65]

Overall, however, local history as a discipline, whether in the guise of a concern with very long-term continuities or of a detailed holistic reconstruction of a region in one given time-period, has failed to produce a convincing model for studying regions or regional identities. In this it shares the more general drawbacks of other historical approaches to territorial identity. The descriptive and inductive methods of historians have led them to focus on the integrative and contextual aspects of identity, describing the institutions and traditions associated with regional identities but failing to provide convincing analysis of two other aspects. The first relates to the narrative dimension of identity. The second, somewhat paradoxical, problem is that historians have focused on describing the attributes of identities and their contexts but failed to deliver a more diachronic model of the formation and emergence of territorial identities. Their focus on the particular and distrust of social theory has militated against a general explanation of the formation of territorial identity.

However, a few historians have adopted a different position on theory. Joyce takes his cue from a reading of post-modernist theory. Citing gender and class, he concluded that identities 'are not the product of an external "referent" which confers meaning on them'.[66] What applies to

---

[62] Edward Royle (ed.), *Issues of Regional Identity*, Manchester, 1998, 4.
[63] Ralph Fevre and Andrew Thompson (eds), *Nation, Identity and Social Theory*, Cardiff, 1999, 247.
[64] Neville Kirk (ed.), *Northern Identities*, Aldershot, 2000, xii.
[65] Adrian Green and A.J.Pollard (eds), *Regional Identities in North East England, 1300-2000*, Woodbridge, 2007, 14.

gender and class identities presumably applies, also, to regional identities. Following this approach, then, regions are a product of regionalism and not the other way around. The object of study then becomes the meanings through which the region is understood and constructed by contemporaries, rather than the social or material forces that formerly were thought to produce the regional consciousness. Furthermore, for the postmodernist, regional identities, and regions too, are very unlikely to be uniform, coherent or homogenous entities but will be 'marked by conflict ... plural, diverse and volatile'.[67]

The move of postmodernist historians to explore issues of ideology and narrative provides an unintended bridge to those regional geographers who, similarly, criticise the fundamental concepts of their colleagues. Of special relevance, Alexander Murphy provided a useful critique of the way other geographers (and social scientists more generally) use the term 'region'.[68] He pointed out how the concept is used as an umbrella term for their more central concepts of place and locale. Place is often defined as a set of attachments for individuals whereas locale is a setting for interaction, a space through which individuals move. In contrast, regions are seen both as sets of attachments and settings for interaction. But this ignores the role of regions themselves as institutional (and ideological) constructions, 'why the region came to be a socially significant spatial unit in the first place, how the region is understood and viewed by its inhabitants, or how and why that understanding has changed over time'.[69] For Murphy, some geographers, like regional historians, still tend to take the regional context for granted, focusing on the attributes of regions rather than the way they are produced. They adopt regional frameworks without recognising the significance of the regionalisation process.

Towards a model of regional production: geographers and the region
The study of regions flowered in the French school of regional geographers and historians around the beginning of the twentieth century. French regional geography took as its central concept the 'pays', an area of countryside determined usually by a particular farming system and by a recognisable landscape. Regions could arise from either shared or polarised activities, as long as these activities gave rise to active links and relationships, and their inhabitants could then proceed to imagine

---

[66] Patrick Joyce, 'The end of social history?', *Social History* 20 (1995), 82.
[67] Joyce, 1995, 82.
[68] Alexander Murphy, 'Regions as social constructs: the gap between theory and practice', *Progress in Human Geography* 15 (1991, 22-35).
[69] Murphy, 1991, 24.

themselves as possessing a shared history. Such a view of regions linked itself to the regionalism that emerged in the second half of the nineteenth century which focused on preserving those aspects of cultural expression – language, dialect, folklore – seen as threatened by modernity.

Culture regions were also central to the work of American cultural geographers of the middle decades of the twentieth century. This body of work was heavily influenced by Carl Sauer and the 'Berkeley School'. Sauer's innovative concept was that of the 'cultural landscape', arguing that landscapes were transformed by culture and could be read as records of human activity.[70] However, the Berkeley School has been subjected to a considerable barrage of criticism from cultural geographers, especially in Britain, since the 1980s. These revolve around two connected points. First, the approach of culture regions is said to reify culture, shifting attention from the individuals and groups who produce culture to a 'super-organic' culture.[71] Second, the concentration on the mapping of cultural traits in the landscape is argued to be unduly restrictive and atheoretical, leading to a neglect of wider political, economic and social structures.

In Britain the concept of the cultural region was always more marginal, with the interesting exception of Wales. The 'Aberystwyth School' of Welsh geographers was concerned to map and understand a Welsh 'culture region' based on the strikingly exceptional (in the British context) cultural trait of the Welsh language. Like the work of regional historians, this provides useful insights into the patterns of regional differentiation as well as a set of conceptual tools for discussing areal patterns, such as the notion of cultural zones of core and periphery.[72] However, also like the regional historians, the predominantly descriptive approach is strong on establishing patterns but less willing to provide a diachronic explanatory, as opposed to descriptive, model for the emergence and reproduction of regions and regional identities.

Dissatisfaction both with what some saw as the descriptive empiricism of traditional regional geography combined with a reaction against the positivist 'objectivism' of the regional and spatial science of the 1960s to

---

[70] Carl Sauer, 'The morphology of landscape', *University of California Publications in Geography* 2 (1925), 19-54.

[71] Peter Jackson, *Maps of Meaning: An Introduction to Cultural Geography*, London, 1989; James Duncan, 'The superorganic in American cultural geography', *Annals of the Association of American Geographers* 70 (1980), 181-190.

[72] For a description of the approach see W.T.R.Pryce, 'The idea of culture in human geography', in E.Grant and P.Newby (eds), *Landscape and Industry*, London, 1982, 131-149.

produce a move to another regional geography discourse in the 1970s. Anne Gilbert described a 'social scientific' regional geography with three strands.[73] These were the 'region as a local response to capitalist process', the region 'as a medium for social interaction' and 'the region as a focus of identification'. The first of these is most associated with the 'new regional geography'. From this perspective, places are consequences of a complex interaction between global processes of uneven development within capitalist accumulation and local uniquenesses. The strength of this approach is that it explains the combination of a changing economy and the continuities of spatial divisions. New products emerge, new techniques are applied but unique places remain. Each round of capitalist investment produces not homogeneity, but a re-formed heterogeneity. The continuing uniqueness of place is always subject to change, 'always already a product of wider contact'.[74] Yet, despite these insights, in practice the new regional geography focused its empirical gaze on localities rather than on regions.

The second strand, the 'region as a medium for social interaction' is heavily influenced by Anthony Gidden's structuration theory. This shifts the focus away from the visible attributes of a region towards the relationship of agents within it, away from structures and towards networks of interaction. Such an approach has obvious affinities with the contemporary 'associationalist' analysis of European regions, which emphasised networks of regional level actors as a possible alternative to hierarchies or markets.[75] But structuration theory and interactionist perspectives still do not clearly conceptualise the region itself either as an institutional or symbolic context, or an agent in its own right. In contrast, it is Gilbert's third strand of social scientific regional geography, the 'region as a focus of identification', that brings us closer to the issue of regional identity. As Gilbert perceives, regions are the result of process, whether socio-economic or cultural.

The role of process in the construction of regions suggests a particular role for historical geographers. However, outside Wales, British historical geographers tended to concentrate on studies of the landscape and its material objects, the geography of field systems rather than class or cultural structures. Its leading landscape studies exponent, H.C.Darby, described this as a 'pragmatic British empiricism'.[76] However, while

---

[73] Anne Gilbert, 'The new regional geography in English and French speaking countries', *Progress in Human Geography* 12 (1988), 208-228.

[74] Massey, 1995, 183.

[75] For a critique see Shahid Amin and Nigel Thrift, 'Institutional issues for the European regions: from markets and plans to socioeconomics and powers of association', *Economy and Society* 24 (1995), 41-66.

interest in landscape remains strong among historical geographers, that interest has changed shape. No longer confined to material structures, geographers have moved onto the political and cultural domains to explain the reproduction of landscapes as symbols and meanings for groups and individuals in society. The agenda of historical geography, even in its traditional guise of a concern with landscape, therefore clearly overlaps with that of cultural geography. This brings historical geography closer to the concerns of historians, producing a potentially fruitful convergence of disciplinary perspectives.

One area to benefit from this convergence was the study of regional identity in the late eighteenth and nineteenth centuries. Marshall had earlier suggested that the 'development, density and shape, of an industrializing region may be fairly easy to trace'.[77] It was no coincidence that the clearest account of the reproduction of regional consciousness in the past was produced by historical geographers and economic historians working on the relatively contained period of the Industrial Revolution.

The implicit traditional view of social historians was that territorial diversity gave way to class-based homogeneity during industrialization. The economic historian Sidney Pollard was already challenging this orthodoxy in the early 1970s. He claimed that economic specialization produced regional societies 'with identifiable features appropriate to a certain stage of the industrial process differing from the stage reached by other regions'.[78] Later, he added more flesh to his concept of industrial regions. The industrial process in the eighteenth century, he argued, was marked by the emergence of a regional system, albeit unstable, containing specialized production regions based on comparative cost advantages.[79] The implication of Pollard's work was that industrialization could co-exist with heightened regional identities, rather than replace regional with class identities.

---

[76] H.C.Darby, 'The relations of history and geography', *Transactions of the Institute of British Geographers* 19 (1953), 1-11 and 'Historical geography in Britain, 1920-1980', *Transactions of the Institute of British Geographers* NS8 (1983), 421-428.

[77] John Marshall, 'Proving ground or the creation of regional identity? The origins and problems of regional history in Britain', in Swan and Foster (eds), 1992, 22.

[78] Sidney Pollard, 'Industrialization and the European economy', *Economic History Review* 26 (1973), 638.

[79] Sidney Pollard, *Peaceful Conquest: The Industrialisation of Europe 1760-1970*, Oxford, 1981.

John Langton, in an important contribution in 1984, picked up on Pollard's concept of the industrial region and proceeded to set out the logic of the causal process through which industrialization led to differentiated regions. Furthermore, he linked this to the production of regional consciousness.[80] Langton's argument was that the process of industrialization intensified the regional differences of pre-industrial England. It was the industrial revolution that led to regionalism. In particular, it was the emergence of waterway-based communications networks in the later eighteenth century that produced 'more specialized, more differentiated ... and more internally unified regions'.[81]

The central thrust of Langton's view of industrial regions was that economic specialization was accompanied by the rise of consistent regional cultural identities. Langton argued that industrial regions gained internal coherence and consistency as their local economies integrated around great provincial cities such as Birmingham, Manchester, Liverpool, Newcastle, Leeds and Bradford. An increasing sense of shared regional economic interests led to an emergent regional consciousness, fostered by provincial newspapers, clubs and societies. The regional novel, working class dialect literature, and antiquarian interest in folk customs all burgeoned in the first half of the nineteenth century and were symptoms of these new regions. At the same time local customs were being synthesized regionally by the emergence of intra-regional specialisms. To sum up, economic specialization produced increasingly internally integrated yet externally differentiated regions, economically, socially and culturally, during the classic period of the Industrial Revolution.

In parallel with historical geographers, economic historians were also re-discovering the region. In 1989 Pat Hudson claimed the region was the 'really important spatial unit' of the early nineteenth century.[82] Hudson's work synthesized that of Langton and Pollard. In the eighteenth century distinct, specialized, internally cohesive industrial regions emerged, linked to national and international markets. 'Sectoral specialization by region' occurred as a growing export trade helped create integrated transport, commercial and financial links within the industrial region, these resting, in turn, on dense social, family and

---

[80] John Langton, 'The industrial revolution and the regional geography of England', *Transactions of the Institute of British Geographers* NS9 (1984), 145-167.

[81] Langton, 1984, 162.

[82] Pat Hudson, 'The regional perspective', in Hudson (ed.), *Regions and Industries: A Perspective on the Industrial Revolution in Britain*, Cambridge, 1989, 5-38.

business networks. Thus, regions were the important spatial unit for capital, labour and information flows. Intra-regional markets and networks for these complemented the extra-regional commodity flows. Industrial regions were 'freer of metropolitan economic, social and political influence than they had been in the late seventeenth and or early eighteenth centuries or were to become from the later nineteenth century'.[83]

Exports went directly from the region rather than through London and regional lobbying and regionally based protest movements indicated growing regional consciousnesses with their epicentres in the larger provincial cities.

However, while providing a temporal framework for the emergence of regional identity, the industrial regions model remains tantalisingly silent on the causal links between economic and social change and the rise of regional consciousness, other than asserting an association between the two. Recognizing this, Marshall called for 'detailed examinations of the growth of regional consciousness' based on Langton's ideas.[84] Nonetheless, such examinations have been slow to appear. Kirk points to the 'considerable gaps in the historical literature dealing with regional and local identities'.[85] In the same volume, Martin Hewitt and Robert Poole suggested that regional identities 'remain a neglected topic', while the period before 1860 'remains something of a wasteland for students of the development, persistence or transformation of regional identities'.[86] Little has changed since.[87]

Meanwhile, work by social and political historians adds extra dimensions to the emerging picture of eighteenth and nineteenth century regions. Dror Wahrman distinguished two cultures in late eighteenth century England, and in doing so set debates on the cultural history of this period within a territorial dimension. He suggested there was a distinction between those attached to 'national' society, a 'gentlemanly bourgeoisie' with London-oriented cultural tastes, and an 'independent bourgeoisie' attached to their communal-provincial culture, valorizing local traditions, customs and practices.[88] There was thus a 'rift within the

---

[83] Pat Hudson, *The Industrial Revolution*, London, 1992, 105.
[84] Marshall, 1996, 47.
[85] Kirk, 2000, x.
[86] Martin Hewitt and Robert Poole, 'Samuel Bamford and northern identity', in Kirk (ed.), 2000, 112.
[87] Bernard Deacon, 'Regional identity in late nineteenth-century England: discursive terrains and rhetorical strategies', *International Journal of Regional and Local History* 11 (2016), 59-74.
[88] Dror Wahrman, 'National society, communal culture: an argument about the recent historiography of eighteenth-century Britain', *Social History* 17

elite' as some reacted against the more ostentatious, London-orientated values of their neighbours to renew an interest in local, more puritan values, especially in the second half of the eighteenth century.[89] This was precisely that period when the contours of industrial regions began to be more clearly perceived.

Wahrman's 'independent bourgeoisie' crystallised around the appropriation and adaptation of the press, associational culture, commercialised leisure activities and around the value of 'independence', asserting their local identities vis-à-vis national society, an assertion that cut across other divides, such as religion. Wahrman claimed to detect growing tensions between the two types of 'middling sort' by the 1770s. It was the 'independent bourgeoisie' that provided the basis for the past-oriented, oppositional, Wilkite radical English, cultural nationalist ideology of the time.[90] This group, more a 'coherent idiom', according to Wahrman, than a class, inhabited the heart of those regional cultures deploying themselves around the centres of eighteenth century regional specialisation. Enlarging on this cultural perspective, Rosemary Sweet has also pointed to the role of the rhetoric of 'independence' and 'local tradition' in the reproduction of provincial loyalties. Concepts of 'civic pride, identity and historical consciousness' were used to maintain and to mobilise local loyalties in borough politics.[91] The work of cultural and political historians therefore re-inserts a sense of contingency and the role of rhetoric and local agency into the formation of regional identities.

These geographical and historical insights do much to identify some of the factors at work in the process of regional creation in the eighteenth and nineteenth centuries. However, to take us further we need to locate these within a more explicit model of the regionalization process.

Regionalization: a dynamic model

We find such a model of the formation of regional identity in the work of Anssi Paasi. He criticises geographers for regarding regions as categories used as instruments of classification and historians for neglecting the wider context of the development of regional systems and not conceptualising the emergence of regions. Instead, they too often provide just a 'detailed and illustrative discussion of the practices occurring in a region during a certain period'.[92] In lieu of this, he offers us the concept

---

(1992), 54.
[89] Wahrman, 1992, 50-51.
[90] Wahrman, 1992, 59-61.
[91] Rosemary Sweet, 'Freeman and independence in English borough politics', *Past and Present* 161 (1998), 115.

of spatial socialisation, 'the discourse in which inhabitants become members of specific products of social spatialization – that is territorially bounded spatial units – and adopt specific modes of thought and action'.[93] Spatial socialization introduces a concept of culture as central to regional production. Regions are the condensation of 'a whole complex of economic, political and social processes into a specific cultural image'.[94] This connects the two dimensions of the material basis of regions and the representational role of regions as 'mediums' of social reproduction. For Paasi, the construction of territoriality involves both mental representations and material practices, discourses as well as divisions of labour.

Central to his understanding is a diachronic approach to regional institutionalization. This takes place in four stages, not necessarily consecutive, during which everyday experiences are given institutional form and result in collective portrayals of a regional territory. The first stage is the development of territorial awareness and shape. Here, the territory is identified as a distinct spatial unit, a process in which power relations play a crucial role in defining boundaries. The second stage is the formation of conceptual or symbolic shape. During this stage territorial symbols are established, giving the inhabitants a means of distinguishing the territory from others and embodying the history and traditions of that territory. But this second stage can only occur alongside the third stage, the emergence of institutions. For Paasi, formal and informal political, legal, educational and cultural institutions are 'the most important factors as regards the reproduction of the region and regional consciousness'.[95] Institutions use territorial symbols and they also reproduce economic and social structures such as the division of labour. Finally, there is the establishment of a territorial unit in the wider regional structure and social consciousness. In this fourth stage the region is widely accepted as having a status in the spatial structure of society, most formally, though not necessarily, through possessing an administrative shell.

A region achieves an identity through the process of institution-alization. However, Paasi crucially distinguishes between the 'regional consciousness' of the inhabitants of a region and the 'identity of a region', both of which come together to make up a 'regional identity'. Regional consciousness is produced in what Paasi terms 'structures of expectations'. This is a concept close to Raymond Williams' 'structures

---

[92] Paasi, 1991, 242.
[93] Paasi, 1996, 54.
[94] Paasi, 1991, 241
[95] Paasi, 1986, 121.

of feeling' or Bourdieu's 'habitus', that taken for granted context of everyday experience.[96] Structures of expectations can arise from 'factual', face to face relations within communities or from 'ideal' relations, mediated through local or non-local newspapers, political institutions and discourse. Structures of expectations give rise to collective portrayals of place, portrayals that might be 'real, imagined or even mythical'.[97] These usually look to the past, towards the history and tradition of that region. In contrast, the 'identity of the region' is more directed to 'becoming' than to the past. Images of the region may be produced either by insiders or outsiders and combine to make up the 'identity of a region'. Figure 1.2 illustrates this framework.

Over the course of his writings Paasi added two further concepts to his model of the institutionalization of regions. First, he pointed to the importance of generation in mediating between regions and place. Generations 'provide people's spatial consciousness with common cultural elements, identity and frames for interpreting experiences'.[98]

Figure 1.2 Paasi's model of the formation of regional identity

factual ideal ideas of community	insiders outsiders
structures of expectation	images of region
regional consciousness of inhabitants	identity of the region
regional identity	

The second concept is that of boundaries. Borders are 'manifestations of socio-spatial consciousness' and Paasi's own empirical work on the Finnish-Russian boundary focuses on the iconography of boundaries and the social construction of this by groups and classes. Boundaries and territorialisation are seen as 'two sides of the same coin', reproduce the spatial limits of identity and construct a 'them' in opposition to 'us'.[99]

---

[96] Raymond Williams, *The Long Revolution*, London, 1961, 48-71; Pierre Bourdieu, *Outline of a Theory of Practice*, Cambridge, 1977, 71-79; Paasi, 1986, 122.

[97] Paasi, 1986, 122.

[98] Anssi Paasi, 'Constructing territories, boundaries and regional identities', in Tuomas Forsberg (ed.), *Contested Territory: Border disputes at the edge of the former Soviet Empire*, Aldershot, 1995, 55.

[99] Paasi, 1995, 43 and 1996, 27-28.

IDENTITY AND TERRITORY

However, boundaries also mediate contacts between social communities and cultures as well as mark the edges of those cultures.[100]

Paasi thus provides a rich set of concepts and a broad framework with which to work through the formation of sub-state territories and their identities. Of particular use is his view of regional identities as the product of historical contingency, the role of institutional construction in this history and the emphasis on discursive as well as material practices, and culture in addition to economics. Together, these provide a much more dynamic and less narrow approach to regional identity formation than the industrial regions model.

However, it still has problems. In one of the few attempts to operationalise Paasi's approach in a British context, Gordon Macleod applied it to issues of governance in twentieth century Scotland. For MacLeod, while Paasi's model can help develop 'comparative studies of particular places' its main weakness is its 'relative silence on the territorialization of social and political life into two distinctive geographical scales: the regional and the national'. As he points out, the identity politics associated with these scales use differing discourses. He feels, as a result, that there is a lack of theoretical guidance from Paasi as to how competing narratives of place can 'vie for hegemony within any given space'.[101]

Moreover, there remains another problem with such a project. How do we represent this complex spatial and temporal process, invoking the national and local perspectives that constitute and are constituted by each other in practice?[102] Put simply, in what form does the author write up this complexity? Paasi himself adopts historical layers in his study of the institutionalisation of Finnish territory, investigating temporal cross-sections of territorialisation.[103] This book takes an alternative approach, discussing a series of thematic geographical layers of Cornwall over the period 1750-1870.

In this chapter I have established the components of a working definition of identity. I also reviewed some influential approaches by historians, geographers and others to territorial identity, focusing on approaches to a regional scale. In the course of this review I emphasized

---

[100] Paasi, 1996, 213.

[101] Gordon MacLeod, 'In what sense a region? Place, hybridity, symbolic shape, and institutional formation in (post)-modern Scotland', *Political Geography* 17 (1998), 839-840. see also Bernard Deacon, 'Proto-regionalisation: the case of Cornwall', *Journal of Regional and Local Studies* 18 (1998), 27-41 for a preliminary application to Cornwall.

[102] Paasi, 1996, 75-76.

[103] Paasi, 1996.

the particular salience of Paasi's work on regionalisation as providing a framework for understanding the emergence of regional identity. Both the components of my definition of identity and Paasi's model re-appear throughout this study to help give shape to a discussion of Cornish identity. However, first, we must ask how Cornwall has been imagined by historians and social scientists.

Chapter Two
Cornwall, Cornishness and the academy

Most academic approaches to Cornwall are structured by one of two assumptions. The first assumes Cornwall to be a local place, occupying the same semantic space as an English county and viewed as an integral, if perhaps distinctive, part of England. The second assumes Cornwall is a Celtic country, or even nation, and approaches Cornwall in terms of its comparative standing vis-à-vis the other 'Celtic' nations of the British Isles and France. Such an approach has produced an (intermittent) recognition of a Cornish ethnic identity in pre-modernity and a picture of a Celtic identity largely manufactured during late modernity. However, the argument advanced here is that both these approaches lead to oversimplified and insufficiently comprehensive understandings of the Cornish identity. In addition, neither approach manages to provide a coherent explanation or even, sometimes, description of the Cornish identity, either in the present or the past. In this chapter I take the position that adopting an explicit Cornish Studies approach offers further insights into the history of the reproduction of the Cornish identity.

Cornwall as local place
If Cornwall is read as local it is also often read as marginal or parochial. This has the effect, either intentionally or unintentionally, of downgrading the Cornish experience. For example, in explaining nineteenth-century Cornwall's status as 'an emigration region comparable with any in Europe', Dudley Baines curiously includes 'parochialism' as one of the reasons.[1] In discussing regional languages and dialects in the later middle ages Ralph Griffiths argues that Welsh was seen by the English as 'wilfully foreign'. Yet Cornish, presumably as 'wilfully foreign' as Welsh, is described as 'quaint', with all its extra connotations of oddness and strangeness.[2] From such a perspective, profound misunderstandings are liable to occur when confronted by

---

[1] Dudley Baines, *Migration in a Mature Economy: Emigration and Internal Migration in England and wales, 1861-1930*, Cambridge, 1985, 159.
[2] Ralph Griffiths, 'The later middle ages', in Kenneth Morgan (ed.), *The Oxford Illustrated History of Britain*, Oxford, 1984, 166-222.

unexpected expressions of Cornish identity. Bernard Crick, for example, when discussing foreign hotel registers and their meaning for the concept of nationality, wrote: 'once I read "Cornish" but I suspected, correctly, that it was a wag and not a nut'.[3] Unwilling, or unable, to believe that anyone could represent their Cornishness as a national identity Crick took refuge in the comfortable assumption that it had to be either jest or madness.

Such explicit incomprehension is rare. Much more common is silence. Keith Robbins' mention of Cornwall's place in the formation of England in the medieval period serves to highlight Cornwall's absence from many other historical texts.[4] We might go further. In the same way as nineteenth-century colonists constructed the peoples they met as 'primitive', people without history, so Cornwall and the Cornish were often positioned as timeless, their history below the horizon of visibility. The logical extension of Cornwall as a marginal place is thus an idealised temporal construct of 'timeless Cornwall', or even 'vanished Cornwall', as the essential attributes designated to this place become more difficult to find on the ground.

Those writing the 'new' British history do not generally say much about Cornwall. Hugh Kearney admits that it deserves more attention but John Morrill, on the other hand, in a discussion of Englishness, Welshness and Scottishness in the early modern period has no place for a sense of Cornishness. For him, Cornwall was just part of England by this time, incorporated in a 'strong sense of regional identity' that had emerged among the English as early as 1300.[5] In contrast, Steven Ellis argues that Englishness before 1500 encompassed a variety of different meanings. Within this matrix of Englishness cultural groups were separate from political subjects. Thus, the English King's subjects included the Welsh, Irish, Scots, French, Flemish and anyone else who happened to live within the realm. However, in the sixteenth century this changed. 'Perceptions of English identity changed quite significantly, and Englishness was more narrowly defined'.[6] In the process the ethnic

---

[3] Bernard Crick, 'An Englishman considers his passport', in Neil Evans (ed.), *National Identity in the British Isles*, Harlech, 1989, 23.

[4] Keith Robbins, *Great Britain: Identities, Institutions and the Idea of Britishness*, Harlow, 1998, 8-9.

[5] Hugh Kearney, *The British Isles: A History of Four Nations*, Cambridge, 1989, 1 and 105; John Morrill, 'The British problem, c.1534-1707', in Brendan Bradshaw and John Morrill (eds), *The British Problem, c1534-1707: State Formation in the British Archipelago*, London, 1996, 1 and 6.

[6] Steven Ellis, 'Civilising Northumberland: Representations of Englishness in the Tudor state', *Journal of Historical Sociology* 12 (1999), 104.

space for the non-English within the territory of England became more constricted and such groups tended to be marginalised. The modernist notion of one ethnic group for each national space made an early appearance on the historical stage of seventeenth century England. During this cultural (and political) shift Cornish ethnicity suffered a loss of status.

Cornwall as Celtic place
Robbins has noted how Cornwall was 'exceptional in its "Celtic" inheritance within England', an inheritance that guaranteed the Cornish formally equal status, as one of the four constituent parts of the 'island of Britain' in medieval times.[7] But in the religious and political turmoil of the sixteenth and seventeenth centuries this status dissipated. Mark Stoyle has argued that in the Civil War period the Cornish still acted from a sense of ethnicity based on 'a culture under threat, of embattled Cornishness' and that the Cornish should be seen as one of the units of the 'war of five peoples' in the seventeenth century.[8] However, even Stoyle appears to accept that, with the continuing decline of the Cornish language, there was a concomitant weakening of Cornish ethnicity.[9] Cornish ethnic identity, based on its separate language, is therefore viewed as a feature of medieval and (more debatably) early modern British history. But it fades away as we move into the modern period.

Relatively unusually for someone who is not a Cornish Studies specialist, Adrian Hastings addresses the Cornish case directly in his historical work on ethnicity, religion and nationalism. He points out that Cornwall is 'an interesting but little considered case'.[10] His own reading of its history suggests it was 'fully integrated into England despite its different language' at a relatively early date, 'quietly absorbed more than it was conquered' by English rulers who, in contrast to the later Normans, were not 'dynamically oppressive' and instead enjoyed 'relatively pacific' relations with their Celtic neighbours.[11] This 'relatively successful integration' occurred because England 'as a whole' was still in an embryonic state, so Danes, English and Cornish could all contribute

---

[7] Robbins, 1998, 8-9.

[8] Mark Stoyle, '"Pagans or paragons?": Images of the Cornish during the English civil war', *English Historical Review* 111 (1996), 323 and 'The last refuge of a scoundrel: Sir Richard Grenville and Cornish particularism, 1644-6', *Historical Research* 71 (1998), 51.

[9] Mark Stoyle, 'Cornish rebellions, 1497-1648', *History Today* 47 (1997), 22-28.

[10] Adrian Hastings, *The Construction of Nationhood: Ethnicity, Religion and Nationalism*, Cambridge, 1997, 66.

[11] Hastings, 1997, 44.

to a wider 'Englishness'. Indeed, Cornwall 'participated in the institutional development of England at every point'. He agrees that it was the Reformation that challenged this Cornish location, as a group with a clear identity, but one firmly absorbed into an implied multi-ethnic England. Echoing Stoyle, he concludes that the rapid decline of the Cornish language that followed was accompanied by a decline 'of the singularity of the Cornish ethnic identity within England. The springboard for any pursuit of independent nationhood was effectively removed'. Yet Hastings immediately qualifies this apparent ethnic disintegration by suggesting that 'nevertheless, there remained a stronger sense of separate identity and common purpose ... among the people of Cornwall than in any other southern shire ... Such politicisable ethnicity could hardly be found elsewhere'.[12]

Hasting's account of the benign attitude of Saxon kingdoms towards their Celtic neighbours might be open to some debate.[13] However, his assertion that Cornwall was a case of a 'successful integration' of a distinct ethnicity is broadly echoed in Philip Payton's account of the medieval period: 'Cornwall was formally annexed to England and yet was not part of it, either ethnically or in terms of territorial absorption'.[14] But the real significance of Hastings' account lies in the crossing of that divide between pre-modern and modern and the proposal of a continuing sense of ethnicity through into the modern period, despite the loss of its Celtic language.

Like Hastings, other writers occasionally note the continuing maintenance of the historic identity of Cornwall into the period of modernity. Robbins, for example, has suggested that the 'retention of a sense of difference' in Cornwall was a result of geographical isolation into the nineteenth century.[15] Drawing the opposite conclusion but employing the same logic, Michael Hechter argues that the 'relative weakness of Celtic ethnicity in nineteenth and twentieth century Cornwall is due, in part, to the fact that the integration of this region into the English economy had occurred prior to 1600'. This led to substantial economic 'inter-group exchange' with neighbouring areas occurring in the 'relative absence of cultural discrimination'.[16]

---

[12] Hastings, 1997, 67.
[13] For an interpretation that questions the notion of 'full integration' see Bernard Deacon, *Cornwall's First Golden Age*, London, 2016.
[14] Philip Payton, *The Making of Modern Cornwall*, Redruth, 1992, 46.
[15] Keith Robbins, *Nineteenth Century Britain*, Oxford, 1988, 25.
[16] Michael Hechter, *Internal Colonialism: The Celtic Fringe in British National Development, 1536-1966*, London, 64-65.

For Robbins and Hechter, isolation produces a sense of difference, but for others loss of 'isolation' might be the cause of a heightened sense of difference. It was the late nineteenth century when, according to Philip Dodd, Cornwall was constructed as 'Celtic'. This was an example not of a traditional identity surviving modernisation but, in contrast, the 'bestowal of identity by the core on the periphery'.[17] James Vernon also focuses on this period, noting that 'the only way the Cornish subaltern could speak itself as a nation was by appropriating this English romance with the Cornish labouring poor'. True, there was a 'a continual traffic in the tropes and narratives of the Cornish and English national imageries' across the Tamar, but clearly the weight of influence was from the east. Vernon concludes that the instability of nationalist imaginations in both Cornwall and England in the later nineteenth century undercuts and 'problematises the "four-nations" model of British national identity, one that tellingly ignores Cornwall or conflates its alterity within Englishness'.[18] However, Vernon uses the Cornish case primarily as a vehicle for investigating Englishness rather than understanding Cornishness. Local actors seem trapped within the structures of larger discourses, such as romanticism or nationalism. Meanwhile, the 'primitive', ordinary 'folk' of Cornwall are passively constructed by other classes and groups both within and outside Cornwall. They have no agency of their own. Vernon's account, with its focus on language and culture, also ignores the economic aspect of these cultural changes, exchanging the economic reductionism of writers like Hechter with a cultural reductionism.

Historians of Britishness, therefore, either focus on pre-Reformation Cornwall where the Cornish possessed a recognisable, if only occasionally visible, ethnic identity, or the post-railway period, when a revived Cornish identity is constructed within the structures of a wider English/British Romanticism and imposed on a passive periphery. The period between, roughly, the mid-seventeenth and the late nineteenth centuries is not so well documented by such approaches.[19] It is more usually ignored.[20]

---

[17] Philip Dodd, 'Englishness and the national culture', in Robert Colls and Philip Dodd (eds), *Englishness: Politics and Culture 1880-1920*, London, 1986, 1-15.

[18] James Vernon, 'Border crossings: Cornwall and the English (imagi)nation', in Geoffrey Cubitt (ed.), *Imagining Nations*, Manchester, 1998, 169.

[19] For some insights into the late seventeenth century see Mark Stoyle, *West Britons: Cornish Identities and the Early Modern British* State, Exeter, 2002.

[20] This despite an outpouring of work on Britishness and Englishness by an angst-ridden English intellectual elite. See Krishan Kumar, *The Making of*

Social scientists and Cornwall

Again, in most of the influential texts by social scientists on ethnicity or regionalism Cornwall is not mentioned. In those cases when it is the approach is familiar. The work of the Oxford School of social anthropologists such as Malcolm Chapman or Maryon McDonald on issues of ethnicity and identity, for example, adds little to that of modernist historians on 'invented traditions' or postmodern historians on the role of language and discourse.[21] In his deconstruction of the idea of 'the Celt' Chapman makes little explicit mention of the Cornish Celt, other than to wonder what 'ordinary local people' were up to when Cornish Celtic revivalists were busy celebrating the Summer Solstice.[22] Chapman (and McDonald in the Breton context) focus on the artificiality of notions of the 'Celt', contrasting it against the ordinariness of material life in 'Celtic' countries. Seduced by the re-workings of the past on the part of revivalists in pursuit of the construction of 'a new Cornish identity',[23] 'post-Celticist' social anthropologists ignore the existence and formation of other and older Cornish identities. In these anthropological accounts there is an implication that modern Cornish ethnicity is contrived, inauthentic, even false, an imposition by non-indigenous processes. Such accounts suffer from an over-concern with the more dynamic but, nonetheless, minority Celtic revivalist movements. In doing so, the spatial identities of the mass are rendered indistinct: indeed, they are lost to sight in another version of the 'vanishing Cornwall' discourse.

Even this interest in the 'new Cornish identity' of the revivalist movement is lost in writings on contemporary regionalism. For Ken Shaw, contemporary Cornish cultural nationalism is not vigorous 'but remains in the antiquarian phase', stuck in the conservative regionalism of the early twentieth century.[24] The non-appearance of a creative cultural elite is interpreted as meaning there is no 'distinctive Cornish

---

English National Identity, Cambridge, 2003 and *the Idea of Englishness: English Culture, National Identity and Social Thought*, Farnham, 2015 or Michael Kenny, *The Politics of English Nationhood*, Oxford, 2015.

[21] Malcolm Chapman, *The Celts: The Construction of a Myth*, London, 1992; Maryon McDonald, *'We are not French!': Language, Culture and Identity in Brittany*, London, 1989.

[22] Chapman, 1992, 223.

[23] Maryon McDonald, 'Celtic ethnic kinship and the problem of being English', *Current Anthropology* 27 (1986), 341.

[24] Ken Shaw, 'Elements in the notion of peripheral identity', in Michael Havinden, J.Queniart and Jeffrey Stanyer (eds), *Centre and Periphery: Brittany and Cornwall & Devon Compared*, Exeter, 1991, 226.

identity'. Echoing Hechter, he concludes that Cornwall's historic openness to the market and to the metropolis undermined the 'original Cornish identity' which has meant that it 'was less able to retain a remote fastness where a peasantry could retain a timeless identity'. Leaving aside the glaring contradiction here between the notion of an essential identity and a social constructivist nod towards the role of local elites, by denying the existence of a phenomenon (distinctive identity) worth investigating then the problem of explaining its historical formation is neatly shelved. Also writing from within what might be termed a 'denial' perspective on Cornish identity, Jeffrey Stanyer at least distinguished between Cornish nationalism and Cornishness. However, he focuses on the former, which is 'tiny', 'very minor', 'weak' and 'oscillates around the threshold of political visibility'. Tantalisingly, Stanyer hinted that 'if Cornishness is important it is because it influences those who are not separatists'.[25] Yet there is no attempt to investigate that Cornishness, its historical formation, nor the ways in which it does or does not articulate with cultural nationalism.

Payton has pointed out that the approach of these regionalists 'led to serious underestimation of the strength of Cornish ethnic identity (and the factors that have led to its perpetuation)'.[26] In particular it appeared entirely to miss the enhanced expressions of 'difference' that accompanied socio-economic change in Cornwall after the 1960s.[27]

The contemporary Cornish identity has attracted nothing on the scale of Ronan Le Coadic's study of Breton identity.[28] This, conducted from a position on the margins, draws out the complex articulations of Breton self-identity with representations of Brittany and Bretonness through an ethnographic survey as well as an in-depth discussion of relevant historical and literary evidence. Nevertheless, there exists some limited ethnographic work on the modern Cornish identity. Mary McArthur interviewed a small number of Cornish people in west Cornwall as part of a study of Cornish ethnicity in the late 1980s. She concluded that

---

[25] Jeffrey Stanyer, 'The Janus-faced periphery: Cornwall and Devon in the twentieth century', *Policy and Politics* (1997), 93.

[26] Philip Payton, 'On centre and periphery', *Journal of Interdisciplinary Economics* 4 (1992), 207.

[27] For these, see Payton, *Making*, 1992, 192-239; Bernard Deacon and Philip Payton, 'Re-inventing Cornwall: culture change on the European periphery', in Philip Payton (ed.), *Cornish Studies One*, Exeter, 1993; Bernard Deacon, 'And shall Trelawny die? The Cornish identity', in Philip Payton (ed.), *Cornwall Since the* War, Redruth, 1993, 200-223; Philip Payton, *The Cornish Overseas*, Fowey, 1999, 391-399.

[28] Ronan le Coadic, *L'Identite Bretonne*, Rennes, 1998.

ethnic identity was not weak: 'most Cornish people were very sure of their Cornish identity'.[29] But Cornish identity, like all territorial identities, is multi-faceted, fluid and heavily context dependent. As McArthur reported, in day to day life, 'consciousness of ethnic difference can range from being non-existent on the part of both Cornish and English (in Cornwall) to being very important'. Neil Kennedy and Nigel Kingcome also reconstruct a sense of Cornishness that is marked by fluidity and diversity rather than fixity.[30]

It is these subtleties that have not been addressed in the sparse references to Cornish identity in the 'mainstream' literature. Neither the heightened sense of difference proposed by Cornish scholars, the diversity of identities within (post-industrial) Cornwall nor the comparative strength of the Cornish identity when compared with English regions have received much attention.[31] Obviously, there is something to explain, but explanations cannot rest on the broad but vague grounds offered by some regional scientists. As an example, Alan Philip claims that 'the much stronger local identities, typically to be found in counties such as Somerset, Cornwall or Durham, ... reflect administrative (and socio-cultural) divisions which go back one thousand years'.[32] Such an explanation is close to the local history perspective that, rather confusingly, places Cornwall in a 'cultural province' - the 'South

---

[29] Mary McArthur, 'The Cornish: a case study in ethnicity', unpublished M.SC. thesis, University of Bristol, 1988.

[30] Neil Kennedy and Nigel Kingcome, 'Disneyfication of Cornwall – developing a Poldark heritage complex', *International Journal of Heritage Studies* 4 (1998), 45-59. A voluminous body of work has more recently appeared on the Cornish identity. For an extended critical review see Bernard Deacon, *From a Cornish Study*, Redruth, 2017, chapter 4. In particular, note Neil Kennedy's *Cornish Solidarity*, the work of Joanie Willett on the politics of identity and the quantification of the identity by Kerryn Husk.

[31] John MacDonald, *The Lack of Political Identity in English Regions: Evidence from MPs*, Glasgow, 1979, 23-24 notes that Cornwall accounted 'for most of the sub-regional bias in (Parliamentary) speeches from the South West Planning Region' in the late 1970s. Similarly, MPs and an MEP could argue in the late 1990s that the Cornish should be regarded as an 'official' ethnic group, along with Scots, Welsh and Irish, thus again illustrating Cornwall's distinctive position within the UK (Home Office, 1999). This was belatedly recognised in 2014 when the Cornish were given the status of a national minority under the Framework Convention for the Protection of National Minorities. The translation of recognised equal status into practical outcomes is now keenly awaited.

[32] Alan Philip, 'Regionalism in the United Kingdom', in Peter Wagstaff (ed.), *Regionalism in Europe*, Oxford, 1994, 111.

British Sea' - which includes Devon and parts of west Dorset but then promptly states that Cornwall is a sub-division of this province, 'distinguished for obvious cultural reasons' from its immediate neighbour'.[33] In short, none of the writers reviewed here offer much purchase on the period between the seventeenth and nineteenth centuries, that period after the de-construction of ethnic Cornwall but before the re-construction of Celtic Cornwall.

The new Cornish Studies[34]
In contrast, the academic discipline of Cornish Studies is rooted in the periphery, in Cornwall itself. Out of Cornish Studies came, at the end of the last millennium, attempts to synthesise and contextualise the Cornish experience.[35] Payton identified this academic work as the beginnings of a 'new Cornish historiography and the new Cornish social science'.[36]

While there is no key text setting out the basis of the new Cornish Studies, the centrepieces of the project were a 'new Cornish historiography' and a search for difference. Payton located the 'new Cornish historiography' in the writings of the 'new British history'.[37] This 'Four nations' approach to the history of the British Isles has precipitated 'what is in effect a major review of how that history might

---

[33] Charles Phythian-Adams (ed.), *Societies, Cultures and Kinship 1580-1850: Cultural Provinces and English Local History*, Leicester, 1993, 15. For a similar assertion about the cultural importance of the Tamar see Edward Royle (ed.), *Issues of Regional Identity*, Manchester, 1998, 3.

[34] For convenience, the term 'new Cornish Studies' will be adopted here. Payton himself wavered between the descriptions 'new Cornish Studies', 'new Cornish social science' and 'new Cornish historiography'. At the same time, it should be noted that, while Cornish Studies could be defined as including natural sciences such as geology and botany there were no claims from geologists or zoologists to be a part of the 'new Cornish Studies'. So, the latter clearly refers to a project restricted to the humanities and social sciences.

[35] The principal works are Payton, *Making*, 1992 and *Cornwall*, Fowey, 1996. For an early attempt to apply a new Cornish Studies perspective see Bernard Deacon, 'The Cornish Revival: an analysis', unpublished paper, 1986. For a more extended summary of the new Cornish Studies and a retrospect see Chapters 1-4 of Deacon, 2017.

[36] Philip Payton, *ICS Associates Newsletter* 4 (1995), 5 and 'Post-war Cornwall: A suitable case for treatment' in Payton (ed.), 1993, 11-12.

[37] See J.G.A.Pocock, 'British history: A plea for a new subject', *Journal of Modern History* 47 (1975), 601-628 and 'The limits and divisions of British history: In search of an unknown subject', *American Historical Review* 87 (1982), 311-336; Kearney, 1989; Bradshaw and Morrill (eds), 1996.

be written and read'.[38] Within it there may be more space for consideration of Cornwall's contribution to British diversity, as one of the 'five peoples' of these islands, although, as I have pointed out above, the actual production of the New British History reserves a disappointingly small space for Cornwall.

Second, new Cornish Studies was concerned with issues of diversity and difference. For Payton, it was propelled by a concern to explain Cornish difference: 'when all is said and done it is this Cornish "difference" that is at root the raison d'être of Cornish Studies as an area of academic inquiry'. But this is a 'difference' that exists not in 'parochial isolation' but is 'an integral part of that wider pattern of European cultural and territorial diversity'.[39] Specifically, this concern raises questions about identity formation, questions central to this book.

However, in concentrating on 'difference', the new Cornish Studies displayed its continuity with the 'old'. At one level, to assert that Cornwall is different is a truism. All places are 'different'; they are all products of unique histories interacting with general social processes. Moreover, in some ways all places also have similarities with some other places. Therefore, a focus on difference could be read as a continuation of the 'local patriotism' of the old Cornish Studies. The charge levelled at Cornish Studies in the past was that it was over-concerned with its own special case, and as a result concentrated in a narrow fashion on finding empirical proof for 'difference'.[40] The pursuit of 'difference', while a not unexpected response to the 'vanishing Cornwall' trope of much mainstream writing, was too vulnerable to such criticisms of parochialism to be a central foundation for the new Cornish Studies.

If neither a search for 'difference' nor the 'new Cornish historiography' provide a sufficiently robust organising framework for Cornish Studies, then what does? One relevant question to ask is what gives modern Cornwall its unity. As we shall see, in the early nineteenth century that unity was constructed and imagined to a large extent through the domination of metal mining in the regional economy. However, it is not economics that gives Cornwall its unity at the beginning of the twenty-first century. 'Cornwall' is now imagined through the notion of a coherent identity and heritage. The emphasis has therefore shifted from economics to culture. The central concern of Cornish Studies therefore might be representation and culture in the broadest sense.

---

[38] Philip Payton, 'Cornwall in context: The new Cornish historiography', in Philip Payton (ed.), *Cornish Studies Five*, Exeter, 1997, 11.
[39] Payton, *Cornish Studies One*, 1993, 2-3.
[40] Glanville Price, *the Languages of Britain*, London, 1984, 141-142. And see comments of Charles Thomas, *Old Cornwall* 7 (1971), 337-349.

Studying the competing myths of identity and heritage, how they are received, how they relate to people's actual activities and what forces and processes – physical, economic, social, local and global – constrain them and allow for change provides a broader framework for the new Cornish Studies. This arena permits a wide range of social science and humanities studies to be marshalled yet still endows Cornish Studies with a central unifying concern, one close also to cultural studies. The concern of the latter with the diversity of cultures within the British Isles and the limitations of the concept 'British' is an obvious connection.

If a potential organising theme is cultural studies (in the broadest sense) then understanding the changing myths and interpretations of Cornwall requires a greater engagement with concerns about meaning and language. The importance of symbolic, in addition to material, issues in providing insights and in arriving at a fuller understanding of modern Cornwall should be clear. Cornwall, partly because of its attractions for artists and novelists, partly because of the marketing of the tourist industry, and partly because of dominant 'home county' imageries and ideologies, floats in a veritable sea of symbols, buffeted by waves of signifiers and storms of competing meanings. Coming to grips with all this is not just a matter of analysing quantitative data but also requires an interpretative approach that is sensitive to the role of discourse and language. Despite the erosion of its institutional academic base, Cornish Studies is still potentially neatly poised to add to the growing corpus of work on power, place and identity, at the same time generating an understanding of the situation of contemporary Cornwall and deconstructing powerful discourses of place.[41]

Deconstructing discourses of place, for the Cornish Studies practitioner, is not just a theoretical issue. It is now widely recognised that social researchers do not merely discover some pre-existing 'reality' but are themselves implicated, to a lesser or greater extent, in the making of that reality. Scholars are not passive, allegedly neutral observers of the world but instead are 'actively involved in processes of construction and ... always ideologically involved, even when we assert objectivity'.[42] The least the researcher can do is to recognise his or her part in this social construction of reality.

In this respect there is an often understated but distinctively normative basis to Cornish Studies that requires foregrounding. Academics can help to reproduce hegemonic structures of power or, alternatively, they can

---

[41] For more on the practice and potential of the new Cornish Studies see Deacon, 2017.

[42] Peter Jackson and Jan Penrose (eds), *Constructions of Race, Place and Nation*, London, 1993, 9.

challenge them. There is a 'politics of position' to their work. The politics of new Cornish Studies was summarised by Payton in the introduction to his synthesis of Cornish history: 'Until recently, our history has been so often the history of Cornwall without the Cornish people, and it is time that we offered a corrective'.[43] Here, there are echoes of Gwyn Alf Williams' approach to Welsh history or the feminist position that asserts 'the right to name ourselves, to act as subjects rather than objects of history'.[44]

New Cornish Studies set out to put Cornwall into a comparative context and identify the differences from and similarities with other people in other places. By reinterpreting Cornwall and setting out to deconstruct some dominant paradigms of Cornwall it also opened up new possibilities for local actors. It recognised that Cornish Studies was part of a struggle for place. It is part of a discourse that asserts the Cornish no longer wish to be marginalised, casually misrepresented or appropriated for other agendas. Cornish people are not just passive constructions of outside discourses. In contrast, Cornish Studies sets out to challenge the self-definition of centres and dominant discourses of place. It helps to deconstruct cultural sovereignties and is itself part and parcel of the recovery of 'progressive articulations of place and the politics of identity'.[45]

Restating the major themes

The new Cornish Studies thus provides the ontological basis for this book, while the definition of identity advanced in Chapter 1 gave us a framework for the study of late eighteenth-century and nineteenth-century Cornwall. We saw there how the five general elements of identity formation – integration, distinction, process, narrative and context – are all present in territorial identities. Integration concerns those elements that bind groups together, distinction those that set them apart. These may be economic, social or cultural activities, such as occupations, religion or dialect. These can and will be described and their spatial distributions mapped and discussed. But integration and distinction, in relation to identity, are primarily imagined. An occupation or religious affiliation only becomes part of a collective identity when it is woven into the memories of individuals and when those individuals

---

[43] Philip Payton, *Cornwall*, Fowey, 1996, vi.
[44] Geraint Jenkins, *The People's Historian: Professor Gwyn A.Williams (1925-1995)*, Aberystwyth, 1996, 7.
[45] Michael Keith and Steve Pile (eds), *Place and the Politics of Identity*, London, 1993, 225.

equate the activity with themselves via a desired identity. This implies that studying identity is not just a matter of isolating activities. It also involves looking at issues of process and narrative. Anssi Paasi's model of the regionalisation process provides a handy set of concepts for thinking through the former and this will be used, not in a prescriptive way, but as a series of signposts to help us recover the reproduction of the Cornish identity in the late eighteenth and the nineteenth centuries. To investigate narrative, we will have to investigate the discourse of Cornishness and, at least in a preliminary way, begin to unravel the way it appealed to men and women in Cornwall in this period.

Identities and the discourses that lie at their heart do not exist and are not created in a vacuum. They are in turn constrained by wider processes and structures. In short, all identities have a context, a specific spatial and temporal combination that sets limits on them and yet provides opportunities for their reception, negotiation and reproduction. Therefore, studying the Cornish identity involves placing it into its wider context, and putting Cornwall into a comparative context.

Finally, territorial identities have one extra dimension, that of scale. In relation to scale all too often Cornwall and the Cornish identity seem to disappear down a conceptual and historiographical crevasse, neither a region nor a nation. Writers on nationalism prefer to see Cornwall as a region, albeit a region where 'the Cornish are fortunate to be able to paint their regional discontents in the attractive colours of Celtic tradition, which makes them so much more viable, even though it leads some of them to reinvent a language not spoken for 200 years' [sic].[46] Conversely, other observers equate Cornwall uncritically with the older nations of Europe. According to Townsend and Taylor this was the reason why, in the 1970s, 'Ulster, Scotland, Wales and perhaps Cornwall command greater attention than English industrial areas'.[47] The relevant point here is that Taylor and Townsend do not unequivocally see Cornwall as a region; for them it is more like a nation.[48]

While conceptually indistinct, 'Cornwall' also has temporal gaps. As I have argued in this chapter, hitherto the historical focus has been on the medieval and the modern, pre 1650 or post 1870. The period between these dates contains its own academic semantic vacuum, because it is

---

[46] Eric Hobsbawm, *Nations and Nationalism since 1780*, Cambridge, 1992, 178.

[47] A.R.Townsend and C.C.Taylor, 'Regional culture and identity in industrialized societies: the case of north-east England', *Regional Studies* 9 (1975), 379.

[48] For a more detailed account of this conceptual ambiguity see Bernard Deacon, 'County, nation, ethnic group? The shaping of the Cornish identity', *International Journal of Regional and Local Studies* 3 (2007), 5-29.

both more and, at the same time, less familiar than the periods before and after. More familiar in that Cornwall appears to share a general experience of industrialisation. Less familiar because the particular features of that industrialisation are not widely understood. As a result, these years come to be seen as merely a 'prelude' to something else, a period when industrialisation produced a steady acceleration in cultural integration. Cornwall's 'most vital period' becomes 'also the period when it was most like England'.[49]

The argument advanced here is that this fundamentally misrepresents the cultural history of Cornwall in its industrial period. It has been suggested that the Cornish identity as it had emerged by the late nineteenth century was marked by hybridity in more than the obvious sense of being heterogeneous like all identities.[50] Cornwall was a proto-region, almost, but not quite, engendering a clear regional consciousness along the lines of the industrial regions studied by Langton and Hudson. But it was also a proto-nation, with a history of separate ethnicity that provided the raw materials for a nationalist re-invention after the 1890s. To understand the complexity of the hybrid modern Cornish identity, therefore, we have to investigate the institutionalisation of the Cornish region in the period between the 1760s and the 1860s. This period was critical for the emergence of a popular sense of spatial identity based on the entirety of Cornwall. This had been produced by the third quarter of the nineteenth century and it continued to reproduce itself, although not in isolation, into the later decades of the twentieth century.

The chapters that follow begin by unpacking aspects of the identity of Cornwall and its people in this period. We then identify some of the institutions and groups involved in the production of regional identity before moving on to the economic context. Finally, we turn to the less formal social institutions of community, workplace and chapel and the way they intersected with identity formation.

---

[49] Jane Korey, 'As we belong to be: The ethnic movement in Cornwall, England', unpublished PhD thesis, Brandeis University, 1992, 25.

[50] Bernard Deacon, 'Proto-regionalisation: the case of Cornwall', *Journal of Regional and Local Studies*, 18 (1998), 27-41.

Chapter Three
Images of Cornwall and its people

In this and the following chapter we explore some narratives about Cornwall and its people. These helped to construct both the distinction and the integration central to identity claims. Following Anssi Paasi, the imaginations of Cornwall and its people that had emerged by the early nineteenth century can be seen as part of the symbolic shaping of the region.[1] The emphasis of this chapter is on the identity of the territory and on those narratives, symbols and images associated with Cornwall. After briefly reviewing some historical and anthropological approaches to Cornish identity I re-assert the role of social context in the production of representations of Cornwall. I then review in turn perspectives on Cornish landscapes, discourses of industrialisation and the role of the Cornish language and dialect in the production of new symbols of distinctiveness in the first half of the nineteenth century.

When they did occur, towards the end of the twentieth century, accounts of Cornwall and the Cornish identity tended to focus on the period after the 1860s when railways, artistic fashions and tourism brought the English intelligentsia face to face with Cornwall.[2] The period before the 1870s, in contrast, remained obscure and ignored. For example, James Vernon, in an otherwise perceptive contribution, makes no mention of mining, Cornwall's dominant industry before the 1870s.[3] Dazzled by the semantics accompanying the meta-narrative of late nineteenth century cultural re-positioning, such writers stumble backwards into the earlier nineteenth century with a severely impaired vision. The result is that they tell us little about how Cornwall was imagined by its own inhabitants in the early part of the nineteenth century. But, seen from the inside, this is precisely the critical period that

---

[1] Anssi Paasi, 'Europe as a social process and discourse: considerations of place, boundaries and identity', *European Urban and Regional Studies* 8 (2001), 17.
[2] Philip Dodd, 'Englishness and the national culture', in Robert Colls and Philip Dodd, (eds), *Englishness: Politics and Culture 1880-1920*, London, 1986, 14-15.
[3] James Vernon, 'Border crossings: Cornwall and the English imagi(nation)', in Geoffrey Cubitt (ed.), *Imagining Nations*, Manchester, 1998, 153-172.

requires analysis, those years during which a popular sense of Cornish identity was being re-moulded. That re-fashioning created a sense of self which melded with more general aspects of regional British working-class cultures in the late nineteenth and early twentieth centuries to produce what has been termed the 'classic' Cornish identity. This persisted, albeit residually, well into the late twentieth century, and helps explain aspects of the contemporary Cornish condition.[4]

'Mainstream', language-centred accounts of late nineteenth century Cornwall neither offer a description or explanation of the sense of territorial identity extant during Cornwall's industrial period before the 1870s. In contrast, materialist perspectives produce suggestions more relevant to this period. John Langton claims a new kind of mass regional consciousness began to take shape in the 'new' industrial regions after the 1760s.[5] Nevertheless, as we saw in chapter 1, writers on emergent eighteenth-century industrial regions do not expand very far on the link between industrialisation and territorial identity.[6] In particular, neither economic historians nor historical geographers have explained the way such identities were imagined, reproduced or contested. Moreover, in a direct contrast with idealist accounts, the impression is conveyed that territorial identities in the industrial regions were constructed entirely by insiders.

Language and social contexts
As the work of postmodern social historians suggests, social identities cannot simply be 'read off' from social structures. However, we should also avoid a mirror image cultural 'reductionism'. So, meanings cannot also be entirely unstable, entirely autonomous. Just as language itself is a structure, with rules and continuities, so the imaginations that make up social identities exist within a structure of meanings. Meanings are 'negotiated, contested and maintained or transformed' by social

---

[4] Bernard Deacon, 'And shall Trelawny die? The Cornish identity', in Philip Payton (ed.), *Cornwall Since the War*, Redruth, 1993, 200-223; Bernard Deacon and Philip Payton, 'Re-inventing Cornwall: Culture change on the European periphery', in Philip Payton (ed.), *Cornish Studies One*, Exeter, 62-79. The best account can be found in Neil Kennedy, *Cornish Solidarity: Using Culture to Strengthen Communities*, Portlaoise, 2016, 98-107.
[5] John Langton, 'The industrial revolution and the regional geography of England', *Transactions of the Institute of British Geographers* NS9 (1984), 155-162.
[6] See Pat Hudson, 'The regional perspective', in Pat Hudson (ed.), *Regions and Industries: A Perspective on the Industrial Revolution in Britain*, Cambridge, 1989, 5-38.

processes. The plurality of meanings is finite, interpretations being 'constructed by interpretative communities ... most interpretations will be constrained to some degree by their relation to that which is interpreted'.[7] Such imaginations of place therefore cannot exist entirely independently of historical, social and political processes.

In the Cornish context, as elsewhere, the content and form of dominant or hegemonic representations of place and people are constrained by certain social parameters. Of course, these parameters are not confined to Cornwall itself. Indeed, representations of Cornwall can be and were produced outside Cornwall and may in that case owe much more to cultural processes and pressures being worked out elsewhere. This possibility of simultaneous insider and outsider production of images is recognised by Paasi. He divides the identity of a region into two parts, the 'subjective' images held by the inhabitants, demarcating their place from others, and the 'objective' images held by outsiders, classifying regions in broader social consciousness. Both insider and outsider, internal and external images are essential parts of the dynamic process of regional identity creation and reproduction.[8] This might seem to provide us with a possible classification of place images. However, insider and outsider representations overlapped and intertwined so considerably in Cornwall that this proves to be an unworkable division. The description of outsider images as 'objective' also carries a debatable implication and implies an unwarrantable distinction between 'insider' and 'outsider' views.

We should also note the danger that the demands of a linear text constrain and seriously over-simplify the shifting web of identity. In particular, Paasi emphasises that identities cannot exist independently of institutions and these institutions emerge and change in parallel with the content of identities.[9] Nevertheless, we will confine this section to an identification of aspects of the identity of Cornwall and will leave the institutions that reproduce them for later consideration.

Landscapes: symbols of place
Agents from outside Cornwall have always, in the modern period, heavily influenced images of Cornwall. Cornwall's place on the

---

[7] James and N. Duncan, '(Re)reading the landscape', *Environment and Planning D* 6 (1988), 119-120.

[8] Anssi Paasi, 'The institutionalization of regions: a theoretical framework for understanding the emergence of regions and the constitution of regional identity', *Fennia* 164 (1986), 133.

[9] Paasi, 1986, 125.

periphery of England and its fascination for members of the literate, metropolitan classes has led to an avalanche of works on its special character, its mystique and its attractions. In this deluge, representations of the landscape have been of major importance and, for these reasons, outsiders have articulated some dominant views about the Cornish landscape.[10]

Traditional academic approaches to landscapes saw them as 'expressions of material culture'; landscapes were the result of human endeavour as different economic needs resulted in their own unique landscapes.[11] This approach to landscapes as material products, however, ignored their symbolic aspects. Landscapes are, indeed, created by productive forces, but they also have meanings for people and are interpreted within shifting cultural norms and fashions. They are thus symbolic as well as material. Landscapes can be seen as visual expressions of identity, certain landscapes acting as the symbols of particular places.

For example, the importance of rural landscapes to notions of Englishness is now well recognised. During the later eighteenth century a taste for the picturesque and a fashion for landscape gardening helped to establish a dominant vision of the countryside, producing what Wendy Darby terms 'unpeopled landscapes'.[12] Wild picturesque nature gave way during the early nineteenth century to tamed and ordered pastoral landscapes, arboreal, small scale and neat, producing a dominant domesticated 'south country' image of the English countryside for the twentieth century.[13] As these images continue to be institutionalised and commercialised through the activities of English Heritage, the National Trust and the mushrooming garden centres of suburbia 'nowhere else (than in England)', in David Lowenthal's words, 'is landscape so freighted as legacy'[14]

---

[10] Ella Westland (ed.), *Cornwall: The Cultural Construction of Place*, Penzance, 1997.

[11] Alan Baker, 'Introduction: on ideology and landscape', in Alan Baker and Gideon Biger (eds), *Ideology and Landscape in Historical Perspective*, Cambridge, 1992, 6-7.

[12] Wendy Darby, *Landscape and Identity: Geographies of Nation and Class in England*, Oxford, 2000.

[13] Stephen Daniels, *Fields of Vision: Landscape Imagery and National Identity in England and the United States*, Cambridge, 1993. See also David Matless, 'Definitions of England, 1928-89: preservation, modernism and the nature of the nation', *Built Environment* 16 (1990), 179-191.

[14] David Lowenthal, 'European and English landscapes as national symbols', in David Hooson (ed.), *Geography and National Identity*, Oxford, 1994, 20.

The recognition that landscapes are symbolic led to complex new approaches to them, part of a more humanistic approach within the social sciences. Various metaphors have been employed to make sense of landscape, from icebergs to theatre to dance.[15] One of the more credible is the metaphor of landscape as text, something that is read and through which meanings are produced.[16] In addition, landscapes encode certain, usually dominant, ideologies, making them concrete. Thus, their reception and decoding can be seen as part of an inherently political process linked to power. 'Whether examined as forms of discourse, representations or physical reality, landscape and territory are embedded in relations of power and knowledge'.[17]

If we adopt the metaphor of landscape as text, at least three readings of the Cornish landscape may be discerned around the beginning of the nineteenth century. First there was a landscape of power. It was the landscape of ordered design, parks and country houses, symbols of landownership and wealth. This was the landscape within which travellers and visitors moved and inside which the local gentry spent a large proportion of their lives. The Cornish landed gentry may not have been so thick on the ground as in the south east of England but there was still a visible landscape of power stretched across Cornwall, protected behind its park walls and its plantations. This landscape sometimes starkly contrasted with surrounding industrial landscapes, as at Clowance in Crowan or Tehidy at Illogan.

A second reading was the landscape of nature, one influenced by romantic readings of the countryside as a primitive and timeless arcadia, read in opposition to the growing presence of urbanisation and industrialisation.[18] This can be illustrated by early guidebooks with their references to places such as Land's End or Kynance Cove: wild, picturesque places usually on the coast. A good example of this reading is presented by Cyrus Redding's *Illustrated Itinerary of the County of Cornwall*, published in 1842. Interestingly, Redding was an insider, originally from Truro. He wrote of the 'charm of some of the most romantic and sublime scenery in the Empire. Cornwall is the land of the wild, the picturesque and the imaginative'.[19] However, while this was later to become the dominant representation of Cornwall, it was

---

[15] See Baker, 1992, 8-9.
[16] Duncan and Duncan, 1988.
[17] Darby, 2000, 15.
[18] Daniels, 1993.
[19] Cyrus Redding, *Illustrated Itinerary of the County of Cornwall*, London, 1842, 3. For an earlier example see John Paris, *A Guide to Mounts Bay*, Penzance, 1816.

relatively subdued in the early nineteenth century and competed with another reading.

In contrast to this romantic reading, for many visitors in the eighteenth and early nineteenth centuries Cornwall seemed a dismal place. Caesar Thomas Gooch wrote back to his family in Norfolk in 1754:

> I have now seen a great deal of Cornwall and think it upon the whole a dismal country to live in ... the inland dwellings are a vast distance from neighbours, everywhere surrounded with rocky mountains, and the prospects chiefly over barren lands.[20]

Later in the same century, another East Anglian visitor, Thomas Preston, summed up the country from Bodmin to Truro as 'the most dreary possible, a complete moor with scarce a dwelling visible, you may travel for miles over a swamp and see nothing but a few men at work at what is called "stream work"'.[21] While inland Cornwall seemed to be a desolate waste, the fishing villages on the coast were to be avoided as far as possible. John Wesley found their attractions marred by 'the perfume' of pilchards and conger-eels.[22] Before the 1820s the dominant reading of the Cornish landscape was not that of the picturesque despite the emergence of Romanticism.

Perhaps the most striking example is provided by William Gilpin who, in the 1780s, had been a key figure in popularising the picturesque aesthetic in relation to mountain scenery in Wales, the English Lake District and the Scottish Highlands.[23] On one of his last tours, travelling through western England around 1800, he reached Launceston Castle and found it 'picturesque'. However, twenty miles further into Cornwall, having crossed the 'coarse, naked country' of Bodmin Moor, Gilpin decided to turn back to Devon instead of continuing to the Land's End, as was his original intention. 'To travel over deserts of dreariness in quest of two or three objects seemed to be buying them at too high a price; especially as it is possible they might have disappointed in the end'. Instead of the 'picturesque', Gilpin had discovered a landscape that was 'heavy, unbroken and unaccommodating', one where the views 'wanted the most necessary appendages of landscape, wood and water, but even form'.[24] The words of the Reverend Richard Warner echo this representation of the Cornish landscape current at the turn of the

---

[20] Caesar Gooch, 'A journey to Cornwall in 1754', *Old Cornwall* 6 (1962), 58-61.
[21] Thomas Preston, 'A Cornish tour', *Old Cornwall* 7 (1972), 481-490.
[22] John Wesley, *Journal*, London, 1864, 327.
[23] Darby, 2000, 60.
[24] William Gilpin, *Observations on the Western Parts of England*, London, 1808, 190-197.

nineteenth century; 'however valuable it may be in a commercial point of view, it can offer no claim to the praise of the picturesque or beautiful'.[25]

A further reading becomes, therefore, the most relevant in the present context. This was the landscape of industrialisation. In stark contrast to the emerging view of pastoral rurality in south-east England, the most commonly remarked landscape features of Cornwall were created by its industry. (While landscapes of nature and industrialisation are identified as separate representations here there was clearly an overlap; descriptions of the industrial landscape were more than often couched in the language of romanticism, as we shall see below.)

On a visit in the 1760s Thomas Kitchen observed that 'as the county abounds in mines, the air is filled with mineral vapours'.[26] In fact, at the time Kitchen was writing, Cornwall as a whole did not 'abound in mines'. Mining in the 1760s was still relatively localised; the bulk of copper ore production was accounted for by just seven parishes from Gwennap in the east to Gwinear in the west and John Rowe has claimed that 'practically the entire (copper) mining region was within eight miles of the summit of Carn Brea'.[27] While it must be noted that tin mining was more widely spread, until the last decades of the eighteenth century there was not much underground mining east of Truro. But, although the mining landscape was confined to only a part of its territory, Cornwall was already being represented by mining, the dynamic factor in its landscape.

This was because the mining districts of Cornwall imprinted on outsiders their most vivid impressions. An intrepid visitor to Redruth in the 1790s found that 'it is in a cloud of smoke, which was the reason we did not breakfast'.[28] In the same decade William Maton described the appearance of the sand dunes near Hayle as 'truly dismal. The immense volumes of smoke that roll over it, proceeding from the copper houses, increase its cheerless effect, while the hollow jarring of the distant steam engines remind us of the labours of the Cyclops in the entrails of Mt. Etna'.[29] The volcanic metaphor also crops up in the writings of Warner.

---

[25] Richard Warner, *A Tour through Cornwall in the Autumn of 1808*, London, 1809, 346.

[26] Thomas Kitchen, *England Illustrated: Cornwall*, London, 1764, 89.

[27] John Rowe, *Cornwall in the Age of the Industrial Revolution*, Liverpool, 1953, 66.

[28] Cited in I.D.Spreadbury, *Impressions of the Old Duchy: Book 1, through Cornwall by Coach*, Mevagissey, 1971, 11.

[29] William Maton, *Observations on the Western Counties of England VI*, Salisbury, 1797, 235.

Travelling on the edge of the mining country to the north west of Penryn, he described it as 'a district filled with extinguished volcanoes, which, having exhausted their fury, could now only be traced in the universal desolation they had occasioned'. For Warner, this was the 'remarkable feature of Cornwall'.[30] These landscapes of fire fascinated the visitor unused to the impact of industrialisation. 'The dismal scene of whims, suffering mules, and hillocks of cinders, extends for miles. Huge iron engines, creaking and groaning, invented by Watt, and tall chimneys, smoking and fuming, that seem to belong to 'Old Nicholas's' abode, diversify the prospect', wrote a visitor to the Consolidated Mines at Gwennap during the 1790s.[31] It was the mining landscape that, for outsiders, made Cornwall different. One jaded traveller, George Lipscomb, who meandered across southern England in the 1790s, in an increasingly frustrated search for the 'interesting', finally found it at Polgooth Mine near St Austell: 'Now we had arrived at a spot which was truly interesting - at a kind of new country of which we had previously formed no tolerable idea'.[32] Here, finally, for him was a landscape markedly different from those to the east.

The significance of the mining landscape was that it then coloured representations of Cornwall as a whole. As early as the 1760s the dominant representation of Cornwall was being derived from its mining sector. As this representation strengthened its hold on later writers, they went further, interpreting the non-mining landscapes of Cornwall in the light of its mining landscapes. When William Maton was still in the 'bleak country' between Looe and Fowey in the 1790s he began to fancy himself 'already arrived in the mining country, and that we had bid adieu to fertility and picturesque beauty'.[33] In a similar fashion, Robert Fraser, in his *General View of the County of Cornwall* (1794), prepared for the Board of Agriculture, discussed the mines of Cornwall before what was intended to be the substantive subject of his treatise, farming. For him it was the mines, 'to which so great a part of its capital and industry is directed' that were central for understanding late eighteenth-century Cornwall.[34] The farmer, by the 1790s, played second fiddle to the miner in representations of Cornwall. It was the industrial landscape that most impressed outsiders, at a time when industrial society was transforming the lives of insiders.

---

[30] Warner, 1809, 106.
[31] *Mining Journal*, 22 February 1840.
[32] George Lipscomb, *A Journey into Cornwall*, Warwick, 1799, 249.
[33] Maton, 1797, 137.
[34] Robert Fraser, *General View of the County of Cornwall*, London, 1794, 14.

So far, I have identified an all-pervasive landscape of industrialisation that outsiders were, by the 1820s, finding it impossible to ignore. To a considerable extent, as we shall see below, this imagery mirrored dominant insider representations of Cornwall in its industrial period and marked a convergence of outsider and insider imageries. However, there is another landscape reading, a more restricted native reading, the landscape of Cornishness. The spectacular results of industrialisation were a part of this landscape but in a more intimate and less escapable way. In the mining districts the people were living their lives in what was described in 1855 as:

> a hungry landscape, everywhere deformed by small mountains of many-coloured refuse; traversed in narrow paths and winding roads, by streams of foul water, by screaming locomotives with hurrying trains; white wheels and whims, and miles of pumping rods, whirling and vibrating, and the forest of tall beams, make up an astonishing maze of machinery and motion.[35]

This landscape of Cornishness included more elements than just the artefacts of industry. For instance, it would also have 'seen' the grid of small chapels that had been superimposed on the Church of England's parochial geography between the 1740s and the 1840s. Along with the chapels, often isolated and serving a dispersed rural population, were the settlements of that population - scattered towns, villages, hamlets and single cottages with no clear urban focus. Around these settlements were the small fields comprising the holdings rented by miners. And interspersed with these elements were the engine houses and the burrows of the mining industry. The prime motif of this landscape was a decentralised, even egalitarian, aspect; a rural-industrial network itself reflecting the complex ties of community, work and kinship that bound together industrial Cornwall. These settlement features, moreover, were not confined merely to industrial communities. This was the landscape that insiders 'saw', a landscape that was a product of their endeavour, a distinct cultural landscape and a symbol of 'Cornwall'.[36]

---

[35] Cited in Paul Newman, *The Meads of Love: The Life and Poetry of John Harris,* Redruth, 1994, 27.

[36] This landscape is familiar from the pages of late nineteenth century Cornish novelists such as H.D.Lowry, *Wreckers and Methodists,* London, 1893 and *Wheal Darkness,* London, 1906 and in early twentieth century texts such as Lawrence Maker, *Cob and Moorstone: The Curious History of some Cornish Methodist Churches,* London, 1935 and Jack Clemo, *Wilding Graft,* London, 1948.

'A peculiar people': discourses of differentiation
We can turn from the way in which the Cornish saw their landscape to images of the Cornish people. Two non-native voices provide a window into Cornish self-representations. In 1877 Bishop Benson, relatively recently installed as bishop of the new Cornish diocese, wrote, with a hint of irritation, 'the Cornish are never weary of saying, "Since they are a most peculiar people": it is quite the truest thing which I have heard them say'.[37] In fact, one of the main claims made during the long campaign for a separate diocese for Cornwall, a campaign that began in the 1840s, was that the Cornish were in a 'peculiar and very interesting condition', because of their reliance on mining and fishing. This 'renders them an independent, and intelligent, and a self-relying people'.[38] It was not just clerics who were using this discourse by the 1850s. Herman Merivale, a barrister who had acted as Recorder at Penzance, Falmouth and Helston in the 1840s, and who was later to become Under-Secretary of State for India (in 1859) wrote of the 'the profound attachment professed for it (Cornwall) by its own children'.[39]

So, we have a population that apparently saw themselves as different and combined this with an attachment to 'Cornwall'. But how did they and others represent this Cornwall? One possibility was 'West Barbary', a lurid and dramatic place populated by food rioters and heavy-drinking roisterers who lived most of their lives underground. A.K.Hamilton Jenkin reported one visitor from London in 1775 as writing that the 'natives' of Cornwall were happiest when:

> they can sit down to a furze blaze, wringing their shirts and pouring the mud and water out of their boots. But the common people here are very strange kind of beings, half savages at the best. Many thousands of them live entirely underground, where they burrow and breed like rabbits. They are as rough as bears, selfish as swine, obstinate as mules, and hard as the native iron.[40]

Such representations went on to claim that in their spare time these troglodytes sallied forth to lure innocent mariners onto the rocks of their inhospitable land. In this representation of a primitive periphery by someone from the civilised centre we have Cornwall as 'the Other', populated by a barbarian and uncouth tribe of people, who exhibited characteristics diametrically opposed to those doing the labelling. In any

---

[37] Cited by P.S.Morrish, 'History, Celticism and propaganda in the formation of the Diocese of Truro', *Southern History* 5 (1983), 256.
[38] Morrish, 1983, 246-247.
[39] Herman Merivale, 'Cornwall', *The Quarterly Review* 102 (1857), 289.
[40] A.K.Hamilton Jenkin, 'Cornish mines and miners', *Old Cornwall* 1 (1925), 13.

case, by the final decades of the eighteenth century another contrasting representation was fast emerging.

In the 1760s the visitor Thomas Kitchen identified three 'peculiarities' distinguishing the inhabitants of Cornwall 'from those of other counties'. These were their 'former' [sic] language, their sports of wrestling and hurling and their 'tinners'. These latter were 'in many respects a community distinct from the other inhabitants of the County'.[41] This was echoed later by Lipscomb, who focused in the 1790s on the miners as:

> a race of men distinct from the common class of British subjects; they are governed by laws and customs almost exclusively their own ... they are separated from the manners of modern improvement, and resemble the primitive possessors of an uncultivated soil, rather than kindred brethren of a great and enlightened nation.[42]

Clearly, Lipscomb was leaning towards a West Barbary imagery here. But his view of the miners as a distinct class was supported by Warner in 1808:

> We observed a few circumstances in their character as a body, which appeared to distinguish them from all other tribes of workmen that had fallen under our notice. These peculiarities naturally arise from the nature of their employment, which is altogether unlike that of the labouring classes in general throughout the kingdom.[43]

Cornwall's industrialisation provided a context for presenting its people and others with new representations of the Cornish people. In its new role as one of the leading centres of late eighteenth century capitalism, Cornwall could be dressed in new imageries. Insiders such as William Pryce, a Redruth surgeon, were clearly mesmerised by deep metal mining. Claiming that Cornwall produced 'more tin in one year than Devonshire has done in half a century', he proceeded to argue in 1778 that 'this little province of Great Britain deserves to be ranked amongst the first principles of this island, as a nation and people whose very name ... is derived from Bratanack, which signifies the Land of Tin [sic]'.[44] The publication of Pryce's *Mineralogia Cornubiensis* was itself a tribute to the role of mining in late eighteenth century Cornwall. By the 1820s mining had suffused the whole of Cornish society. According to Thomas Preston, by 1821:

---

[41] Kitchen, 1764, 107-108.
[42] Lipscomb, 1799, 262.
[43] Warner, 1809, 297.
[44] William Pryce, *Mineralogia Cornubiensis: A Treatise on Minerals, Mines and Mining*, London, 1778, preface.

the mines of Cornwall occupy the attention of the principal inhabitants. As you advance to the west, so you hear them more and more talked about till you arrive at Truro; there their whole ideas are immersed in the value of the shares of such and such a mine; if you go to Redruth, then it is the weight of a piece of ore or the quality of what was raised or dug up yesterday.[45]

Even the efficiency of steam engines was of sufficient interest to warrant its own newspaper (*Lean's Engine Reporter*) from 1811, devoted to detailing the duties achieved.

In the late eighteenth century, therefore, transfixed by the experience of industrialisation, the preferred local myth became one of progress from darkness to light, from 'West Barbary' to 'Industrial Civilisation'.[46] This narrative of achievement both fitted the rationalist, science-based discourses of technical progress that were dominant in industrialising Cornwall and was encouraged by Wesleyan Methodism, which claimed for itself the credit for this moral revolution (see chapter 9 below).

At first sight, the adoption of such a myth would seem to be the opposite of a 'discourse of differentiation'. After all, industrial civilisation was a generalised representation and one that could be applied to several other regions. In addition, the social upheavals that accompanied it seemed to many observers to be erasing old customs and producing uniformity. Nevertheless, the way the global process of industrialisation was experienced in Cornwall was itself interpreted as part of a local discourse of differentiation. Conscious attempts to create this discourse had already appeared in Cornwall by the 1820s. Industrialisation and the change to 'Industrial Civilisation' had produced its own 'peculiarities' – not so dramatic as those representations of the peoples of the western periphery as West Barbary perhaps, but 'peculiarities' that were used as a representation of the group and a basis for self-identification.

Three main elements were involved in this representation of 'industrial civilisation'. First, the Cornish were 'independent'. Independence was an attribute ascribed generally to industrial populations and prized by working class communities. Aspects of pre-modern local society may have especially reinforced this representation in Cornwall. John Hatcher showed how a lack of manorialism, the influence of the political institution of the Duchy, conventionary leasehold tenures, and the tinning industry had combined to produce an independent and mobile tenant

---

[45] Preston, 1972, 489.
[46] For the culture of industrialisation in Cornwall see Philip Payton, *The Making of Modern Cornwall*, Redruth, 1992, 77 and A.C.Todd, *Beyond the Blaze; A Biography of Davies Gilbert*, Truro, 1967.

farming class as early as the fourteenth century.[47] This tradition of an independent tinner-farmer group was reinforced in west Cornwall by early industrialisation which may have led to greater sub-division of holdings as the population grew.[48] Some access to land continued as wastes were cultivated in smallholdings let out on the three life leasehold system, a factor that, together with other collateral aids, removed a proportion of labour from total dependence on market relations in the workplace.[49] These powerful enabling factors helped reproduce the myth of independence. Moreover, that myth is best seen as an ideological process, partly because independence was generalised to include the Cornish as a group (whether or not there was access to land); and partly because it was naturalised.

> Among the prevailing propensities of the Cornish, there are some striking features in their character, which seem to arise from their natural courage, and from that proud spirit of independence, which no revolution, either in politics or morals, has hitherto been wholly able to subdue ... their spirit of independence not only pervades their general actions, but it enters into their various views, and incorporates itself with their conflicting opinions.[50]

Indeed, 'independence', with two other aspects - 'combination' and 'enterprise' - had come together to make up a coherent ideology of 'the Cornish as industrial civilisation' by the 1820s.

Independence could also be expressed as individualism, producing a 'promptitude of decision, which frequently degenerates into obstinacy, that among the lower orders sometimes terminates in quarrels, and among those who can bear the charges, in tedious and expensive litigation'.[51] Methodist secessions and sectarianism after 1815, disagreements over proposed railway routes in the 1840s, the rivalry and competition between the small Cornish towns and the absence of trade unions could be and have been all interpreted as consequences of this

---

[47] John Hatcher, *Rural Economy and Society in the Duchy of Cornwall 1300-1500*, Cambridge, 1970, 52, 60-61, 70, 220 and 'Non-manorialism in medieval Cornwall', *Agricultural History Review* 18 (1970), 1-16.

[48] David Cullum, 'Society and economy in west Cornwall, c.1588-1921', unpublished PhD thesis, University of Exeter, 1993.

[49] See Damaris Rose, 'Home ownership, subsistence and historical change: The mining district of west Cornwall in the late nineteenth century', in Nigel Thrift and Peter Williams (eds), *Class and Space: The making of an Urban Society*, London, 1987, 108-153 and below, chapter 8.

[50] Fortescue Hitchins and Samuel Drew, *The History of Cornwall*, Helston, 1824, 710.

[51] Hitchins and Drew, 1824, 710.

individualism. 'Never was a small people more curiously and readily divisible into factions, or more disinclined (we are sorry to say it) to really useful co-operation'.[52] However, the individualist side of the independence coin received more emphasis at the end of the nineteenth and into the twentieth centuries when it became a convenient scapegoat for the difficulties caused by de-industrialisation.[53]

In contrast, any tendency to individualism in the early nineteenth century was tempered by the second component in the ideology of the Cornish as industrial civilisation - a willingness to combine. The motto 'One and All' was already in common use by the 1820s. By the 1850s it was being described as 'the watch word and battle cry of the Cornish ... of great antiquity'.[54] A 'conspicuous' feature of the Cornish, according to Samuel Drew, was the:

> warmth and ardour with which they undertake an enterprise, and persevere in its prosecution. Accustomed to associate in bodies, they mutually encourage each other to perseverance, even on occasions when all rational hopes of success have taken their leave. Hence 'One and All', accompanied with three huzzas, will ... infallibly reanimate their drooping spirits, in the midst of a doubtful exploit.[55]

Merivale also noticed what he called a 'spirit of aggregation', which 'rather finds a vent in camp-meetings, temperance parties and monster tea drinkings'. Merivale again notes how this aggregation was marked by a 'tendency to the enthusiastic', echoing the insider Samuel Drew's 'warmth and ardour'.[56] The revivalist aspect of Cornish Methodism was here helping to underpin this representation of enthusiastic combination.

Myths of 'independence' and 'one and all' combined with a third component, 'enterprise', to make up the trilogy of the industrial ideology of Cornishness that had appeared by the 1820s. 'Few', argued Drew, 'are more active, more enterprising, or more persevering' than the Cornish.[57] This 'restless aspiration after change' had made 'the Cornishman one of the most locomotive of mankind', wrote Merivale, attributing the emigration patterns of the Cornish to their enterprise.[58] Here we have the representation of Cornish emigration as that 'high point of Cornish

---

[52] Merivale, 1857, 311.
[53] See for example A.K.Hamilton Jenkin, *The Cornish Miner*, London, 1927.
[54] Roger Burt (ed.), *Cornwall's Mines and Miners: Nineteenth Century Studies by George Henwood*, Truro, 1972, 231.
[55] Hitchins and Drew, 1824, 711.
[56] Merivale, 1857, 311.
[57] Hitchins and Drew, 1824, 708.
[58] Merivale, 1857, 317.

achievement' that Philip Payton has noted.[59] George Henwood, Cornish mine captain and *Mining Journal* correspondent in the late 1850s, neatly combined enterprise, emigration and Cornish pride:

> The Cornish are remarkable for their sanguine temperament, their indomitable perseverance, their ardent hope in adventure, and their desire for discovery and novelty; hence their wide distribution all over the world, in the most remote corners of which they are to be found amongst the pioneers; and to this very cause has science to boast of so many brilliant ornaments who claim Cornwall as their birthplace.[60]

It was not just the Cornish who represented themselves in this way. To Warner what was noticeable was the miners' progressive and industrial spirit; the employment relations in the mines 'keeps their spirits in an agreeable agitation, renders their minds lively and alert, and prevents that dullness which generally characterises the English labourer'.[61] Other outsiders echoed this perception. As early as the 1790s Fraser was reporting that 'the people of Cornwall also possess a great degree of perspicacity and acumen; they attend to new improvements; if they find them successful, they are not slow in imitation'.[62] What is also noticeable here is that the qualities of the mining population were being extended to the whole population, just as the landscape of industrialisation was colouring representations of Cornwall as a whole. As the miners were now so large a proportion of the population, the inhabitants of Cornwall generally were considered all to be 'marked by peculiar features of character'. However, though labelled as peculiar, in the sense of being different, these peculiarities were themselves gendered in decidedly familiar ways. Thus, as Warner commented, 'its men are sturdy and bold, honest and sagacious; its women lovely and modest, courteous and unaffected'.[63]

Outsiders, aware of the possible representation of the periphery as barbarian, were inducted quickly into the locally preferable alternative. Joseph Farington seemed slightly relieved and surprised to find in 1810 that, far from having a 'savage character', as he had been led to believe, the Cornish miners were 'civil and obliging and not at all of the description supposed. Lord de Dunstanville said when assembled in bodies they are rough when moved by some occasion, but individually are sufficiently peaceable'.[64] As a result, for most bourgeois visitors as

---

[59] Payton, 1992, 113.
[60] In Burt, 1972, 232.
[61] Warner, 1809, 298.
[62] Fraser, 1794, 13.
[63] Warner, 1809, 348.

well as Methodist insiders, the Cornish working class became paragons of industrialisation, ingenious, inventive, civil, well-mannered and alert. In the account by the conservative commentator J.D.Tuckett in 1846 we find the Cornish miners in particular presenting 'by many degrees the brightest picture we have met with, of the condition of any considerable body of the labouring class in England at the present day'.[65] By the time that J.R.Leifchild visited Cornwall in the early 1850s he could state, without too much fear of contradiction, that 'the Cornish miners hold a high rank amongst English workpeople for their general conduct'.[66] Representations of the miners as a barbarian race of primitives had been exchanged for the equally overdrawn opposite picture. The Cornish miners had metamorphosed into a body that was:

> highly intelligent, compassionate, hospitable, industrious, speculative and brave. Among themselves they use the greatest familiarity, expressing their ideas without flattery or fear. On many occasions their language abounds with lively sallies of poignant wit, and their sarcasms are frequently keen and pointed, without being always low or vulgar. To strangers they are civil in a high degree: being always ready to communicate the information they desire, and sometimes they astonish those with whom they converse, by the promptitude of their replies, and the quickness of their apprehension.[67]

In this representation the beershops, drunken brawls and occasional rioting that continued to be part of life in the mining districts into, at least, the 1840s, faded into the background. These aspects were difficult to interpret as part of 'one of the most orderly and civilised societies in the world', as indeed were the few examples of strike action after the 1840s. As a result, they tended to be conveniently ignored.

Yet, paradoxically, representations of industrial civilisation and narratives of achievement required a point of origin and comparison. The older representation of Cornwall as barbarian 'Other', as West Barbary, was perfectly placed to provide this. In the re-telling of the myth of industrial civilisation in the nineteenth century West Barbary became more barbarian as Industrial Civilisation became more civilised. Without West Barbary Industrial Civilisation could not thrive, so insiders adopted West Barbary in retrospect, embellishing it to re-affirm the alternative to

---

[64] James Greig (ed.), *The Farington Diary, Volume 6*, London, n.d., 133.
[65] J.D.Tuckett, *A History of the Past and Present State of the Labouring Population, Volume 2*, London, 1846, 537.
[66] J.R.Leifchild, *Cornwall: Its Mines and Miners*, London, 1857, 148.
[67] Hitchins and Drew, 1824, 727.

the newly dominant industrial discourse. The image of West Barbary was one constantly referred to by insiders:

> In the scale of intellect, and in the improvements that have been made in the effects which have resulted from mental cultivation, the inhabitants of Cornwall hold out an example worthy of imitation, to those who still affect to call them the barbarians of the west ... a comparative revolution may be said to have been accomplished in the morals and manners of the inhabitants of Cornwall.[68]

One of the best examples of this need for insiders to re-affirm West Barbary as opposition is seen in the vigorous and idiosyncratic writings of Francis Harvey, a Cornishman from Hayle who emigrated to Natal in 1850 and wrote his autobiography in the 1860s. Harvey was a local preacher and an auctioneer who expressed, in forceful language, his sense of Cornishness. Not the least of this was the outrage he aimed at the 'West Barbary' image:

> More monstrous stories of the fearful doings of Cornish wreckers have been manufactured by the 'penny-a-line dreadful accident makers' in one London low newspaper in one winter, than ever really happened in Cornwall since the time when Noah's ark was stranded, ... [In contrast] as to the general relative moral character of Cornish men, amongst whom the too common infamies of inland English counties, such as burglaries, poachings, murders, incendiary burnings, treasonable irruptions have not been known, it is indeed a matter of just pride to be a Cornishman![69]

Old traditions, new peculiarities
Industrial virtues were only part of the emerging discourse of Cornish 'peculiarity' in the early nineteenth century. The local literate classes were casting around for other 'peculiarities', ones that were less bound to the social relations created by industrialisation. For, as well as creating new, albeit subtle, differences, industrialisation was destroying old ones. The social upheavals accompanying it seemed to many observers to be erasing old customs and producing uniformity. In 1817 Thomas Heard noted that 'these local habits which might once have been deemed unconquerable, have almost completely disappeared'.[70] Hitchins and Drew's *History of Cornwall*, written around 1820, catalogued a long list

---

[68] Hitchins and Drew, 1824, 727-728.
[69] Francis Harvey, *Autobiography of Zethar: St Phillockias, Cornu-waille, England*, Durban, 1867, 25.
[70] Thomas Heard, *Gazetteer of Cornwall*, Truro, 1817

of dying customs, from church ales to Christmas plays, from maypoles to mock mayor processions:

> In some places a few vestiges of these customs still remain; but more generally they have been so far neglected or forgotten, as to leave scarcely their original names as a memorial behind them. And even in those places where they still exist, the more enlightened grow ashamed of them, and the procession is consigned over to the conduct and management of the illiterate and vulgar ....[71]

What appears to be a pattern of growing uniformity has, however, to be qualified. First, writers such as Drew were themselves writing from that dominant discourse of 'Industrial Civilisation' and Methodism that left little room for irrational pursuits. Second, when, after the mid-century, other writers turned their attention to re-discovering 'old customs' they seem to have managed to find them without too much difficulty.[72] And third, there always seemed to be new candidates for extinction, new 'differences' on the verge of dissolution.[73] The spirit of industry may have been erasing difference, but it was much slower in its task of creating uniformity. Merivale could still write in 1857 that:

> strong local peculiarities ... (will be) replaced by that uniformity of thought and action, and extinction of mere local influences, which seems destined to be the ultimate result of our present course of improvement ... Whatever sentimental regrets we may entertain for the past, we cannot doubt that anomalies of this kind do substantially act as so many obstacles, so much unnecessary friction, in the way of the machinery of civilisation, and that the power of combined action on the one hand, the power of human thought itself on the other, will gain enormously by their entire removal.[74]

The point to note here is that after at least 100 years of industrial change and the dynamic growth of mining there were still 'local peculiarities' waiting to be 'extinguished'.

Indeed, the parallel growth of regional self-assertiveness accompanying industrialisation led to increasing valorisation of these older peculiarities as well as the appropriation of new symbols of

---

[71] Hitchins and Drew, 1824, 722.
[72] William Bottrell, *Traditions and Hearthside Stories of West Cornwall*, Penzance, 1870; Robert Hunt, *Popular Romances of the West of England: The Drolls, Traditions and Superstitions of Old Cornwall*, London, 1871.
[73] Cf. Malcolm Chapman, *The Celts; The Construction of a Myth*, London, 1992, 138-139.
[74] Merivale, 1857, 328.

'peculiarity', new banners around which the 'imagined Cornish community' could be proclaimed as somehow different from others. The differences were sometimes real, sometimes invented. This distinction is not perhaps as important as it might seem, as both 'real' and invented differences gave meaning to the experience of living at a time of profound change. Charles Dellheim has shown how, by the 1860s, writers in Lancashire and Yorkshire had, in a similar way, evolved a discourse about their counties that allowed them to express a county pride. In that discourse, differentiation was stressed, differentiation from southerners in general and differences between Lancashire and Yorkshire in particular.[75]

In the early nineteenth century what struck outside observers was that the mining industry, even with its own local peculiarities, had also helped to produce a supremely rational population. Warner wrote in 1809 that 'the miners of Cornwall are free from the shackles of these terrors of the imagination'.[76] At around the same time Daniel Carless Webb concluded that the people's 'manners bear no striking difference from those of large towns in general, arising from the influx of strangers and the facility of travelling'.[77] However, fashions were changing. Merivale, writing in the mid-1850s, could still suggest that superstitions were relatively unimportant in Cornwall. In contrast to Ireland 'Cornish superstitions have been less "exploités" for the market, partly because less known, and partly because less attractive from what we have termed the essentially unpoetical spirit of the people, which has never invested them with any kind of legendary interest'.[78] But his mention of the market was percipient.

Some local writers, influenced by the general fashion for Romanticism and antiquarianism, were already before mid-century representing the Cornish as superstitious. This became part of a deepening discourse of differentiation in the first half of the nineteenth century. For example, the Reverend Richard Polwhele, with his roots firmly in the small gentry class, concluded in 1806 that, because of its 'intercourse with other provinces, if (the manners) of the Cornish were in any way peculiar, it could only have been in former ages'.[79] Yet, thirty years later, Polwhele was busy pinpointing Cornish peculiarities, from a supposed adherence

---

[75] Charles Dellheim, 'Imagining England: Victorian views of the north', *Northern History* 22 (1986), 216-230.

[76] Warner, 1809, 303.

[77] Daniel Webb, *Observations and Remarks during Four Excursions made in Various Parts of Great Britain*, London, 1812, 132.

[78] Merivale, 1857, 325.

[79] Richard Polwhele, *The History of Cornwall, Volume 7*, London, 1806, 133.

to superstitions to a predilection for saffron buns. Moreover, the superstitions of Cornwall, he argued, 'assimilate in a surprising manner' to those of Scotland, Ireland and Wales.[80] In this Polwhele was anticipating the Anglican, Tory Celticists of the early twentieth century Cornish Revival.[81]

By the 1860s, for some this romantic representation of Cornwall had become as important as the industrial representations. For example, even Max Muller, that early debunker of 'Celtic Cornwall', opened his account of 'Cornish antiquities' in 1867 with the words 'it is impossible to spend even a few weeks in Cornwall without being impressed with the air of antiquity which pervades that county, and seems, like a morning mist, half to conceal and half to light up every one of its hills and valleys'.[82] Here, those widespread views within England of the countryside as a place of stability and a reservoir of timeless certainty, in contrast to the uncertain futures and the social problems generated in the large cities, were being applied to Cornwall. Of course, in this imagery the social changes of the countryside were absent: changes in land-ownership patterns, enclosure and rural depopulation were forgotten in the imagining of a spiritual timelessness. From such a perspective, superstitions, with their apparent link to pre-modern modes of thought, had an obvious place. The further removed from the centre, from the heartland of rational logic, the more one was likely to meet the superstitious 'Other', pursuing ways of life abandoned years ago in the centre but clung to tenaciously in the 'traditional' periphery. As such images of the timeless countryside took hold, and a nostalgic desire to preserve old ways in the face of rapid change gripped the antiquarian classes of mid nineteenth century England, the search for superstitions spread into every nook and cranny of the periphery. Despite the strength of the parallel imageries of industrialisation, Cornwall was no exception. Indeed, although superstitions and industrial imagery seem strange companions, they could co-exist quite amicably as representations of Cornwall. For example, Robert Hunt combined a scientific interest in Cornish mining with his pursuit of customs and folk tales.[83]

---

[80] Richard Polwhele, *Reminiscences in Prose and Verse, Volume 1*, London, 112 and *Volume 2*, 8 and 163.
[81] Bernard Deacon, Dick Cole and Garry Tregidga, *Mebyon Kernow and Cornish Nationalism*, Cardiff, 2003, 14-18.
[82] Max Muller, 'Cornish antiquities', *The Quarterly Review* 123 (1867), 35.
[83] Robert Hunt, 1871 and *British Mining: A Treatise on the History, Discovery, Practical Development and Future Prospects of Metalliferous Mines in the UK*, London, 1887.

The Cornish language
Other 'peculiarities' were less a response to either of the demands of an outside market or dominant representations of peripheral places. For example, William Pryce appended to his largely technical treatise on mining in 1778 a list of Cornish language terms. He did this because 'the idioms and terms of Cornish miners are mostly derived from the ancient Cornish British dialect, and therefore not easily intelligible to gentlemen unaccustomed to Mining, who may have occasion to converse or correspond with them'.[84] The Cornish language itself was a relic of a former pre-industrial society, but not something that could easily be ignored.

Although marginalised both socially and geographically since the mid-seventeenth century, the language had been used as a vernacular, along with English and Cornu-English, throughout the early modern period to the end of the eighteenth century. By the early 1700s it was restricted to the coastal parishes of West Penwith and the Lizard, and to the poor and the older generations. Outsiders writing about Cornwall in the late eighteenth and early nineteenth centuries would give it a passing mention and note the consequences of its loss. As we have seen, Kitchen in the 1760s viewed the Cornish language as one of the three 'peculiarities' of Cornwall. But, as Warner wrote in the 1800s, 'with the disappearance of their language, the Cornish have lost almost all those provincial peculiarities in customs and amusements, which distinguished them from the inhabitants of other English counties'.[85]

Nevertheless, the Cornish language did not just disappear on the passing of the final generation of vernacular speakers in the last decades of the eighteenth century. It remained important in two ways in images of Cornwall. First, as the example of Pryce shows, it could not easily be ignored by antiquarians and writers on Cornwall in the late eighteenth century. Three decades earlier than Pryce's compilation of Cornish mining terms, William Borlase, in pursuing his explanation of the antiquities of Cornwall, had also found it necessary, for equally instrumental reasons, to acquaint himself with the meanings of placenames. The fact that over 80 per cent of placenames in Cornwall, with the highest frequencies in the west, originated in the Cornish language meant that the death of the spoken language could not erase its memory. In addition, the starting point for nineteenth century writers, especially indigenous writers, was often Richard Carew's *Survey of Cornwall*. Yet, this had been written at the very end of the sixteenth

---

[84] Pryce, 1778, i.
[85] Warner, 1809, 359.

century, at a time when Cornish was still spoken widely in mid and west Cornwall. Although not himself a Cornish speaker, Carew had devoted a section of his book to the language.[86] Therefore, later writers were presented with this reminder of the existence of the language. This meant that Cornish retained the potential to be employed as a factor of territorial differentiation.

The second way the language remained important was less instrumental. For example, in 1748/49 Borlase wrote that 'it will be a kind of duty in us Cornishmen to gather together the remains of our departed language'.[87] There is more than a hint here of the injunction almost 200 years later by the cultural revivalist Morton Nance to Old Cornwall Societies to 'cuntelleugh an brewyon us gesys na vo kellys travyth' (collect the fragments that remain so that none might be lost).[88] And it was hardly for instrumental reasons that such an enthusiast for the new industrial age as Davies Gilbert arranged a series of Cornish placenames in alternate rhyming stanzas in 1828. As he commented, the sounds of the placenames, even though the meanings had largely been lost, 'cannot fail to affect a Cornish heart with that peculiar sort of pleasing melancholy which is excited by the portrait of a dear departed friend'.[89]

This was the same Davies Gilbert who had welcomed the end of the Cornish language as a colloquial vernacular in 1826: 'no one more sincerely rejoices ... that the Cornish ... language has ceased altogether from being used by the inhabitants of Cornwall'.[90] Brian Murdoch regards it as curious that the 'demise of Cornish as a language of everyday discourse was actually welcomed in some respects, especially in the nineteenth century'.[91] But the curious thing is not the welcoming of the end of a spoken language that was seen as separating Cornwall from the progressive endeavours of an industrialising England. This, articulated by an outward looking bourgeoisie, was surely to be expected. The curiosity lies more in the nature of the welcoming. In Gilbert's case the language's demise was celebrated in an introduction to one of its preserved texts, in the form of an edition of the last miracle play, 'Gwreans an Bys' [The creation of the world]. In forgetting it, it was being remembered. Moreover, in the 1820s, this remembering was taking a much more nostalgic, romantic form than the remembering of those

---

[86] Richard Carew, *Survey of Cornwall*, London, 1811, 150ff.
[87] Cited in Peter Pool, *William Borlase*, Truro, 1986, 118.
[88] Robert Morton Nance, 'What we stand for', *Old Cornwall* 1 (1925), 3.
[89] Anon., 'The Cornish cantata', *Cornish Magazine* 3 (1828), 199.
[90] Davies Gilbert (ed.), *The Creation of the World*, London, 1827, v.
[91] Brian Murdoch, *Cornish Literature*, Cambridge, 1993, 142.

local small gentry who, in the later seventeenth and early eighteenth centuries, had tried self-consciously to 'write a modern Cornish' and preserve the fragments of what was still (just) a living, spoken language.[92]

Thus, for insiders the language was taking on a symbolic meaning almost as soon as it had been detached from its social base. It was a local example of that nostalgia for 'pre-industrial cultural variants' that Langton has identified.[93] But it was also one that, in an emerging world of nation-states and nationalisms, had a potential for mobilising future generations. This made it qualitatively different from the usual run of local customs.

Cornu-English: the Cornish dialect
The Cornish identity did not intersect only with language in the form of a recently deceased Celtic vernacular. Patrick Joyce identifies two roles for language in fostering group identities. First, it bears the values and ideas of the group; and second, it has itself a symbolic meaning, standing for the desires, beliefs and associations of that group.[94] The renewed interest in the Cornish language identified above carried a symbolic meaning but the language itself could no longer bear values, at least not values accessible to the vast majority of people in the early nineteenth century. For a combination of these roles - as symbol and as a carrier of ideas - we need to focus on a more relevant linguistic register, that of Cornu-English dialect.

Joyce argues that in the north of England dialect literature, which emerged in the 1840s, and enjoyed its heyday from the 1860s to the 1920s, played a crucial role in constructing and elaborating the identities of working people. This literature was a continuation of the older oral tradition and ballad broadsheets, at first written by a 'literary intelligentsia' (schoolmasters, clergy and the like) but addressed to a wider audience. Moreover, in Lancashire and Yorkshire especially, the major dialect writers of the second half of the nineteenth century were themselves members of the working class or the sons (apparently only very rarely daughters) of the working class. A 'mass dialect literature' emerged, a literature of the 'working poor', in which the values of northern working-class communities were played out. Of particular

---

[92] See Murdoch, 1993, 127-142; Oliver Padel, *The Cornish Writings of the Boson Family*, Redruth, 1975.
[93] Langton, 1984, 157.
[94] Patrick Joyce, *Visions of the People: Industrial England and the Question of Class 1840-1914*, Cambridge, 1991, 279.

significance to this study, this was the means through which regional pride was expressed.[95]

Outside the north, Joyce submits, dialect literature was less widespread, its writers more respectable, its themes more paternalist. In the north, 'popular ... dialect developed primarily out of the cultural resources of the working poor'.[96] The implication is that outside these regions an extra-proletarian dialect literature represented the world of the working poor from the outside. Although many dialect writers were of Liberal and dissenting backgrounds and were sympathetic to the plight of the labouring poor, real empathy was difficult and the role of dialect literature more limited.

However, Joyce's conclusions concerning the 'extra-proletarian' dialect literature outside the north are drawn from limited sources and suffer to some extent from a failure to apply in practice his own observation that 'to a considerable extent regional diversity was more marked than is often thought'.[97] Specifically, Cornish dialect literature is noted only in passing and then as part of a 'westcountry' regional framework. Having suggested that class and culture do not exist before language but are 'actively constituted by language' it seems strange that Joyce then takes a 'westcountry' region for granted.[98] Like other academics writing within the dominant territorial discourse, Joyce fails to differentiate Cornish dialect literature from a general rural literature, the principal themes of which concerned the small farmer and agricultural labourer.

Oddly enough, despite seeing Cornwall as a unit distinct from the 'westcountry', Vernon's reading of Cornish dialect echoes that of Joyce. He prefers to emphasise its 'reification of the peasantry as a pastoral and deeply moral people' and its role in constructing a '"primitive" folk' as the 'source of Cornish national identity'.[99] However, this insufficiently deconstructs both the content and the reception of Cornu-English texts in Cornwall. In contrast, we might suggest that Cornish dialect literature, while in some respects fitting Joyce's broad model of 'extra-proletarian dialect literature', occupied an intermediate position between the 'high' upper-class dialect literature of rural southern England and the 'mass' dialect literature of northern England.

The timing of the emergence of a popular dialect literature in Cornwall, popular in the sense of being consumed by a wide market, is remarkably

---

[95] Joyce, 1991, 279-301.
[96] Joyce, 1991, 268.
[97] Joyce, 1991, 312.
[98] Joyce, 1991, 10 and 265-268.
[99] Vernon, 1998, 154-155.

similar to that outlined by Joyce for Lancashire and Yorkshire. In 1846 William Sandys, a solicitor born in London and educated at Westminster School, edited *Specimens of Cornish Provincial Dialects* under the pseudonym 'Jan Trenoodle'. As its title suggests, this, published in London and with its introduction explaining Cornwall and its dialect to the reader, was clearly aimed at a non-Cornish audience. Most of the stories in it were reprints of the work of Charles Fox, who was born in 1749 in Falmouth but who died at Bath in 1809. Fox was a member of one of the branches of a gentry family which had considerable involvement in industrial enterprises in Cornwall yet one, with its Quaker connections, somewhat marginalised from the mainstream of local landed society. Sandys' publication, however, was soon followed by the emergence of a new generation of dialect writers, the most prolific of whom were John Tabois Tregellas and William Bentinck Forfar. Tregellas was born in the mining parish of St Agnes in 1792, became a merchant and mines purser, introducing a cast steel borer into his mines in 1848, before taking up lecturing 'on the peculiarities of the Cornish dialect' to literary and mechanics institutes across Cornwall.[100] His stories were published widely in the 1850s and 1860s. Forfar was a solicitor, born in Breage, another mining parish, around 1800.[101] Other important figures in the explosion of dialect publishing which occurred around mid-century were the brothers James and Edwin Netherton, printers and publishers at Truro. From 1854 James Netherton began to publish *Netherton's Cornish Almanack* on an annual basis. Thus, the social origins of those involved in the early phase of Cornish dialect literature was, as Joyce and Vernon suggest, middle and upper class in status, professionals and businessmen. Some clerics were also involved, for example the Reverend Francis O'Donoghue, Irish born and incumbent of Godolphin in the early 1850s, who published *St Knighton's Kieve, A Cornish Tale* in 1864, but none of the farmers' sons that Joyce links to rural higher-class dialect writing can be identified.

Nevertheless, the themes of this dialect literature had their own regional characteristics. Differences lay in the content rather than the tone of the writing which was, as elsewhere, comic and ironic, and took as its subject the events of daily life. Fox's early stories were, if anything, more realist than some of the writings of Tregellas half a century or more later. In dualogues such as 'Saundry Kempe and Mall Treloare', 'Jan Knuckey and Graacey' or 'Gracey Penvear and Molly Treviskey' the

---

[100] *West Briton*, 20 March 1863; Maurice Bizley, *A Friendly Retreat: The Story of a Parish*, Truro, 1955, 130.

[101] George Boase and William Courtney, *Bibliotheca Cornubiensis*, London, 1874, 158.

characters discuss the day to day details of employment and personal relations, the quality of ore, the violent and drunken husband.[102] Some of Tregellas' writings are more obviously comic caricature, as in 'The St Agnes Bear Hunt' and the 'Perran cherrybeam' and are clearly aimed at entertaining a lecture audience.[103] However, the 'gullible fools' of these stories, a device that no doubt fed on the intense parochialism of community rivalries within Cornwall, are also joined by the 'wise fools', a common motif of dialect writing. In the title story of *The Adventures of Rozzy Paul and Zacky Martin*, Tregellas tells the tale of two illiterate miners who go to London to give evidence at an election lawsuit. Their earthy and direct manners led to a series of mishaps when they arrived. The pretensions of London society are contrasted with the injured pride, but also stubborn independence, of the two heroes. Finally, inevitably, the wise fools win the day. They go to Parliament

> And made the folk with laughter roar;
> How brazen barristers were vex'd,
> And lawyers with their words perplex'd;
> Suffice to say, they gained the case,
> And bragging Bullion lost his place.[104]

Rozzy Paul and Zacky Martin were miners, as were most of the characters who appear in early and mid-nineteenth century Cornish dialect literature. Fox's earlier stories, more often than not, also took miners as their subjects and stories are littered with mining terms even if miners are not the ostensible subjects. William Bentinck Forfar's first published story in 1850 was also titled, significantly, '"The Bal" or "Tes a bra keenly lode"'.[105]

These stories, dense with mining references, reinforced the connections of the industry with the region. Just as dialect literature in Lancashire concentrated on the textile industry, Cornu-English writers in Cornwall focused on mining. The interests of mining were identified with the interests of Cornwall. Indeed, it was, according to Sandys in the 1840s, only 'in the mining districts' and other 'parts most remote from traffic and intercourse with strangers' that the 'Cornish provincial dialect' was

---

[102] Jan Trenoodle, *Specimens of Cornish Provincial Dialects*, London, 1846, 22-26, 38-42, 43-46.

[103] John Tregellas, *The Adventures of Rozzy Paul and Zacky Martin; The St Agnes Bear Hunt; and the Perran Cherrybeam; Three Comic Cornish Poems*, Penzance, 1853.

[104] Tregellas, 1853.

[105] William Forfar, *The Bal or 'Tes a bra keenly lode'*, Helston, 1850.

'to be heard in its full richness'.[106] It was not therefore, a pastoral peasantry who were being reified by Cornish dialect writings, as Vernon claims, but a mining 'folk' community.[107]

The mining communities occupied the centre of Cornu-English literature in its early period. That literature, through ignoring real variations in spoken dialect within Cornwall, helped to construct a uniform region where mining was the ascendant and inescapable presence. (The major dialect difference in Cornwall lay between the Cornu-English of mid and west Cornwall and the 'Wessex' dialect, shared with Devon, Somerset and Dorset, of east Cornwall. This reflected in turn a long-lasting isogloss in mid-Cornwall between the Cornish and English languages from the thirteenth to sixteenth centuries.) Regional pride crystallised around the idea of a local monopoly of mining knowledge. In Tregellas's tale 'The London Director, Hannibal Hollow, at Wheal Blue Bottle', the subject of the story visits a Cornish mine and, because he does not understand the dialect, ends up completely confused.[108] The frontispiece of the booklet reinforces the message:

> When copper and tin no longer are found,
> And Owld Gwennap lodes turn up no more ore,
> When London directors do work underground,
> Oh then, Captain Stephen, love mining no more

Only the Cornish knew how to mine: outsiders, particularly London investors, were the gullible fools soon to be parted from their money as the insiders surveyed the industry with a confidence born of practical knowledge. Here is something more than the 'wise fool' of the dialect stories. This is the knowledgeable expert expressing local pride and independence.

These stories, which welded representations of Cornwall and the Cornish to the mining industry, reached a considerable audience. John Tregellas' booklet *The Adventures of Rozzy Paul and Zacky Martin* went through seven printings in the three years after its publication at Penzance in 1853. *The humorous adventures of a Cornish miner at the Great Exhibition* by Jimmy Trebilcock (a pseudonym), printed at Camborne in the heart of the mining district in 1862, sold at least 5,000

---

[106] Trenoodle, 1846, 1.
[107] Vernon, 1998, 155.
[108] John Tregellas, *Farmer Brown's Blunders, including the cayenne pepper story; Captain Hoskin's Battle of Lanterns; and the London Director, Hannibal Hollow, at Wheal Blue Bottle*, London, 1857, 29-43.

copies within two years.[109] Given a far smaller potential market, this suggests sales of a magnitude much higher than those dialect journals and prose works Joyce cites in Lancashire, which regularly reached 10,000 copies in the 1850s and 1860s.[110]

Cornu-English literature in the 1850s and 1860s can thus be regarded as a mass literature although it was not at this stage a working-class literature. It was only later - in the 1890s - that working-class authors appeared but by then the literature was restricted to specific districts and social domains in Cornwall.[111] It remains to be explained why Cornu-English dialect literature occupied this intermediate position in the 1850s, a mass literature but without working class authors. Joyce suggests that dialect literature helped manage the disruption caused by social change by emphasising links to the past and to notions of traditional plebeian culture.[112] But it also required a sufficient degree of literacy to support a commercial market as well as the means to produce and disseminate cheap published material.

We might speculate that in Cornwall the period of most intense change - in the eighteenth century and early decades of the nineteenth - preceded the emergence of a sufficiently literate market. Perhaps there was less space for Cornu-English literature when we consider the hegemonic role played by Methodism, especially in mining communities. As we shall see in chapter 9, it was Methodism, rather than, or in addition to, dialect, that fulfilled the function of continuity in the face of change. Dialect, of course, had a role here, but it was a spoken dialect, in the form of the exuberant sermons of the scores of lay preachers who were scattered across Cornwall, that met the need for continuity before the 1840s. By the time a market for dialect literature and the technology that allowed cheap production and distribution had emerged, another factor was working against the appearance of working class authors. In the 1840s mass emigration began, removing potential authors out of the orbit of the localism that dialect literature thrived on. It is no coincidence that one of Tregellas' best-selling stories was that of 'Hacky Retchatts and Marky Daniels' who, in a number of versions in the late 1850s, pursued their adventures to the New World.[113] While concentrated on mining, the

---

[109] Boase and Courtney, 1874, 1012.

[110] Joyce, 1991, 264.

[111] See William Thomas, *The Socialist's Longing and other poems*, Penzance, 1893.

[112] Joyce, 1991, 281-282.

[113] John Tregellas, *Hacky Retchatts and Marky Daniels' Dangerous Voyage of Discovery*, Plymouth, 1857 and *California and Hacky and Marky*, Truro, 1859.

horizons of Cornu-English literature were drawn towards the global labour market that accompanied mining. This, if nothing else, makes Cornish dialect literature difficult to classify easily in terms of Joyce's 'high' and 'mass' forms.

If the peculiarities presented by Cornwall's mining economy and Methodist culture go some way towards explaining the rather different role of dialect literature in imaginations of the region, the Cornish language added yet another difference. The first edition of *Netherton's Cornish Almanack*, published in 1854, contained five dialect stories along with, among other things, a selective list of 'historical events' and lists of banks, copper ore ticketings, mechanics' and literary institutions and fairs. But also, significantly, it contained over six pages about the Cornish language, including meanings (sometimes rather fanciful) of placenames and specimens of the 'ancient Cornish language', including the names of months, numbers, proverbs and sayings.[114] So, in this journal aimed at a popular readership, readers were being re-presented with the Cornu-English dialect at the same time as being re-introduced to the Cornish language. This suggests that, even at this early stage, the region and its people were not being imagined solely in terms of a dialect literature that looked to past continuities but via a language that had its roots even further in the past. These images prefigured the similar, and sometimes uneasy, combination of dialect and language that marked the Old Cornwall movement of the inter-war period.

Conclusion

Out of the embers of an ethnic identity based on a distinct language, an identity that had occupied a residual status since the 1650s, there emerged in the final decades of the eighteenth century a reformulated identity. While there was some overlap with the earlier sense of identity, this revised territorial identity rested centrally on the symbols of Cornwall's industrial experience.

In this chapter we have seen how, by the 1840s, a dominant ideology of Cornwall as 'industrial civilisation' had emerged, ordered, religious, temperate, one that rested on the three central representations of 'independence', 'one and all' and 'enterprise'. However, such an ideology also required the opposition of West Barbary in order to emphasise the transformation through which the Cornish people had passed. Assertions of identity rested on the achievements of mining and representations that were based on features inherent to that industry. The popularity of Cornu-English dialect stories in the 1840s and 1850s was

---

[114] James Netherton, *Netherton's Cornish Almanack*, Truro, 1854.

one symptom of that. While dialect literature written by working people had not emerged on the lines of the industrial regions of northern England, the wide appeal of this literature ensured that Cornwall was imagined through the icons of mining and the manners of the mining population.

This suggests that the Cornish identity of the early nineteenth century was one primarily forged in the crucible of industrialisation, rather than remoteness. It was one in which, as Langton suggests, insiders were actively involved.[115] Unlike the deconstruction of the 'Celtic' identity that Chapman presents, where the main actors are outsiders imposing a romantic identity upon a basically passive population,[116] we have an example of an actively asserted territorial identity. This merged into a more general cultural process, involving an interest in old traditions and superstitions at the very point at which they were under threat and on the verge of disappearance. But in searching for old traditions people encountered the more unique local aspects of the Cornish language and the institutional structures and customs associated with mining. Eventually, in confronting these, insiders and outsiders would put radically different interpretations on them. However, for a period, in the second quarter of the nineteenth century, where the dominant representation of Cornwall was that of 'industrial civilisation', insider and outsider representations of Cornwall were closer together than at any time since. I have now identified some representations of Cornwall and its people. The next chapter attempts the more difficult task of exploring the territorial consciousness of its inhabitants and assessing the intensity of feeling for the place called Cornwall.

---

[115] Langton, 1984.
[116] Chapman, 1992.

Chapter 4
Cornish consciousness

This chapter offers some evidence for the group consciousness of the Cornish in the period before the 1860s. In doing this we move from the image of the region and its inhabitants to the other aspect that makes up the regional identity – the consciousness of the region's population. Regional consciousness cohered around symbols and can thus be viewed as part of Anssi Paasi's stage of symbolic shaping. However, an important element in regional consciousness is the construction of boundaries between the group and those outside. This boundary creation helps shape the group and is part of the territorial shaping of a region. The argument in this chapter is that, while containing some ambiguous dimensions, the territorial and symbolic shaping in this period was an important stage in the longer-term development of a Cornish territorial identity. This identity can be viewed as a form of ethnic identification which established certain symbols. These took on greater significance later, in the twentieth century. In this sense, we can restore some continuity between Cornwall's 'industrial' and 'post-industrial' phases and challenge those perspectives that see few connections across the economically depressed years of the late 1860s and 1870s.

A self-opinionated people
A clear pride in being Cornish had emerged by the 1850s. One indication of this local patriotism was a growing interest in 'eminent Cornishmen' in the early nineteenth century. A correspondent to the *Royal Cornwall Gazette* in 1811 wrote 'I have been highly gratified (in common, no doubt, with every Cornishman who is alive to the honour of his native county) at perusing in your late papers the substance of the scientific lectures of our excellent countryman Dr [Humphry] Davy.' Asked what reason there could be for producing the *Cornish Magazine* in 1826, the editors responded that 'in the County of Cornwall there existed much talent, indigenous as one may say to the soil (witness the names of Sir Humphry Davy, Woolcott, Opie, Borlase, Polwhele etc., etc.)' (anon, 1826). And even the uncompromisingly dour Methodist journal, *The*

Cornish Banner, ran a series of 'sketches of eminent Cornishmen' in 1847.[1]

As Alan Everitt points out, a gentrified 'county' or 'local' patriotism was not uncommon in the early nineteenth century.[2] But how deeply did this gentry patriotism spread? Francis Harvey, writing in the 1860s in South Africa as an emigrant from the engineering centre of Hayle, leaves us in no doubt about his allegiance. 'Confessedly an enthusiastic lover of my own dear Cornwall, I am proud of the opportunity to justify the manifold excellencies of our 'one and all' 'Tre, Pol and Pen' men against the unworthy attacks of ignorant accusers ... [against] ... England's first, best county!'[3] Harvey was perhaps a special case, remembering Cornwall from a distance. But his pride was also reflected in the glee of the postman who brought the news to John Harris, the Camborne poet, that he had won the Shakespeare Tercentenary Prize in 1864: 'We have beaten them all! Hurrah! Hurrah! The barbarians of Cornwall are at the very top of the tree!'.[4]

Herman Merivale's close observation of the Cornish left him in no doubt. The Cornish, he wrote, were 'considerably self-opinionated ... the thorough Cornishman's respect for his own shrewdness and that of his clan is unbounded, or only equalled by his profound contempt for 'foreigners' from the east ... this feeling increases ludicrously in intensity as we advance further west'.[5] This was not just a factor of peripherality, feelings of Cornishness heightening with distance from England. The geography of this identification reflected the geography of mining, with the areas where industrialisation had progressed furthest being those areas with the greatest intensity of feeling. This suggests that there was a correlation, if not necessarily a direct causal link, between industrialisation and expressions of Cornish identity. The centrality of mining is also illustrated in Henwood's discussion of the phrase 'out of the world, and down to St Ives'. This, he explained, meant 'literally out of the mining world (the "world" of the Cornish)'.[6] In contemporary

---

[1] *The Cornish Banner*, January 1847, 201-205.
[2] Alan Everitt, 'Country, county and town: patterns of regional evolution in England', *Transactions of the Royal Historical Society*, 5th series 29 (1979), 79-108.
[3] Francis Harvey, *Autobiography of Zethar: St Phillockias, Cornu-waille, England*, Durban, 1867, 33.
[4] John Harris, *My Autobiography*, London, 1882, 92.
[5] Herman Merivale, 'Cornwall', *The Quarterly Review* 102 (1857), 316.
[6] Roger Burt (ed.), *Cornwall's Mines and Miners: Nineteenth Century Studies by George Henwood*, Truro, 1972, 316.

internal representations of Cornwall, mining was central and fishing peripheral.

Territorial loyalty was much more than an abstract allegiance to an imagined community. It could have repercussions for its members in terms of group solidarity and instrumental aid. Cornwall's peninsular geography had led Richard Carew to suggest in the late sixteenth century that the Cornish gentry were all 'cousins', with a strong sense of kinship and complex inter-marrying binding them together.[7] However, in 1822 Richard Polwhele reported in a letter that 'yesterday, in a conversation respecting "Cornish cousins" ... we observed with regret, that the fellowship of affectionate kinsmen was now almost done away with'.[8] This would seem to suggest that the interconnected bonds of kinship and geography among the gentry were weakening. Certainly, there was an increased tendency for the sons and daughters of the very wealthy to marry outside Cornwall after 1775.

Table 4.1: Location of marriage partners of Cornish greater gentry families (%)

	Cornwall	Devon	elsewhere	(N)
1675-1725	40	35	25	(20)
1725-1775	73	7	20	(15)
1775-1825	45	9	45	(22)
1825-1875	50	4	46	(24)

Source: Based on Joseph Polsue, *Lakes' Parochial History of Cornwall*, Truro, 1867-73.

In the mid-eighteenth century there was a sharp decline in marriages to partners in Devon. In the first 50 years of the industrialisation period, 1725-75, the marriages of the greater gentry became more endogamous, perhaps reflecting a consolidation of mineral rights in this period as deep mining for copper grew rapidly. It was only after the 1770s, by which time Cornwall had emerged as a specialised mining region, that more partners were sought from further afield. Wider social contacts then replaced the limited interaction with families just across the county border that appears to be the norm in pre-modern Cornwall.[9]

---

[7] Richard Carew, *Survey of Cornwall*, London, 1811, 179.
[8] Richard Polwhele, *Traditions and Recollections, Domestic, Clerical and Literary*, London, 721.
[9] See also Anne Duffin, *Faction and Faith: Politics and Religion of the Cornish*

Nevertheless, around 1836 Hugh Tremenheere, himself born in Bath and brought up outside Cornwall, could still be surprised when, 'not long after joining the western Circuit' he was visited by William Arundell Harris when at the Launceston Assizes 'reminding me that we were Cornish cousins'. Tremenheere was introduced to others as of 'good Cornish stock'.[10] This might suggest that lineage was deemed important when defining group boundaries.

There is evidence, too, that a sense of companionship on 'ethnic' grounds existed among the smaller gentry. For example, in 1812 Richard Polwhele received a letter from his son who was at Calcutta. There he had met a Captain Stevens from Penzance: 'Captain Stevens, as soon as I was introduced to him as a Cornishman, shook me by the hand, and you cannot conceive how glad he was to see me ...'.[11] For Stevens, who insisted that the young Polwhele lodge with him rather than at a Calcutta inn, being from Cornwall clearly had a special meaning. Furthermore, Stevens had been living in India since 1785. The role of exile had here produced a conscious self-identification.

It was not just the landed class, in cultural terms hardly distinct from their equivalents across the Tamar by the nineteenth century, who valued their lineage. The mining population, wrote Henwood, had a 'certain pride of ancestry, a boast of descent, and a veneration for heirlooms ...'.[12] Yet, most of the limited evidence we have about self-identification comes from men. Women on the margins are usually even more invisible, territorial identities also being gendered identities. It was the male underground miner rather than his female counterpart on the surface who became the referent of Cornishness; 'Cousin Jack' bound the imagined community together. In constructions like this the space for women became unstable. In this context the story that Walter White recounted about Mary Kelynack (a Cornish woman who walked to the Great Exhibition in 1851) may be significant in suggesting the self-identification of Cornish working class women.

> Burnard, struck by the expression of character in her face, requested leave to take her bust. She replied, with a hearty laugh, 'Oh, bless your heart, my dear! If you be a Cornishman you may do what you like with me; for I'll stick up for the Cornish as long as I've a drop of blood left in my body!'[13]

Gentry before the Civil War, Exeter, 1996, 30-31.
[10] Hugh Tremenheere, *Memorials of my Life*, London, 1885, 26.
[11] Polwhele, 1826, 650.
[12] Burt (ed.), 1972, 220.
[13] Walter White, *A Londoner's Walk to the Land's End: and a trip to the Scilly Isles*, London, 1855, 204.

Note that the context for this tale was set by a trip to London. For it was when away from home that the territorial identity was more likely to be articulated.

Samuel Drew, born the son of a tin streamer and smallholder near St Austell in 1765, began work at the age of eight as a buddle boy in a stream works and was later apprenticed to a shoemaker. Drew became a Methodist and a respected writer on theology and history. His writings betray no particular sense of Cornish identity until 1819. But in January of that year he took a post as an editor of a magazine at Liverpool. It is then, in a letter home to his wife, that he refers to his Cornish identity. On refusing to acquiesce to his employers' wish for him to work a twelve-hour day he wrote 'I would rather stand on the ground of honour than suffer the independent spirit of a Cornish author to wear a shackle'. In similar vein, he reported a sermon he had given where the crowd, 'many of whom came, I suppose, to hear a Cornishman'.[14] Whether they did or not must remain in doubt, but the important thing here is that Drew felt that they did. Here, he was using his identity as Cornish to represent himself and other people's reactions to him.

Meanwhile William Lovett, the Chartist, recounts how, at almost the same time, in 1821, he migrated from Newlyn to London. He at first moved within a circle of fellow Cornish acquaintances: 'one evening on my return to my lodgings I met with three countrymen, carpenters by trade. They were, however, strangers to me, but coming from the same county, we soon became acquainted'.[15] Here, ethnic bonds were being utilised to ease the transition to new communities, these no doubt reinforcing and interacting with other networks based on family, kinship and neighbourhood.

Lovett also represented himself in 'Cornish' terms even when involved in what historians might view as an aspect of class conflict. When cheated by an employer, this proved 'a little too much for my Cornish blood (and) was repaid by a blow that sent him to a respectful distance'.[16] Both Drew and Lovett were defining themselves with reference to their territorial identity in their early days in exile and this despite their well-known religious and class identities respectively. The bonds of ethnicity and a broader regional consciousness had, through migration, made people such as Drew and Lovett more conscious of their Cornishness in ways not relevant at home in Cornwall. In this, their response resembled other migrating ethnic groups: 'to be Welsh in Wales was unremarkable:

---

[14] J.A.Drew, *The Life, Character and Literary Labours of Samuel Drew*, London, 1834, 272.

[15] William Lovett, *The Life and Struggles of William Lovett*, London, 1876, 20.

[16] Lovett, 1876, 23.

to be Welsh in Liverpool was to be visible, and to be conscious of that position'.[17]

Clearly, the explicit sense of Cornish identity would vary from individual to individual. For instance, Humphry Davy in his writings rarely referred to his Cornish identity in the sense that Drew and Lovett did, although he wrote romantic poems about Cornwall.[18] Nevertheless, self-identification as Cornish had a wide social currency by the 1810s and provided one possible identity that Cornish people from differing social groups could adopt. By the second quarter of the nineteenth century, if not earlier, this group identification was also becoming of striking instrumentalist benefit in networks associated with the emigration process.[19]

County identity, national identity, regional identity?
Spatial identities sometimes become enmeshed in disputes over the appropriate label to give them. The Cornish identity is particularly prone to this; its hybridity has produced concurrent descriptive labels, including county, regional, ethnic and national identity, used both by insiders and outsiders.[20] However, the question of what label we give it is one which can take on more significance in the early twenty-first century than it did for early nineteenth century contemporaries, who just identified themselves as Cornish. Cornish nationalists might note with some relish the observation of Wilkie Collins in 1850: 'a man speaks of himself as Cornish in much the same way as a Welshman speaks of himself as Welsh'.[21] Or they could point to Pryce's description of Cornwall as a 'nation' in 1778 that we met in the previous chapter. However, this does not imply an all-embracing Cornish national consciousness. When we turn to the writings of other insiders we find a telling absence of explicit references to 'nation'. While eighteenth century writers occasionally apply the term 'nation' to the Cornish,[22] there was little reference to

---

[17] R.M.Jones and D.B.Rees, *The Liverpool Welsh and their Religion*, Liverpool, 1984, 34.
[18] John Davy, *Memoirs of the Life of Sir Humphry Davy 1778-1829*, London, 1836. Similarly, there is much evidence of Methodist and English self-identification but no mention of Cornwall in K.M.Burall (ed.), *Cornwall to America 1783: From the Journal of Paul Burall (1755-1826)*, London, n.d.
[19] See Philip Payton, *The Cornish Overseas*, Fowey, 1999.
[20] For further thoughts on this see Bernard Deacon, 'County, nation, ethnic group? The shaping of the Cornish identity', *The International Journal of Regional and Local Studies* 3 (2007), 5-29.
[21] Wilkie Collins, *Rambles beyond Railways*, London, 1852, 70.
[22] See William Borlase, *Natural History of Cornwall*, Oxford, 1758, 304;

'nationality' as such in the first half of the nineteenth century. That had to await the self-conscious articulation of Cornishness associated with the Cornish Revival at the very end of the nineteenth century.[23]

As we have seen, place and ethnic identities are often associated with stereotyping an opposing 'Other'. The nature of this 'Other' can, perhaps, tell us something about the labelling identity. For instance, people in Redruth might identify themselves in opposition to the 'Other' in the neighbouring town of Camborne. At a very different scale, the emergence of both English and British nationalism in the eighteenth century has been linked to the stereotyping of a French 'Other'. So, who did the Cornish define as the 'Other'? At one level the term 'foreigner' was used for stranger; 'the description of a non-Cornish person as a "foreigner" continued to be standard practice in Cornwall'.[24] But this use of the term can be seen as the older dialect meaning of 'non-native, unfamiliar, strange' as well as 'person of a different country', 'country' here referring to something closer to the French concept of *pays* or the Welsh *bro*. Indeed, this use of the term 'foreigner' was hardly unknown in dialects east of the Tamar.

While the common use of 'foreigner' was too vague and contained insufficient stereotypical attributes to be useful, there were two clear candidates for the Cornish 'Other' at this period - Londoners and Devonians. The opposition to Londoners was splendidly articulated by Francis Harvey who ascribed the 'West Barbary' myth to Londoners:

> Thus truly 'the one and all men' even in play were true and faithful. These 'West Barbary Barbarians' and 'not of England', as many scapegrace, evil-minded Cocknies have derisively in their stupidity, falsely named us, were, thank God! too sternly honest and noble, to learn the vile strategy, or imitate the viler doings of their slimed accusers. As superior in the moral sense to their weak brained revilers, as in the might of their muscular arm, to those mere distortions of humanity, creeping and limping in debased Cockneydom.[25]

Whilst 'other inland traducers' may also have contributed to these false images of Cornwall, Harvey's spleen is reserved for this one named group, Cockneydom. Harvey was not alone. Polwhele echoed this antipathy to Londoners: 'these London tradesman are of all vulgar

---

William Pryce, *Mineralogia Cornubiensis*, London, 1778, preface.

[23] See the work of novelists such as Charles Lee, *Paul Carah; Cornishman*, London, 1898.

[24] Philip Payton, *The Making of Modern Cornwall*, Redruth, 1992, 92. And see Burt (ed.), 1972, 231.

[25] Harvey, 1867, 35-36.

cockneys the most vulgar ... the present race of illiterate prigs and coxcombs'.[26] In contrast to this, Devonians came off rather more lightly, being viewed merely as 'savage', 'brutal' and 'muleish' by Harvey, their sins crystallised by the Devon style of wrestling, which allowed 'the cruel and barbarous usage of unmanly "kicking shins" ... so long a disgrace to Devonians'.[27] Devonians were seen as backward and slow, in contrast to the scheming and altogether less trustworthy Londoners. However, the important aspect of this is that 'the Other' was represented by groups within England and not 'the English' as a group. In this context the Cornish identity resembled that of Lancashire and Yorkshire, sharing a conventional provincial suspicion of Londoners in particular, along with a competitive attitude to their near neighbours.

Writers such as Harvey, however, were aware of other possible representations of Cornwall that did not apply to English counties. Cornwall was sometimes represented as 'not of England'. Harvey himself strongly rejected this as a production of outsiders. Yet at times, feeling marginalised by metropolitan opinion, Harvey came close, in his own confusing way, to accepting this labelling and reversing it:

> it is a fact that in Cockneydom, and may be elsewhere, where other blunderers have grown up, Cornwall the brave and truly great, has been of mere slander called 'West Barbary' and 'not of England'; well be it so, Cornishmen can well afford to smile at all this slang and stupid malignity; may be, Cornwall may justly be proud, as being in all her history, in her internal priceless worth, and in the glorious elements with which she has served and aided, and honoured every valuable interest of the nation; of being in truth, if 'not of' yet superior by far to England, if really 'not of it'.[28]

Here lay a tension which is still observable within the Cornish identity. Cornish patriotism was expressed in a sometimes intense fashion in the mid-nineteenth century but existed alongside a British or English nationalism. Harvey, for example, began his autobiography with an account of Cromwell's expedition against the Irish in 1649.[29] His Cornishness 'nested' within a Protestant, constitutional English/British nationalism. Cornishness and British nationalism were not contradictory; in fact, the former could appear to be a building block for the latter. As an instance, at a meeting in 1819, when the Mayor and inhabitants of Truro resolved that 'as true Britons, and, especially, as "the faithful Cornish", we are determined "one and all", to support the just

---

[26] Richard Polwhele, *Reminiscences in Prose and Verse*, London, 1836, 101.
[27] Harvey, 1867, 30.
[28] Harvey, 1867, 29.
[29] Harvey, 1867, 1.

prerogative of the Crown, and the authority of the Government; standing firm in defence of the throne and of the Altar'.[30]

What are we left with? The Cornish, revivified by industrialisation, with their own discourse of peculiarity, expressed an assertive self-consciousness by the second quarter of the nineteenth century. But the Cornish identity at this time could be interpreted as a regional identity that operated in a symbiotic relationship with an English/British identity rather than as an ethnic identity in opposition to a civic identity at a larger scale. In some respects, for example in the popularity and themes of dialect literature, this was an identity closer to the emergent cultural identities of the industrial regions of Northern England than the residual and socially conservative county identities of Southern England. That said, there were certainly elements of the latter in Cornwall, particularly among the gentry and inscribed into their institutions. Nevertheless, the intensity of self-identity noted by contemporaries, allied with certain historical symbols (see below) and with material processes such as overseas emigration, always had the potential to produce something much more than a county identity - even though Cornwall was locked into and partly constituted by its administrative, local government framework. Moreover, what made the Cornish identity fundamentally different from English regional identities was an underlying ethnic component, albeit an ethnicity that, at this time, did not produce territorial political demands.

What this and the previous chapter have so far emphasised is the dialectical nature of the processes of identity formation. The self-images of Cornish people were being constructed partly within more global discourses. The 'West Barbary' image was one apparently originating from outsiders, although re-constructed by insiders as opposition to their own self-imagery. 'Industrial civilisation', adopted by Drew and many others, shared a cultural content with broader narratives of progress that were to become dominant by the mid-nineteenth century. Pryce's work on Cornish mining can be seen as part of the emerging scientific discourse of the later eighteenth century. The increasing interest in superstitions can obviously be linked to a Romantic discourse. Finally, we have also seen how articulations of Cornishness were often subject to 'interference' from a more dominant English/British nationalism. However, this does not mean that Cornish people and the early nineteenth century Cornish identity were passively structured by these more general processes. They made choices, they contested those discourses, they negotiated their own sense of identity, they articulated

---

[30] Polwhele, 1826, 584.

their perceived place in the world. One way they did this was by writing their history.

The Cornish and their history

In the nineteenth century there emerged a multitude of historical and archaeological societies that, in turn, reproduced 'provincial pride, identity and consciousness'.[31] People looked to the past for their sense of stability and continuity as contemporary society underwent profound change. History, therefore, provided groups with a sense of their own identity. Sometimes this could be more than that local identity buttressed by the collection of parochial trivia so beloved by the Victorian antiquarian. History, according to Anthony Smith, was the tool by which intellectuals provided 'maps' for ethnic groups, grounding their sense of distinctiveness around common historical memories and myths. For Smith there are two aspects to this process of intellectual production, the creation of myths of landscape, or 'poetic spaces', and myths of history, or 'golden ages'. In the first, monuments were naturalised and treated as a part of the special nature of the territory. In the second, moral exemplars of the ethnic past illuminated the present and provided inspiration for the future.[32]

Gerhard Brunn agrees with Smith that ethnic/national histories have emphasised golden or heroic ages which he contrasts with periods of decline, associated with rule from outside the territory or by another ethnic group.[33] For Brunn, history performs a number of tasks in the process of ethnic formation, uncovering the obscured history of 'history-less' peoples, creating solidarity and inspiring the people to its 'glorious' task. He also distinguishes between two sources of historical consciousness. First, there is the collective, unreflective - we might add 'folk' - memory of the group and second, the deliberate intellectual reconstruction of the group's past, a construction then popularised by the intelligentsia: journalists, novelists, painters, poets and politicians. This second source is the most important in raising the group's consciousness of themselves. These ethnic or national histories have also to be written as counter-histories in direct competition with dominant views of the past which render state-less peoples also 'history-less' by projecting present political arrangements into the past.

---

[31] Charles Dellheim, *The Face of the Past: The Preservation of the Medieval Inheritance in Victorian England*, Cambridge, 1982, 58-59.

[32] Anthony Smith, *National Identity*, London, 1991, 65-70, 91, 127.

[33] Gerhard Brunn, 'Historical consciousness and historical myths', in Andreas Kappeler (ed.), *The Formation of National Elites*, Aldershot, 1992, 327-338.

Was the Cornish past employed as a component of the transformed modern identity? Did it also have its intellectual constructors and 'golden ages'? Morrish identifies the three 'fathers of Cornish history' as Carew, Borlase and Polwhele.[34] The writings of these three, together with those of Samuel Drew, were influential in transmitting representations of Cornwall's past to mid-nineteenth century readers in Cornwall. One essential constituent of any self-respecting ethnic history is an idea of a common and distinct origin for the group. All of the above writers identified a common origin for the Cornish. Borlase wrote of the 'Cornish Britons', who, fleeing before the Saxons, 'retired into Wales and Cornwall' and then into Brittany.[35] Polwhele plagiarised this from Borlase and added that the 'inhabitants of this island ... were dispersed before the Saxon conquerors, they retired into Wales and Cornwall, and thence into Bretagne ...'.[36]

A second constituent of ethnic histories is a clear sense of boundary between the ethnic group and others. For Borlase the early Cornish were seen in clear opposition to the invading Saxons:

> there was a national enmity betwixt the Britons and the Saxons, which Athelstan recognised by excluding the Cornish from east of the Tamar and making 'the Tamar their future boundary, which has ever since been so accounted ... from this time therefore we are to consider Cornwall under the Saxon yoke ... the Cornish Britons ... maintained a perpetual struggle against the Saxons for the full space of 500 years'.[37]

Drew echoed this interpretation in his account of the 'fierce contentions which subsisted between its [Cornwall's] ancient inhabitants and the rapacious Saxons ... so tenacious were the British tribes of their ancient inheritance, that they disputed the encroachments of their invader, and defended their hereditary rights against them for several centuries'.[38] Indeed, Drew constructs the tenth century incorporation of Cornwall into the Kingdom of Wessex in recognisably nationalist terms. This was 'both fatal and final to the independence of the Cornish. This, amidst all the struggles that Cornwall made to preserve her liberty untainted, and that

---

[34] P.S.Morrish, 'History, Celticism and propaganda in the formation of the Diocese of Truro', *Southern History* 5 (1983), 249.

[35] William Borlase, *Antiquities Historical and Monumental of the County of Cornwall*, London, 1769, 40.

[36] Richard Polwhele, *The History of Cornwall*, London, 1806, 25.

[37] Borlase, 1769, 42-44.

[38] Fortescue Hitchins and Samuel Drew, *The History of Cornwall*, Helston, 1824, 12.

her enemies made to rob her of that inestimable jewel, this was the era of the first subjugation of the Cornish by the English'.[39]

However, the clear boundaries drawn by Cornwall's historians between Saxons and Cornish in the first millennium were much more ambiguously constructed in relation to the Cornish and the English of the eighteenth and nineteenth centuries. Sometimes the Cornish were defined by their historians as not English, 'surrounded [sic] as they are by the sea, and reckoning themselves as it were of another and different nation from the English'.[40] But for Drew the centuries that had followed the 'first subjugation of the Cornish by the English' had seen 'both the vanquisher and vanquished ...blended together in one undistinguished mass'.[41] By the eighteenth century the English were no longer those Saxon 'barbarians' of old. Instead they had been civilised by the Normans, to become altogether more cosmopolitan and cultured and, as Polwhele described them, 'friends of literature'.[42] For writers from the gentry-clerical class a desire to stress their Norman roots and the influence of an English historiography (that to some extent had confined the Saxons to England's 'dark ages' and hybridised the racial origins of the 'English') combined to blur the Cornish/English binary by this time.

As the nineteenth century unfolded, the Cornish began to be viewed more explicitly as 'Celts'. Borlase had used the term 'Celt' in the eighteenth century but included within it Scythians, Celtoiberians, Teutons and Germans, all descended from Gomer, a view of 'Celtic' descent common in the later eighteenth century.[43] Nevertheless, Borlase also clearly identified the Cornish, along with the Welsh, Bretons, Cumbrians and Gaels, as 'ancient Britons ... one and the same people, as to origins'.[44] By the 1850s the term 'Celtic' was being used again in the narrower sense proposed by Lhuyd and Pezron a century and a half before. Thus Merivale described the Cornish as 'Cornu-Britons, that small but strongly characterised Celtic people'.[45] While Merivale used the term 'Celtic' in a descriptive way, the Reverend Wladislaw Lach-Szyrma, himself born in Plymouth and the son of a Polish emigré, went much further. He argued in the 1860s that the Cornish were a distinct 'race', 'no contiguous counties in England contain populations so

---

[39] Hitchins and Drew, 1824, 725.
[40] Borlase, 1758, 304.
[41] Hitchins and Drew, 1824, 2.
[42] Polwhele, 1806, 35.
[43] Colin Kidd, *British Identities before Nationalism: Ethnicity and Nationhood in the Atlantic World, 1600-1800*, Cambridge, 1999, 51-52.
[44] Borlase, 1769, 11.
[45] Merivale, 1857, 302.

entirely distinct in race from one another as Devon and Cornwall ... The Cornish ... are mostly Celts'.[46] For Lach-Szyrma, newly fashionable ideas of racial distinctiveness plus Cornwall's linguistic history made the Cornish far closer to the Welsh and Bretons than the English. Here were the beginnings of that Cornish Celtic revival that was to re-construct a more explicit common myth of descent. Here also were the local echoes of nineteenth-century notions of 'purer', racially based identities. Such ideas were to lead to a racialization of the English as having common Anglo-Saxon roots in the 1890s, a move that of course opened up the space for Celtic 'racial roots' for the other peoples of Britain.

By emphasising Celtic and non-English origin myths, intellectuals in Cornwall were constructing a common memory, but it shared the ground with other popular myths. Edward Spender, managing director of the *Western Morning News*, repeated in the 1860s the, by then, common view of Celtic origins. But he also suggested that the popular descent myth 'a generation ago' stated that the racial origins of the Cornish could be traced to the Phoenicians, despite Borlase's explicit rejection of this in the 1760s.[47] Spender added that this descent myth was 'untrue', although the 'Kelts (sic) undoubtedly had an oriental origin', spoke 'a tongue of Aryan origin, and ... worshipped the same gods as the Fire and Sun worshippers of the East'![48] Here we have an amalgam of an older myth of southern or eastern European origin, new views of Celtic origins and the romanticism that was later to envelop the Cornish, creating its own mists of confusion. This representation of Mediterranean origins had two popular variants. The first believed that the Cornish were one of the lost tribes of Israel, a view reinforced by mis-readings of Cornish place-names like Marazion. The second claimed that the Cornish were of Spanish descent; there were many descendants of settlers from southern Spain 'at a very remote period'.[49] This latter was also based on confusion over Cornish surnames such as Pascoe, Jago or Jose.

Francis Harvey's writings also suggest that the popular myth was not exactly coherent:

> "Cornish boys" and "one and all men" terms certainly telling of their nobly bold, and truly united clanism, and sure sympathy, were familiar household words, and every true Cornishman prizes these exclusive titular rights, as valued reliques of the peerless men, who, of all England baffled and nobly withstood the ancient

---

[46] Wladislaw Lach-Szyrma, *The Bishopric of Cornwall: A Letter to W.E.Gladstone*, Truro, 1869, 8.
[47] Borlase, 1769, 13.
[48] Edward Spender, *Fjord, Isle and Tor*, London, 1870, 126-127.
[49] Spender, 1870, 126.

aggressive forces of the north, causing the defeated marauders, when leaving our shores discomfited, and hopeless in their grief, to exclaim "they are only waille," (foreigners), hence "kornuwaille", the horn in the sea, possessed by the foreigners; ....[50]

In this narrative the English of the ninth and tenth centuries were apparently displaced by the Danes. The latter, in fact allies of the Cornish in their battle against the English at Hingston Down in 838, had become their enemies. Regional patriotism had here restructured its past from within a master narrative of English nationalism, a process that was later to cause some despair among twentieth century Cornish revivalists.

Whereas a Celtic origins myth co-existed and competed with a Mediterranean origin myth, it is instructive to note what became accepted much more quickly. In 1825 Robert Stephen Hawker published anonymously his 'Song of the Western Men'. This song, popularly known as 'Trelawny', caught on rapidly and was accepted by Davies Gilbert and other writers as a genuine seventeenth-century popular song. Within twenty years it appears that it had become the Cornish anthem, although penned by a high Church Devonian who was, like Lach-Szyrma, born in Plymouth, and who was based at Morwenstow, in the far northern margins of Cornwall. It commemorated a fictitious near rebellion when the Puritan Bishop Trelawny was imprisoned by James II in 1688. Fictitious or not, Trelawny quickly became a Cornish folk-hero. By the 1850s it could be said, by a Cornishman, that the Cornish 'are particularly proud of their parentage, to a degree almost rivalling that of the Welsh, and refer to King Arthur and Trelawny as demigods and patterns of virtue and patriotism. The soul stirring patriotic and favourite song of 'Trelawny' is still sung by them'.[51]

The creation of the Trelawny myth created another possible 'golden age', combining vague memories of the Cornish rebellions of the late fifteenth and sixteenth centuries (and the Cornish military victories in the 1640s) with the Protestantism that was a feature of the nineteenth. The embarrassingly Catholic and traditional aspects of the Cornish revolts were avoided by the simple device of realigning Cornish sixteenth-century rebelliousness with Protestantism and projecting events of the late fifteenth and sixteenth centuries onto a later period.

There are other potential 'golden ages'. For example, King Arthur, mentioned above, suggests the period of independence before the tenth century. (The time lapse between the tenth and the nineteenth centuries was no real impediment, as the examples of other 'golden ages' show;

---

[50] Harvey, 1869, 29.
[51] George Henwood, in Burt (ed.), 1972, 220. See also *The Cornish Banner*, January 1847, 203-205.

Macedonians looked to the golden age of the Bulgarian tsars in the ninth and tenth centuries and the Irish looked back to early Celtic kingdoms.)[52] Indeed, the period before 1050 became an implied 'golden age' during the long campaign for a separate Cornish diocese that began in the 1840s and culminated in the 1870s. Morrish suggests that this historical argument had a 'community appeal'.[53] This appeal lay not in the details of the historical argument but in its connection to a more generalised desire for Cornish distinctiveness. A sense of identity was here seeking out distinctiveness whilst, at the same time, it was itself created by distinctiveness.[54]

The Chartist missionary Abraham Duncan had in 1839 lamented that the collective folk history of the Cornish people was extremely limited. 'The people have no dreams of the past - no historical epochs to fall back upon, calculated to light the torch and inflame the soul anew for the battle of liberty. They never fought, bled, or died for liberty'.[55] In fact, there were plenty of historical epochs to choose from but they all lay on the far side of two major historical divides that, to some extent, cut the Cornish off from their history. These were, first, the language shift in mid and west Cornwall from Cornish to English during the sixteenth to eighteenth centuries and, second and possibly more important, the divide produced by industrialisation. Industrialisation produced a way of life structured by Methodism and mining plus an associated identity with a dominant ideology of progress. It was a difficult project to match this new self-representation with the potential 'golden ages' that Cornwall's history offered.

At the same time, however, while collective memories were dim and shifting, the Cornish as well as the non-Cornish middle classes, especially clerics, were assiduously re-creating history for this 'history-less' people. For instance, John Wallis, Vicar of Bodmin from 1817 to his death in 1866, reprinted long accounts of the rebellions of the fifteenth and sixteenth centuries, pointing out 'how Cornishmen were mixed up with the stirring events of those unhappy days'. He went further, arguing against administrative centralisation 'on behalf of a County which once had almost regal privileges'.[56] The argument that Cornwall's constitutional history, the Duchy of Cornwall and the

---

[52] Brunn, 1992, 333.
[53] Morrish, 1983, 260.
[54] For the history of Cornwall's first golden age see Bernard Deacon, *Cornwall's First Golden Age*, London, 2016.
[55] Cited in Alf Jenkin, 'The Cornish Chartists', *Journal of the Royal Institution of Cornwall*, NS9, 1982, 31-45.
[56] John Wallis, *The Cornwall Register*, Bodmin, 1847, 15, 124, 129-156.

Stannaries all gave it a special constitutional position was echoed in the Lysons' *History of Cornwall*: 'by its royal privileges, and the retention of its ancient language, Cornwall still continued nevertheless to retain some semblance of a distinct sovereignty'.[57]

Here then we have the outlines of a distinct group history produced by an intellectual class. Golden ages in the late seventeenth century and before the eleventh century, special constitutional privileges, a shared 'Celtic' origin and quasi-mythical folk heroes all combined by the 1850s to make up a consistent group history. This seems different only in content rather than form from other emerging 'ethnic/national' histories of the nineteenth century. Indeed, Morrish points out how the vigour of the historical arguments employed to advance the case for a Cornish Bishopric was much stronger than elsewhere.[58] In other places, such views of history were the basis for claims of nationality. While Morrish's own preference is to describe the Cornish arguments as part of a 'county loyalty and identity',[59] rather than as a national identity, there seems no particularly good reason for this, other than the course of subsequent history and Cornwall's administrative status. This could itself be viewed as the result of historical and geographical contingency, the incorporated territory of Cornwall being just about the right size to be administered as one 'English' county.

An alternative view is to see the myths of Cornish history as the latent resources for a sense of nationality (which it did become for some people later in the nineteenth century and for many more in the second half of the twentieth) but which did not emerge in an explicit form in the period we are discussing. At this time there existed certain material difficulties that constrained the emergence of a 'Cornish nationalist' view of history. Principal among these must be the nature of social class forces in Cornwall. Industrialisation had produced a dynamic class associated with mining and related industries, in the increasingly respectable mine captains and entrepreneurs. However, there remained a social gulf between this predominantly Methodist group and the Anglican clerical antiquarians and historians who were writing and re-writing Cornwall's history. Industrialisation also meant that there was no obvious 'period of decline' with which to contrast the so-called 'golden ages', at least before the later 1860s. The disaffected middle classes, who appeared to be at the vanguard of ethnic consciousness elsewhere in Europe, are

---

[57] Daniel and Samuel Lyson, *Magna Britannia: A Concise Topographical Account of the Several Counties of Great Britain, Volume 3*, London, 1814, iv.
[58] Morrish, 1983, 259.
[59] Morrish, 1983, 256.

difficult to identify in the Cornish context. When de-industrialization did set in, the disaffected had the ready escape route of emigration available to them.

Therefore, while boundaries had been produced and various symbols of distinctiveness created, the Cornish identity remained essentially regional in expression. Cornish intellectuals looked for certainties in the face of industrial change in the same way as some of the middle classes in the industrial cities of the North of England were doing. At the same time other social groups gained their self-identity more from Cornwall's role in industry and mining than from its remote past, although, as we have seen, there were popular myths of a common origin and popular historical folk-heroes. Nevertheless, the work of Cornish historians in this period did produce and reinforce views of the past that helped to structure a sense of difference and these were themselves overlaid by a wider turn to Romanticism later in the century. In the long run, these representations proved more resilient than the way of life based on the economic region. The latter succumbed to a changing global division of labour that was to shatter the base of Cornwall's regional self-confidence, but the identity remained, to be transformed and transmitted by future institutions. But this is to jump too far ahead. First, we must identify some of those institutions that had such an important role in producing and reproducing the emerging Cornish identity in the late eighteenth and early nineteenth centuries.

Chapter 5
Social institutions and elites

In chapters 3 and 4 I focused on the perception of contemporaries when describing the transformation of the Cornish territorial identity in the eighteenth and nineteenth centuries. I emphasised the symbolic meanings ascribed to the notion of Cornwall and some of the ways in which these were produced, articulated and reproduced by different agents over time. In doing this, moreover, I noted the key role of Cornwall's economic structure, in the centrality of its mining industry and the symbols and way of life associated with that industry.

Yet, whether stressing the structures of the mining region or highlighting the perceptions of agents, whether focussing on the context or the narratives of identities, we do not have a fully satisfactory answer to the question of 'territorial shape'. Why Cornwall? After all, there were other possible paths, other territorial identities open to people. The most obvious was an area smaller than the administrative county of Cornwall, perhaps confined to west Cornwall, the heartland of the industrial region and, as will be suggested below, the core zone of the cultural region. It was only with the expansion of mining in east Cornwall in the 1830s and 1840s that some of the cultural features of this zone extended eastwards. Nevertheless, Cornwall and the Cornish were being imagined as a unity well before those decades, at a time when deep mining east of Truro was relatively unusual. Alternatively, why did a much larger area, such as Devon and Cornwall, not become a focus for territorial identity? The growing city of Plymouth, on the border of Cornwall, provided a potential provincial centre which, theoretically, could bind together a broader hinterland. To answer this problem of territorial scale we might profitably return to Anssi Paasi's model of the institutionalisation of regions and to the element of process.

Central to Paasi's model is the way in which symbols are welded onto the territorial framework through the process of institutionalisation. As we saw in chapter 1 Paasi proposes an institutionalisation process involving four overlapping stages. One of his stages is 'the emergence of institutions', standardised, permanent modes of behaviour and fixed roles.[1]

---

[1] Anssi Paasi, 'Deconstructing regions: notes on the scales of spatial life',

These institutions, both formal establishments, such as newspapers or schools, or more informal local and non-local cultural, economic, political, legal and educational practices, link the symbols to the territory. Individuals are socialised into ideas of the region through their membership of such institutions and through the communications of such institutions. For Paasi, the role of social institutions is therefore central. These, defined broadly, will 'eventually be the most important factors as regards the reproduction of the region and regional consciousness'.[2] This chapter therefore begins by identifying some of the cultural institutions which appeared during Cornwall's industrial phase and which carried the idea of 'Cornwall' to succeeding generations. Here we are discussing formal institutions rather than less formal social institutions such as the family or kin or broader cultural practices such as those attached to custom, aspects of which are touched on later in chapters 8 and 9.

Moreover, the process of institutionalisation is inextricably linked to prevailing social hierarchies. Some groups specialise in 'ideas' about the region, helping to create the symbols that are attached to a particular regional territory. We have already noted the role of the Cornish clerical-antiquarian gentry in this respect in the late eighteenth and early nineteenth centuries and others have pointed out a similar role for a metropolitan class of artists and intelligentsia in relation to the changing symbolic vocabulary of Cornwall after the 1870s.[3] Here, we proceed from an identification of Cornwall-wide institutions to investigate the Cornish landed and middle classes, the key groups in staffing such institutions and in reproducing the territorial identity of this period.

The production of Cornish institutions
In our period there were three waves of Cornish institutional production. From the first, in 1792, three initiatives sprang forth. In Truro in September 1792, seven gentlemen met at the Red Lion to discuss the formation of a County Library, Museum and Literary Society.[4] Three

---

Environment and Planning A 23 (1991), 245.
[2] Anssi Paasi, 'The institutionalization of regions: a theoretical framework for understanding the emergence of regions and the constitution of regional identity', *Fennia* 164 (1986), 121.
[3] Philip Dodd, 'Englishness and the national culture', in Robert Colls and Philip Dodd (eds), *Englishness: Politics and Culture 1880-1920*, London, 1-28; Jane Korey, 'As we belong to be: the ethnic movement in Cornwall, England', PhD thesis, Brandeis University, 1992, 141 *passim*; James Vernon, 'Border crossings: Cornwall and the English (imagi)nation', in Geoffrey Cubitt (ed.), *Imagining Nations*, Manchester, 1998, 153-172.
[4] Denise Crook, 'The early history of the Royal Geological Society of Cornwall,

months later at Bodmin another select committee of seven was formed to canvass subscribers for a Cornwall Agricultural Society.[5] Both of these societies were to enjoy long-term success, although the first eventually restricted itself to a library. The third institution was not successful. This was a proposed society 'for the general improvement of mining'.[6]

The second wave of institutions occurred in the 1810s. This included the Cornwall Geological Society in Penzance in 1814 and the Cornwall Philosophical Institution at Truro in 1818, later to receive royal patronage as the Royal Cornwall Geological Society (RCGS) and the Royal Institution of Cornwall (RIC) respectively.[7] These were two of the three 'county' literary institutions that were to dominate the intellectual life of nineteenth century Cornwall. The third society of the 1810s was more short-lived, the Cornwall Physical Institution at Falmouth in 1817 or 1818.[8] Although it did not survive, this institution managed to stake Falmouth's claim to be the home of Cornwall's third major 'county' institution, which was duly established in a third wave of institutional production. In 1833 the Royal Cornwall Polytechnic Society (RCPS) emerged in Falmouth to encourage the self-help and inventiveness of Cornish people. Its historian, Alan Pearson, suggested that its aim was more practical than the earlier two societies, reflecting another institution that appeared in 1832, the Cornwall Horticultural Society.[9] Between the first and second wave of Cornish institutions, a Cornish press had also appeared. In 1800 the *Royal Cornwall Gazette* began to publish. In 1810 the *West Briton* followed suit, established by reforming interests as a reaction against the Tory politics of the *Gazette*. In the nineteenth century, both newspapers, although published at Truro, attempted to provide a Cornwall-wide coverage.

These, then, were the key formal institutions, organised at least in name on a Cornwall-wide basis, that appeared in the 40 or so years from 1792. They both reflected a certain level of 'county' consciousness and articulated this county consciousness through their activities. But they were also, as Paasi reminds us, products of a hierarchical society. The

---

1814-1850', PhD thesis, Open University, 1990, 13-14.

[5] Christopher Riddle, *'So Useful an Undertaking': a History of the Royal Cornwall Show*, Wadebridge, 1994, 3.

[6] 'Rules of Cornish Mining Society'. CRO M255/6.

[7] Crook, 1990, i; Sally Freeborn, 'A history of the RIC and its role in adult education during the nineteenth century', MPhil thesis, Cornwall College, 1986, 66-67.

[8] Crook, 1990, 55.

[9] Alan Pearson, 'A study of the Royal Cornwall Polytechnic Society', MA thesis, University of Exeter, 1973, 26.

earlier institutions, those of the 1790s, were initiated and controlled by elements of the landed gentry. Indeed, Sir Francis Basset of Tehidy was a member of both the select committee of the Cornwall Agricultural Society and one of the promoters of the Cornwall Library and there was much overlap in the subscription lists of these two societies, lists dominated by the landed and clerical-landed class. These gentry-led institutions had been prefigured by the Cornish Club, established in London in 1768 for all 'gentlemen, connected with Cornwall, as might be temporarily or permanently residing in London, to dine together several times in every year'.[10] Sir William Lemon, county MP from 1774 to 1824, was a subscriber to the Cornwall Agricultural Society and promoter of the Cornwall Library in 1792 and also one of the five founder members of the Cornish Club.

In contrast to these successful gentry-led institutions, the proposed society of 1792 to promote Cornish mining, aimed at 'agents, captains and others concerned in mines' failed to establish itself. However, by the 1830s, a few at least of this more middle-class target group were involved in the activities of the Cornish literary societies. More generally, the urban professional and middle classes were increasingly present in the institutions of the second and third waves in addition to the gentry.

Did this mean that the reproduction of the symbolic ideas of Cornwall passed from the landed to the middle classes between 1790 and 1840? Mark Billinge proposes that the new grand bourgeoisie of the industrial regions - businessmen, together with some professional men, particularly surgeons and doctors - established literary and philosophical institutions dominated by a concern for science.[11] The self-identity and status of the bourgeoisie was forged around these institutions.

Was the role of the Cornish literary institutions the same? Did they act in a manner similar to the institutions of the industrial regions of northern England - as foci for an emergent bourgeois culture? It would seem not. Medical men did play a critical role in the Cornwall Geological Society in 1814, in much the same way as they did in the Manchester Literary and Philosophical Society in 1781.[12] But there were major differences between the Cornish societies and the northern 'lit and phils'. The first is one of timing. The Cornish societies emerged at least a generation later than societies such as the Manchester Lit and Phil or the even earlier

---

[10] CRO AD 965/2.

[11] Mark Billinge, 'Hegemony, class and power in late Georgian and early Victorian England: towards a cultural geography', in Alan Baker and Derek Gregory (eds), *Explorations in Historical Geography: Interpretative Essays*, Cambridge, 1984, 35-37 and 45-46.

[12] Crook, 1990, 24; Billinge, 1984, 51.

Birmingham Lunar Society and the Honourable Society of Cymmrodorion in Wales.[13] In Cornwall, such societies were coterminous with similar organisations in provincial and 'county' towns across England. For instance, literary societies were formed in Plymouth in 1812 and Exeter in 1813. Thus, they resembled, in this respect, county literary societies rather than the self-confident urban societies of the industrial regions. This conclusion is reinforced by other differences.

Principal among these was the absence of dissenters in the Cornish societies. Old dissent provided a large proportion of the membership of eighteenth century English literary societies. In contrast, Denise Crook concludes that 'only a small proportion of the membership of the Royal Cornwall Geological Society belonged to one of the dissenting groups, and none of the clergy among the members was from this group'.[14] Crook could identify with confidence only four Methodists among the 65 original members, despite the dominant numerical position of Methodism in west Cornwall by this time (see chapter 9 below). The Royal Institution of Cornwall was similar and even the membership of the Royal Cornwall Polytechnic Society, despite the role the Quaker Fox family played in it, was dominated by Anglicans.

Socially, the Cornish institutions recorded a higher proportion of gentry and a lower proportion of businessmen than the societies of the industrial cities. Table 5.1 overleaf summarises the occupational background of two of the Cornish institutions at selected periods.

Crook notes that in the Manchester Lit and Phil 56 per cent of members were manufacturers and merchants in 1809-11, a proportion matched in similar societies in the Potteries and Yorkshire. The proportion of active businessmen was never that high in the Cornish societies.[15] Although the most numerous social group does appear to have been the professional and business middle classes, unlike their northern counterparts all the Cornish societies adopted a policy of actively encouraging members of the landed gentry to join. Here the role of the clergy and lawyers in mediating between the county gentry on the one hand and the petty bourgeoisie (shopkeepers, small traders and manufacturers) in the towns seems to be along the lines proposed by Dennis Smith in his study of Birmingham and Sheffield.[16] While many were passive patrons, some gentry, like Sir Charles Lemon, were very actively involved in these societies. It seems that, while being broadly

---

[13] Crook, 1990, 1.
[14] Crook, 1990, 71.
[15] Crook, 1990, 63-64.
[16] Dennis Smith, *Conflict and Compromise: Class Formation in English Society 1830-1914*, London, 1982, 8.

middle-class institutions, the Literary Societies in Cornwall were seeking additional status (and additional funds) through their association with the gentry. The search for status drove these societies, as it had driven the earlier societies of the industrial cities, but in Cornwall there was a need to associate with, rather than against, the landed class. This process is also demonstrated in the seeking and attainment of royal patronage.

Table 5.1: Occupations of male members of the Royal Cornwall Geological Society and Royal Cornwall Polytechnic Society, 1818-1856 (%s)

	RCGS 1818	RCGS 1834	RCPS 1856
gentry	26	37	27
business	29	31	30
law and medicine	19	10	13
clergy/army/navy	11	12	12
not known/misc	14	11	19
N	159	94	231

Source: based on Crook, 1990, 58, 166; Report of the Royal Cornwall Polytechnic Society 24 (1856); Kelly's Directory, 1856.

The absence of earlier, more self-confidently independent 'bourgeois' literary institutions in Cornwall can, of course, largely be explained by the absence of a single large and expanding industrial town where professional and business classes could congregate. The small towns of Cornwall also militated against the development of co-operative relations between the 'Lit and Phils'. Indeed, proposals from the RGSC in 1842 that the three senior Cornish societies should unite to form an 'Association of Cornish Societies', with some joint meetings, fell on stony ground following hardly any response from the other two societies.[17] The urban middle classes in Cornwall were unable to overcome their parochial interests to give a clear institutional form to their territorial identity. In terms of institutional formation, their more local place identities seem to have outweighed their Cornish identity.

Finally, how was the pre-eminence of the mining industry reflected in Cornwall's new literary institutions? If we look at the membership, there was a notable absence of those directly involved in mining, despite its central role in Cornish society. Nonetheless, Crook notes that, despite

---

[17] Crook, 1990, 48.

only three per cent of the original members of the Royal Cornwall Geological Society in 1814 being mining professionals, 'more than half the members were involved financially in mining affairs; many more may well have held shares in mining ventures'.[18] The apparent absence of direct links with mining does not mean, therefore, that the Cornish societies escaped the influence of mining. Indeed, this paradox reflects the nature of the 'mining interest' in Cornwall. Moreover, the expanding mining industry had – directly and indirectly – both added to the ranks of the Cornish social elite and undermined its social stability.

Cornwall's merchant bourgeoisie
As early as 1778 William Pryce was noting that 'it is the popular opinion that no real surplusage beyond the charges of mining do arise to the adventurers in general'.[19] Three quarters of a century later J.R.Leifchild was working the same vein of pessimism: 'in Cornwall, as elsewhere, it is known to the well-informed, that mines in the aggregate are a losing concern'.[20] Yet it is possible to find others who were arguing the reverse, that mining offered a profitable investment opportunity to match any other, even as late as the 1850s.[21] Pryce himself was sceptical of the arguments of the pessimists, commenting upon the 'opulent fortunes' made by some, while William Borlase, also writing in the eighteenth century, was conscious of the 'great fortunes [that] have been raised to adventurers'.[22] Other commentators have explained an apparent lack of aggregate profitability alongside continued investment in Cornish mining by pointing to the role of local merchants who were also adventurers. They could profit, even from a failing concern, through monopolising supplies of materials.[23] This view was also implied at the Commons Committee investigating the Copper Trade in 1799 when John Vivian, in giving evidence, went out of his way to argue that merchants did not dominate copper mines[24] Whether they did or not, and Vivian's

---

[18] Crook, 1990, 55.
[19] William Pryce, *Mineralogia Cornubiensis: A Treatise on Minerals, Mines and Mining*, London, 1778, xii.
[20] J.R.Leifchild, *Cornwall: Its Mines and Miners*, London, 18547, 245.
[21] J.A.Phillips and John Darlington, *Records of Mining and Metallurgy*, London, 1857, 197.
[22] Pryce, 1778, xii; William Borlase, *Natural History of Cornwall*, Oxford, 1758, 206.
[23] Roger Burt, *The British Lead Mining Industry*, Redruth, 1984, 80-83. And see Allen Buckley, *The Cornish Mining Industry: A Brief History*, Penryn, 1992, 23.
[24] 'Report from the select committee adopted to enquire into the state of copper

presentation was somewhat disingenuous in its classification of 'merchants', some people clearly did make money, a lot of money, out of Cornish mining. Moreover, the really large gainers were more likely to have diversified portfolios of interests as merchants, smelters and bankers.

By the end of the eighteenth century a group of merchants, along with some of the landed gentry, were major shareholders in copper mining. Foremost among them was the Williams family, originating as tinners in Stithians in the seventeenth century. By the early eighteenth century John Williams (c.1684-1761), who had moved to Gwennap, at the centre of the expanding copper industry, was the manager of Poldice mine and heavily involved in the building of the Great County Adit, a project that opened up a large area of productive ground in the Camborne-Redruth district. Allen Buckley claims that by 1800 the Williams family 'controlled or managed over a quarter of the copper mines in Cornwall'.[25] John Williams' grandson, also named John (1753-1841), moved from mine management into other fields, establishing, in 1822, the partnership of Fox, Williams, Grenfell and Co., later Williams, Foster and Co., which invested in copper smelting in Swansea and opened places of business in London, Liverpool, Manchester and Birmingham. By 1840 the company's capital was £400,000 and John Michael Williams, who left £1.6 million in his will in 1880, was described as 'probably the most wealthy man in Cornwall'.[26]

The Williamses moved from mines management and adventuring in the eighteenth century into smelting, banking and other trades in the nineteenth century. Their counterparts, the Bolithos, equally dominant in tin mining by the 1840s, had moved in the opposite direction. Before 1740, this family had moved from Penryn, where they had been tanners and merchants, to Madron, near Penzance. There Thomas Bolitho (1765-1858) leased lime pits and, by 1805, had joined in a partnership which owned the tin smelting works at Chyandour. In 1810 Bolitho Sons and Co. were involved in tin smelting, shipowning, dealing in hemp, cordage and tallow and the export of pilchards.[27] However, their most significant move was into banking. In 1807 they established the Mounts Bay Commercial Bank and entered into partnership in the East Cornwall Bank, based at Liskeard. From this base they then bought shares in

---

mines and copper trade of the kingdom', British Parliamentary Papers, 1799, X.653, 159-163.

[25] Buckley, 1992, 16.
[26] G.C.Boase, *Collectanea Cornubiensis*, Truro, 1890, 1252.
[27] D.B.Barton, *A History of Tin Mining and Smelting in Cornwall*, Truro, 1967, 24.

various tin mines. By 1885 the family was wealthy enough to be described as the 'merchant princes' of Cornwall.[28]

Other merchants prospered from the general increase in trade associated with mining expansion. The Fox family had moved west from Fowey to the growing port of Falmouth sometime in the early eighteenth century. Making money from pilchard exports and the timber trade, the Foxes had become major investors in Cornish mining by the 1790s, as well as leading a consortium that built an iron foundry at Perranarworthal. They had also helped to form the Portreath Company, which worked Cornwall's first railway, linking the harbour at Portreath to the Gwennap mines. Investing widely in various mines from the 1780s to the 1840s and being the principal financiers for the restarting of Dolcoath in 1799, the Foxes showed considerable foresight in pulling out of mining in the later 1840s.[29]

This pattern, either from mines management and investment into banking and smelting, or from general merchanting into mines investment and smelting and/or banking, was followed by many other families. William Davey of Redruth was a solicitor and manager of Consols Mine in nearby Gwennap in 1819. His sons, Stephen and Richard, major mines adventurers in the 1840s, were cited by John Rowe as an example of the managerial class in mining, 'risen to the highest ranks of county society'.[30] While the Daveys and others followed the first path noted above, from mines management into banking and merchanting, perhaps more common was the second route. Examples include Thomas Daniell, who succeeded to some of William Lemon's business interests around 1760 and became the 'head of the great Truro merchant dynasty'.[31] His successor, Ralph Allen Daniell gained large profits from Great Towan at St Agnes in the late eighteenth century and had 'considerable interests in the Gwennap mines', while remaining 'primarily a Truro merchant'.[32] In the productive copper mining country at St Day, east of Redruth, Collan Harvey (1770-1846), a cooper who diversified his interests to become a grocer, ironmonger, mathematical instrument dealer and flour merchant in partnership with his brother James, also became a successful mines adventurer and a partner in Williams, Foster and Co. for a time, as well as having a concern in

---

[28] *Cornish Magazine and Devon Miscellany*, cited in Boase, 1890, 1332-1340.
[29] D.B.Barton, *A History of Copper Mining in Cornwall and Devon*, Truro, 1961, 112.
[30] John Rowe, *Cornwall in the Age of the Industrial Revolution*, Liverpool, 1953, 24.
[31] Barton, 1967, 22 and Rowe, 1953, 59.
[32] Barton, 1961, 156.

Portreath harbour with the Foxes and Williamses. In turn, his son Richard (1808-70) became a partner in Williams, Harvey and Co, one of the leading tin smelters in Cornwall after 1837. At his death he left 'half of a million of money'.[33] The Fosters of Lostwithiel, tanners, merchants and bankers from 1807, also became involved in smelting - evidence that the fertility of mining could bear fruit even outside the principal mining districts.[34]

The merchant bourgeoisie and the gentry
This merchant middle class was located primarily in and near the towns of Truro, Falmouth and Penzance, together with Redruth and Gwennap. No doubt it was geographical proximity that aided their networking. In the tin mining industry in particular, Denys Barton claimed that by the 1840s the smelters were totally dominant, 'a tightly knit group no outsider could penetrate'.[35] It was also the merchant middle classes in places like Truro and Penryn who were prominent in the signs of 'voter independence' that Ed Jaggard detects in these boroughs before 1800.[36] But, at the same time as this group remained tightly knit in trade, sometimes cementing their commercial alliance by intermarriage, they were also marked by a progressive fusion with landed interests - a fusion made easier by the mercantile source of much of their wealth.

Within three generations at the most, the merchant families we have noted had bought their landed estate, in the process sometimes moving away from the district in which they had made their wealth. The Bolithos did stay in the Penzance area but, in 1866, Thomas Simon Bolitho, grandson of the first Thomas at Madron, bought Trengwainton House, which had been built by Sir Rose Price in 1814 from the profits of Jamaica sugar plantations. Thomas Simon Bolitho's son, Thomas Robins Bolitho, in the 1850s and 1860s enjoyed an education befitting a landed gentleman, at Harrow and Oxford.[37] In the early nineteenth century the Foxes of Falmouth were also busy 'becoming country gentlemen' as they spread across the pleasant south-facing countryside along the Helford estuary, building or buying the houses of Trebah, Penjerrick and Glendurgan.[38] Michael Williams, the second son of the founder of

---

[33] Boase, 1890, 328-330.
[34] Boase, 1890, 258.
[35] Barton, 1967, 76.
[36] Edwin Jaggard, *Cornwall Politics in the Age of Reform*, Woodbridge, 1999, 60.
[37] Boase, 1890, 1332-1340.
[38] Boase, 1890, 160-162.

Williams, Foster and Co., made the symbolic shift away from the Gwennap district in 1854 by purchasing Caerhayes Castle on the south coast. Michael's son, John Michael (1813-80) was educated at Charterhouse and bought landed estates at Grampound, St Columb and Wadebridge. In a similar move Stephen Davey of Redruth had decamped to Bochym Manor in Cury by the 1860s and sent his sons to Harrow and Oxford. Richard Harvey, son of Collan, bought the manors of Galmpton, near Brixham and Greenway, near Dartmouth, both in South Devon and many miles from Pengreep in Gwennap, where his father had died within a mile or two of the mines that had brought the family their fortunes.[39]

The Cornish merchant bourgeoisie in the first half of the nineteenth century were following a familiar path of gentrification, culturally aping the landed gentry, becoming their neighbours, sending their sons to their schools. In Cornwall there was nothing spectacularly new or different about this. This was a path already trodden by the Lemon family, who, in the seventeenth and eighteenth centuries, had gone in three generations from mines adventuring to a seat in Parliament, baronetcy and a country house, via banking and mercantile interests in Truro. Veronica Chesher argued that in the late seventeenth and early eighteenth centuries there were 'probably more nouveau riche ... than in almost any other county' as families such as the Carlyons and Gregors used the money made from tin and trade to ease their way into membership of the landed gentry.[40]

Moreover, this movement from trade to land was not only in one direction. Chesher points out that mining opportunities drew in 'old' families too. These used their resources to invest heavily in non-agricultural activities in eighteenth century Cornwall. The Bassets of Tehidy made £134,000 from mining between 1723 and 1760 while Samuel Enys took £20,000 profit from the same source in 25 years.[41] Chesher concludes that 'the scale of living of both (these) families was lifted on to a new level'. This was no icing on the cake as Chesher's statistics suggest that the Bassets' profits from mining exceeded all their other revenues in the period she examined by around 32 per cent. The involvement of the landed interest in industrial activity suggests an early convergence of economic interest between it and the rising merchant class. This served to ease the status accession of the latter.

Nevertheless, differences remained between the landed gentry and the merchant bourgeoisie in early nineteenth century Cornwall, however much the latter aspired to the culture of the former and the former

---

[39] Boase, 1890, 191 and 330.
[40] Veronica Chesher, 'Some Cornish landowners 1690-1760: a social and economic study', B.Litt thesis, Oxford University, 1957, 11 and 19.
[41] Chesher, 1957, 211.

benefited from the economics of the latter. Most important, most landed gentry remained primarily rentiers. Rents from land or from mining rights were usually their most important source of income. On the other hand, the bourgeoisie, however grand, could always fall victim to bankruptcy when the mining market moved against their investments. For example, the Gundry family built up a major merchanting business in the village of Goldsithney during the later eighteenth century. They became heavily engaged in mining in the Breage and Lelant areas with some interests in smelting and banking. However, the crash of 1814/15 hit them hard and continuing difficulties with the Wheal Vor flotation forced them into bankruptcy in 1820. Even merchant dynasties like the Daniells were not immune. Ralph Allen Daniell's son, Thomas, found himself in financial difficulties by 1828, just two years after serving a term as County Sheriff. To escape bankruptcy proceedings, he was forced to flee to Boulogne.[42] The shadowy presence of the bankruptcy court indicates a continuing distinction in culture and values between the landed and the bourgeois class in early nineteenth century Cornwall. In addition, it acted as an active spur to the latter to evolve a less risk-taking, more diversified resource base, preferably one buttressed by the apparent solidity and prestige of land.

However, in the meantime, the values of the merchant-bourgeoisie - of commerce, market relations (albeit oligopolistic), enterprise and risk-taking – had become the dominant values of Cornish society in the later eighteenth century. By 1812 the 'Associated Tinners' were able to stop landowners leasing smelting houses to unwelcome up-country interests, suggesting that hegemonic power rested with this mercantile class.[43] While gaining this economic dominance the mercantile class had adopted many of the mores of the landed gentry. Yet, at the same time local political power remained firmly with the latter.

John Beckett has suggested that the first step for the ambitious merchant seeking entry into the landed gentry was 'to accept the post of sheriff, a prestigious but expensive and time-consuming position that the local gentry preferred to avoid'. In both Shropshire and Cumberland merchants and traders held this post intermittently from 1725.[44] But in Cornwall the first merchant who can be identified acting as sheriff is Ralph Allen Daniell in 1795. By then of course he was living the life of a country gentleman at Trelissick in Feock. In 1803, Thomas Rawlings, a Padstow merchant, and in 1810 Richard Oxnam of Penzance served as

---

[42] Barton, 1967, 55.
[43] Barton, 1967, 35.
[44] John Beckett, *The Aristocracy in England 1660-1914*, Oxford, 1986, 122.

sheriffs.[45] Both these men were bankrupt by 1820. It was not until much later, in the 1850s and 1860s, that the Williamses, Fosters and Bolithos appeared in the list of sheriffs.

The Cornish merchant bourgeoisie were also slow to gain that other measure of social acceptance and political power, a place on the County bench. It was, according to Beckett, 'unthinkable' before 1850 for an individual to 'remain active in commerce or manufacturing' and be on the bench, although he cites some exceptions to this in areas where the gentry were few, notably Gloucestershire, south Wales and Cumberland.[46] Cotton merchants and masters began to come onto the Lancashire bench in large numbers after 1832, but more usually the proportions of businessmen on county benches were smaller; only 11 per cent of Justices of the Peace in Caernarfon, Derbyshire, Westmorland, Hertfordshire and Somerset were engaged in trade in 1867. In mid-century Cornwall the proportions did not reach even that figure. There were just eleven identifiable merchant-bourgeoisie amongst Cornwall's JPs in 1856, or 8 per cent of the total, heavily outnumbered by the 20 per cent who were clerical magistrates. By this time the Williamses and Bolithos had attained the bench, as had the Davey brothers of Redruth, Richard Foster of Lostwithiel, Joseph Carne, the Penzance banker and merchant, Edward Coode jr, John Magor and Humphrey Willyams - the last three all bankers. By 1873 the proportion of merchant-bourgeoisie had not increased. In fact, numbers stuck at eleven, now representing just 7.5 per cent of the 146 county magistrates. And of these eleven magistrates, the Bolitho and Williams families contributed five.[47]

Thus, while there was considerable fusion of economic interests between the landed class and merchant-bourgeoisie, the power of the latter was exercised mainly in the economic sphere; and even then, only rarely as direct employers of large numbers of workers. Culturally and politically, the Cornish merchant-bourgeoisie can hardly be said to have wrested power away from the landed class. This helps to explain why the landed classes' representations of Cornwall, their 'county' identity, with its formal expressions in the 'county' literary institutions, remained so important. In a similar way, the clerical-antiquarian view of Cornwall also retained a cultural dominance as both merchant-bourgeoisie and small-town professionals and tradesmen adopted and shared the images of the landed class.

---

[45] Joseph Polsue, *Lake's Parochial History of the County of Cornwall*, Truro, 1867-73, supplementary papers, 133-135.
[46] Beckett, 1986, 126 and 122-123.
[47] E.R.Kelly, *The Post Office Directory of Cornwall*, London, 1856 and 1873.

SOCIAL INSTITUTIONS AND ELITES

The mining interest
Indeed, when seeking the most influential groups in the institutionalisation of Cornwall, we are forced back to the concept of a hegemonic mining 'interest' in Cornwall rather than a dominant class or group. Roger Burt defines the 'mining interest' as those 'investing capital made from long standing family connections with the industry' and classifies these separately from smelters and local landowners.[48] However, as Burt also points out, because of the difficulty of distinguishing amongst a 'wide range of interests, held by the same individual or family' ... the 'classification of speculators as smelters, merchants, landowners, traders or industrialists [is] essentially an arbitrary one'.[49] This is an important point as it suggests that the one thing in common to this group of large and small capitalists was an interest in mining. Even if, as was often the case, individual fractions were in conflict – for example smelters against investors in mines or those who made their profits selling to the mines against those who looked to profits from the production of mines - it seems that the mining interest (defined more broadly as a loose alliance of landowners, smelters and other mines adventurers) acted to weld together the different fractions of capital socially and culturally.

Within this broad 'mining interest', the merchant-bourgeoisie were economically dominant, reserving to themselves the bulk of the surplus wealth generated by mining. But socially and culturally, they merged into the background, abdicating social control and political power to the traditional landed gentry in the countryside and to the professionals and petty bourgeoisie in the towns. Nevertheless, by the 1840s the expansion of mining, together with the institutionalisation of Methodism, was helping to produce a new, more genuinely self-confident and self-contained, middle class.

Mine captains - the making of a Cornish middle class
As mines became larger and more capitalised, the need for a managerial class became greater. Mine agents, in Cornwall called mine captains, fulfilled this role. Samuel Drew summed up their duties in 1824:

> The subordinate management of the mines is consigned to the care of captains; the number of whom increases in proportion to the size of the concern. It is their business to inspect the various departments of the work; to see that the men employed are properly distributed; to notice their industry or idleness; to

---

[48] Burt, 1984, 70.
[49] Burt, 1984, 60.

observe the increase or the decline of the prospects before them; to regulate the price of labour according to the hardness or softness of the ground; and to mark the variations which appear. It is also their business to see that the more dangerous parts are sufficiently propped with timber; that some men are employed in making new discoveries, while others are raising ore to meet the common expenditure; to notice the consumption of candles and gunpowder, and the injury done to the working tools; to see that the stopes and levels are fairly worked; that the channels conveying the water are in a state of repair, and that they conduct their various streams to the engine shaft, from which it is raised from the mine; to observe that there is neither a deficiency nor an unnecessary waste of materials; and to take care that no fraud is committed in the private distribution of the ore that is broken. It must be obvious that these captains sustain offices of high responsibility.[50]

By the second quarter of the nineteenth century this subaltern class, given a large amount of autonomy and with control over the labour process, occupied a strategic position, not just in mines management, but also in wider Cornish society. As Burt points out, captains played a patriarchal role in mining communities. Becoming a mine captain was the main avenue of social mobility open to an ambitious working miner in the period of mining expansion. However, because of their origin as working miners, they retained a blunt, down-to-earth straightforwardness.[51]

Mine captains, with their own experience of social and geographical mobility, espoused an ideology of personal independence, buttressed by their widespread allegiance to Methodism. They practised a rough form of social egalitarianism, but one welded to authoritarian and hierarchical relations with the working miners. This distinctiveness (personally independent, socially egalitarian, yet patriarchal) clearly resonated closely with the representation of Cornwall as 'industrial civilisation' that was identified in chapter 3.

Indeed, whereas the merchant-bourgeoisie had melded fairly unproblematically with the landed gentry in a mutually beneficial compromise, relations between mine captains and the landed/merchant-bourgeoisie coalition tended to be pricklier. Two case studies can be used to indicate the nature of these relations. The first is a painting. In 1786 John Opie completed a portrait showing Thomas Daniell, the Truro merchant and smelter and a 'Captain Morcom'. This was entitled 'Gentleman and a Miner' (This painting is used on the back cover of

---

[50] Fortescue Hitchins and Samuel Drew, *The History of Cornwall*, Helston, 1824, 613-614.
[51] Burt, 1984, 109.

Rowe, 1993. The original is at the Royal Cornwall Museum). Daniell holds in the palm of his hand a large lump of ore. Morcom stands, finger pointing. He may be making a reference to the engine house silhouetted in the background, smoke belching from its stack. Or he may be emphasising a technical or geological point to Daniell. Morcom, however, is the dominant figure, dynamic and direct, apparently fixing Daniell with his gaze. Daniell, on the other hand, looks past Morcom passively. The relations suggested by Opie show no hint of deference. Daniell may be a gentleman but Morcom is represented as approaching him in the same way that he would, presumably, approach anyone who needed to be told something about mining. The two share the painting but they do not engage with each other: Daniell gazes into the future and the family mansion at Trelissick along the quiet waters of the Fal, preferring to look away from the source of his wealth, the engine house and away from the eager, pushy Morcom.

Figure 5.1: 'Gentleman and a Miner', by John Opie, 1786.

The failure of easy communication between merchant-bourgeois and mine captain implied in Opie's painting echoes the relations of the two social classes within the county institutions of the late 1830s and 1840s. The low numbers of mining professionals joining the county societies was a subject of regret for the Royal Geological Society of Cornwall in 1841: 'the contributions of our intelligent mine agents and miners, both to the Society's museum and to its transactions, have been unusually few'.[52] As a result the society offered a premium for 'information of new and interesting facts connected with the mines'. But in 1843 it was reported that these 'have not drawn from the agents or from the miners the communications which the Society has been anxious to obtain'.[53] In 1847 the Society introduced a 'second class' membership, 'to enlist into their service the practical portions of our mining population'. However, despite the fact that 'since that time no efforts have been spared to induce such persons to join us in carrying out the intentions of the society ... our efforts have had only partial success'.[54] In 1849, a success was finally reported:

> The council have also to report the reception of some communications on the mineral deposits of the county, from persons whom they are particularly desirous of encouraging - the working miners, many of whom, from the nature of their occupation, must possess much valuable information. The council gladly welcome these communications; but, in doing so, they would intimate that they are much more anxious to obtain facts than theories. The latter can be useful only when they are based on a large accumulation of facts; but they are more likely to retard than to aid the progress of science, when they have only a few insulated facts for their foundation.[55]

Mine captains, therefore, could communicate but within certain limits. Sticking to facts was acceptable. Theory was reserved for the first class of members and was for gentlemen only! The Royal Geological Society seems to have had a genuine inability to realise that its implicit assumptions about social class were inhibiting its dialogue with the mine captains. The Society was unable to overcome the constraints of its social class assumptions.

A few years before this, Charles Lemon in 1838 had suggested a mining school should be established, an idea first floated by John Taylor in 1829. Lemon 'contacted mining agents with a proposal that he would bear the expenses of such an institution for two years'.[56] The Royal Institution of Cornwall at Truro made its premises available for the use of the School. However, a succession of mine agents initiated resolutions

---

[52] *Transactions of the Royal Geological Society of Cornwall* (1841), 15.
[53] *Transactions of the Royal Geological Society of Cornwall* (1843), 24.
[54] *Transactions of the Royal Geological Society of Cornwall* (1848), 19.
[55] *Transactions of the Royal Geological Society of Cornwall* (1849), 15-16.
[56] Burt, 1984, 126; Patrick Keane, 'Adult education and the Cornish miner: a study in Victorian initiative', *British Journal of Educational Studies* 22 (1974), 261-291.

against a proposed tax of a farthing in the £ on metallic materials to fund the school and the plan failed. The agents' opposition may have been connected with the proviso of Sir Charles that 'the college should be essentially a Church of England establishment'. This, and the location of the classes at Truro, at a distance from the main mining districts, guaranteed its collapse.

Other attempts by the RIC in the later 1850s were equally unsuccessful. It was only after the intervention of Robert Hunt and Robert Were Fox, of the Royal Cornwall Polytechnic Society, that eventually a Mining School was successfully launched. The difference this time was that a new organisation was to run it, and not one of the county societies. That organisation was itself to be managed by the mine captains. The inaugural meeting, significantly enough in the central mining district itself, at Camborne in October 1859, established a Mining Association of Cornwall and Devonshire, which went on to 'promote classes in elementary sciences connected with mining'.[57]

The story of the formation of the Mining Association is well known. But what previous commentators have failed to address is the formal title of the Association. Why Cornwall and Devon? In this instance the borders of the institution most closely linked with the mining industry were not coterminous with the borders of Cornwall. An explanation for this might be tentatively offered. The mine captains may have been ambiguous about the dominant historical idea of Cornwall, reproduced by the literate elite, one linked to the landed clerical-intelligentsia and the existing county societies. By encompassing Devon, even though in practice 'the Association was to be almost entirely a Cornish venture', the mine captains were doing two things.[58] First, they were distancing themselves from the county elite who thought only in 'county' terms. And second, by including Devon they were saying that the mining region was larger than Cornwall alone. Indeed, mining did spill over the border into Devon. The mine captains were staking a claim on that west Devon part of the industry but, and here the name of the institution - Cornwall and Devon - implies the relationship, one in which Cornwall was very much the senior partner. The still expanding industry of mining was not to be limited to old historical boundaries. County boundaries were assumed to be irrelevant to the new economic region. In saying this the mine captains came closer to the idea of Cornwall as an 'industrial region', something that will be explored further in the next chapter, than

---

[57] Keane, 1974, 275.
[58] Keane, 1974, 289.

did either the old county landed elite or its newer partners, the merchant-bourgeoisie.

Conclusion
I have argued in this chapter that, between the 1790s and the 1830s, new cultural institutions appeared in Cornwall. These institutions helped to reproduce ideas of Cornwall. In terms of Paasi's model they were instrumental in giving 'symbolic shape' to Cornwall. Yet, within them the landed gentry and their values continued to play a large, indeed dominant, role. This was despite the emergence of a recognisable Cornish 'merchant-bourgeoisie' during the eighteenth century. However, this merchant class, although gaining considerable economic power, did not confront local landed interests. On the contrary, by the early nineteenth century there was a growing fusion between merchant-bourgeoisie and gentry, with the former undergoing a process of gentrification and the latter using profits from mining and commerce to supplement their rent rolls. In this respect, the Cornish merchant bourgeoisie did not occupy the same social role as the self-confident business classes of industrial regions in the north of England. In Cornwall before the 1840s, formal political power remained in the hands of the traditional landed elite, albeit an elite with especially porous boundaries.

However, I have also suggested that a potentially more distinctively Cornish middle class emerged at the end of the eighteenth century. At its core were the mine captains, occupying a strategically important supervisory role, controlling labour in the dominant mining industry. Patronised by the landed class and their urban agents in the professions, mine captains were themselves discovering an institutional voice by the 1850s. Moreover, as we shall see in chapter 9, this added to their central role in another formal institution, the Wesleyan Methodist Connexion and its various offshoots, an institution that had a more pervasive effect upon the lives of local communities than the county literary institutions or their small-town imitators.

It was this social group, together with other industrial families, that spawned a new generation who, towards the end of the century, played a leading role in the new regional framework (Paasi's final stage) of diocese and County Council. However, the self-confidence of this incipient Cornish middle class was heavily dependent on the fortunes of the industry that begot it – mining. By taking a step back and looking in more comparative detail at Cornwall's economic history in this period we can both provide a context for the emergence of this class and the modern Cornish identity and place Cornwall's industrial period into a wider comparative perspective.

Chapter Six
Mines and mining: capital formation in Cornwall

In the previous three chapters we saw how Cornwall began to be imagined in new ways in the late eighteenth century. At several points in the creation of the symbolic shape of Cornwall the mining industry made an appearance. Indeed, the geography of identity mirrored the geography of mining. The language in which the Cornish identity was asserted, the ideology of 'industrial civilisation' and the institutions of the early nineteenth century did not, therefore, occur in a vacuum. There was a context and the facts of Cornwall's economic history make up part of that context. Adopting Dror Wahrman's insight, we can state that the economic framework provided a 'space of possibilities' within which representations of Cornwall could be produced and reproduced.[1] While Cornwall's mining economy did not determine the way it was imagined it did provide the parameters within which those imaginations took root.

This chapter asks how accurate it is to describe our 'industrial Celts' as 'industrial'. How did Cornwall's experience of industrialization compare with other regions? In asking these questions I review some approaches to Cornwall's economic history in this period before proposing a framework for understanding the economic background to identity formation. Historical perspectives on proto-industrialisation and industrial regions will be employed to discuss aspects of the Cornish economy between 1740 and 1870.

Framing the Cornish economy
Economic historians and regional geographers provide two perspectives on the Cornish economy in this period. These can be summarised as 'Cornwall as pastoralized margin' and 'Cornwall as industrial region'. According to Maxine Berg, 'manufacture was by no means new to the eighteenth century; cottage industries were widespread over the Scottish Highlands, west Wales, the Yorkshire Dales, the Derbyshire and Cornish countrysides'. But competition from more efficient industrial areas meant that these rural margins experienced a 'new pastoralization', the

---

[1] Dror Wahrman, *Imagining the Middle Class: The Political Representation of Class in Britain, c.1780-1840*, Cambridge, 1995, 6 and 8.

destruction of their cottage industries and a pauperisation of the communities dependent on them. That led to a 'long period of resistance to technology in many such communities'.[2] Berg shares her argument with Eric Richards who sees Cornwall as a part of the 'margins' of the industrial revolution. Along with such diverse regions as the west and north of Ireland, the Hebrides and Australia, Cornwall was 'drawn into the widening economic network on terms which seemed to be dominated by the more industrial, more populated and more dynamic centres' and 'condemned, at least in the early phase of industrialisation, to a greater dependence on non-industrial output'.[3] This view also lies behind Julian Hoppit's explanation of the relatively low bankruptcy rate he discovered in eighteenth century Cornwall. This was because Cornwall was 'on the periphery of the national economy, away from the main flows of internal and external trade'.[4]

There are two major weaknesses in this account of Cornwall as a margin. First, unambiguous empirical evidence for this pastoralization, or de-industrialisation, of the countryside is hard to find, at least for the late eighteenth and early nineteenth centuries. In the west, a process of de-industrialisation of rural cottage industry, if it did take place, had occurred much earlier. Lewis commented in 1907 that the low wages of tinners in west Cornwall in the later seventeenth century was partly because 'no clothing trade existed to serve as a by-employment'.[5] This claim has been borne out by more recent work. In west Penwith, an area of early tin mining, David Cullum found that domestic textile production equipment became less common in inventories during the later seventeenth century, indicating a shift from domestic production to the consumption of imports. He concludes that this tin-producing region, although part of a geographical periphery, also saw an early importation of consumer goods through the growing port of Penzance.[6] However, any de-industrialisation of local craft industries was offset by the parallel expansion of tin mining. What this suggests is a decline of rural textile

---

[2] Maxine Berg, *The Age of Manufactures, 1700-1820: Industry, Innovation and Work in Britain*, London, 1994, 6.

[3] Eric Richards, 'Margins of the industrial revolution', in Patrick O'Brien and Roland Quinault (eds), *The Industrial Revolution and British Society*, Cambridge, 1993, 204.

[4] Julian Hoppit, *Risk and Failure in English Business, 1700-1800*, Cambridge, 1987, 62-63.

[5] G.R.Lewis, *The Stannaries: A Study of the Medieval Tin Miners of Cornwall and Devon*, Boston, 1907, 221.

[6] David Cullum, 'Society and economy in west Cornwall, c.1588-1750', PhD thesis, University of Exeter, 1993, 293.

industry as early as the seventeenth century in the western, mining areas of Cornwall but the avoidance of net de-industrialisation through the concurrent expansion of mining employment.

If rural de-industrialisation did take place in the late eighteenth century, it would have been in the non-mining areas of east Cornwall. Thus, *Heard's Gazetteer* remarked: 'before the late war, the clothing business flourished' in Liskeard, but had disappeared by the date of publication.[7] Similarly, in Michaelstow in north Cornwall the published Census of 1801 claimed that 'the domestic manufacture of spinning obb yarn has been much injured by the introduction of machinery'.[8] This hints that some de-industrialisation took place during the Napoleonic war period, although more research is required in order to confirm or deny such a process.

The second weakness of the view of Cornwall as a de-industrialising and poverty-stricken margin is its difficulty in incorporating the mining industry into the picture. Sometimes the contradictions are unresolved. Berg, for example, after describing the Cornish countryside as an arena for new pastoralization, 'major dislocation' and the destruction of cottage industry, at the same time argues that 'early and rapid growth' in Cornwall produced 'the basis for one of the most advanced engineering centres in the world'.[9] The relevant aspect here is the timing of these two processes – the decline of rural, domestic industry and the expansion of the (also rural) mining industry. Richards allows that Cornwall had been part of an 'older core' but appears to suggest that it became de-industrialised after 1815 when 'rural, low-productivity domestic industries' were swept away by the low-priced goods of modern factory industry.[10] However, this date is certainly too late for the decline of domestic industry in the mining districts of west Cornwall and possibly too late also for their decline in the non-mining eastern districts. But, as a date for de-industrialisation, it is, as we shall see below, also far too early, as it anticipates the peak of mining production by about half a century. In fact, at the very point when, according to Richards, Cornwall was beginning its economic decline, mining, the dominant sector of the Cornish economy, was poised on the brink of 40 years of almost uninterrupted growth.

While the classification of late eighteenth and early nineteenth century Cornwall as a pastoralized margin lacks credibility, precisely because of the growth of metal mining, another perspective takes that growth as

---

[7] Thomas Heard, *Gazetteer of Cornwall*, Truro, 1817.
[8] Census, *British Parliamentary Papers* (140),.VI.8.13, 1801, 47.
[9] Berg, 1994, 6 and 112.
[10] Richards, 1993, 211 and 215.

central and argues that Cornwall was one of Europe's early industrial regions. We met this perspective in Chapter 1 in the converging work of historical geographers and economic historians on the industrial region. That work was part of a broader critique of the dominant aggregate approach to Britain's industrialisation that argued it was marked by continuity rather than revolution.[11] Maxine Berg and Pat Hudson, in particular, proposed a new agenda for the economic history of the industrial revolution which moved beyond this dominant interpretation.

Their approach has obvious attractions to anyone trying to make sense of the details of Cornwall's industrial period. According to their perspective, in the eighteenth century distinct specialised, internally cohesive industrial regions emerged, linked to national and international markets. 'Sectoral specialisation by region' occurred as export trade helped to create integrated transport, commercial and financial links within the industrial region. These in turn rested on dense networks of social, family and business links. Exports went directly from the region rather than through London and regional lobbying or regionally based protest movements had their epicentres in the larger provincial cities.[12] I will return to this model of industrial regions below and use some of its concepts to contextualise aspects of Cornwall's economic history. However, before doing this we require a more robust narrative for that history.

Narrating Cornwall's economic history
We might identity four phases. First, the period to 1750 was one of transition, as the foundations of extensive growth were established. Second, the long period from the 1750s to the 1830s contained the classic growth phase, when the contours of a specialised industrial region became apparent, but one with striking elements of continuity from the earlier period. Third, the two decades from the 1840s to the 1860s may be viewed as a distinct period of modernisation, when structural changes began to set Cornwall on a path of convergence with other more typical industrial regions. However, this trajectory was in turn abruptly arrested in the 1870s, pitching Cornwall into a fourth period, of de-industrialisation.

---

[11] Nicholas Crafts, *British Economic Growth During the Industrial Revolution*, Oxford, 1985.
[12] John Langton, 'The industrial revolution and the regional geography of England', *Transactions of the Institute of British Geographers*, NS9 (1984) 145-167; Pat Hudson, *The Industrial Revolution*, London, 1992, 102-108.

1) Transition

Roger Burt set out the circumstances in which the non-ferrous metals industries grew from the seventeenth century. New non-recyclable uses led to a widening and deepening of the markets for lead, copper and tin. Early expansion of the firearms industry stimulated lead production. This was followed by a growing market for brass wire in the woollen industry and for tin from the China trade. These produced supply side responses in an institutional context of a tradition of free market exploitation and private property rights in minerals lacking in other parts of Europe. Organisation in Cornwall was small-scale, lower cost, un-proletarianized and therefore more flexible, able 'to slide smoothly back into production, assisted by a continuing "subsidy" to labour costs from the agricultural by-employment of their labour force'.[13]

Output of Cornish tin rose during this transitional phase. Burt argues this was achieved through a multiplication of small units of production in the later seventeenth century, worked by 'semi-independent part-time miner/farmers, albeit with a greater degree of application of intensity'.[14] As he acknowledges, this picture reminds us of the proto-industrial model of the origins of industrialisation. Traditionally, this model, focusing on dispersed production in domestic units, has ignored or dismissed mining, seen as organised around centralised plant. However, if Burt is right then the assumption that metal mining at this period was centralised is itself flawed. Instead the usual unit was the small underground working involving a handful of people, perhaps even families, and with very limited capitalisation, one that was the mining equivalent of the cottage workshop.[15]

Does it help to view late seventeenth and early eighteenth century Cornwall as a proto-industrial economy? The poverty of Cornish tinners in the sixteenth and seventeenth centuries has been variously commented upon. It implies a group of workers who were relatively easily attracted to tinning if required, only to be discarded when demand receded.[16] For

---

[13] Roger Burt, 'The transformation of the non-ferrous metals industries in the seventeenth and eighteenth centuries', *Economic History Review* 48 (1995), 31.

[14] Roger Burt, 'The international diffusion of the non-ferrous metals industries in the seventeenth and eighteenth centuries', *Economic History Review* 44 (1991), 249.

[15] Roger Burt, 'Proto-industrialisation and the "stages of growth" in the metal mining industries', *Journal of European Economic History* 27 (1998), 85-104.

[16] Lewis, 1907, 221; Julian Cornwall, *Wealth and Society in Early Sixteenth Century England*, London, 1988, 80.

Burt this produced an 'independent and occupationally mobile society'.[17] It was also one where production costs were subsidised by other activities such as farming or fishing. This produced a labour force similar to the kelp, linen and straw-plaiting workers who Gilbert Schrank identifies as proto-industrial in eighteenth century Orkney. As a result, 'there were few fixed labour costs, a very low remuneration rate for the producers, who were members of a dominated group, and the ready expansibility and contractability of the work force in a widely fluctuating global market'.[18]

Franklin Mendels' original formulation of proto-industrialisation, seen as a stage between pre-industrial and industrial society, emphasises four aspects. First, rural industry grows as an income supplement for peasant farmers who become part-time workers. Second, its products are marketed outside the region. Third, proto-industrial activity stimulates and accompanies the emergence of commercial agriculture. Finally, the towns in the region spawn the merchants who provide the necessary circulating capital.[19] To some extent all these factors apply to seventeenth century Cornwall, with the possible exception of the knock-on effect on agriculture, although even here Burt notes the import of food into Cornwall by the eighteenth century and the demand from the mines for horses for transport.[20] Furthermore, both some of the preconditions for proto-industrialisation and some of its implications are applicable to Cornwall. The early disintegration of feudalism, weakness of manorialism and lack of access to common rights that are cited as necessary for proto-industrialisation have all been identified in Cornwall.[21] At the same time earlier marriage ages and high rates of population growth seem to be found in the tin-mining districts in the seventeenth century.[22]

However, there are also problems. Basing his criticism on the implication that proto-industrialisation is also a theory of proletarianisation, Cullum rejects its application to seventeenth century Cornwall on the grounds that the tin-mining farmers of West Penwith

---

[17] Burt, 1991, 267.

[18] Gilbert Schrank, 'Crossroad of the north: proto-industrialization in the Orkney Islands, 1730-1840', *Journal of European Economic History* 21 (1992), 368.

[19] Franklin Mendels, 'Proto-industrialisation: the first phase of the industrialisation process', *Journal of Economic History* 32 (1972), 241-261.

[20] Burt, 1998, 93-94.

[21] John Hatcher, 'Non-manorialism in medieval Cornwall', *Agricultural History Review* 18 (1970), 1-16.

[22] Cullum, 1993, 272-273; James Whetter, *Cornwall in the Seventeenth Century: An Economic Survey of Kernow*, Padstow, 1974, 8-10.

were not wage labourers. Instead, they were shareholders 'in a co-operative or a venture capitalist' rather than 'a proto-industrial worker'.[23] To an extent the differences between Burt and Cullum rest on the different versions of the proto-industrial model which they each articulate. Some versions emphasise proto-industrialisation as producing proletarianisation; others see it as remaining part of a feudal mode of production where surplus labour exists, although not necessarily proletarianised.[24] This suggests more general difficulties with the concept of proto-industrialisation, used to describe some very different conditions.

Those using it more recently tacitly accept this, emphasising the importance of proto-industrialisation more broadly in terms of directing our approach to the social context of industrialisation and the relationship between labour organisation, culture and production. If we accept the point of Berg et al. that proto-industrialisation should be placed 'within a broader context of social transformation, which was polymorphic, varying greatly between regions, branches of industry and time' then we have a more modest, more descriptive and more relativist use of the term.[25] As industrialisation based on greater levels of fixed capital and changes in the family economy evolved in Cornwall, especially with the explosive growth of copper mining after the 1730s, much of the identity of the later industrial region - notably the tradition of the 'independent' tinner - was moulded by its earlier experience of industrialisation, whether or not we bestow the title 'proto' on it.

Therefore, Cornwall before 1750 may fruitfully be seen as a variant of a proto-industrial region. Berg points out how proto-industrial regions 'connected much more significantly to the metropolis, and through this to international markets', than did later industrial regions.[26] The role of London merchants in the tin market in Cornwall in the early eighteenth century,[27] and that of the Duchy and Crown in Cornish tin extraction, illustrates the way Cornwall was locked into metropolitan-dominated circuits before the 1750s. In this way Charles More sees even nineteenth-century Cornwall as an example, along with London, of an older industrial region, distinct from the new industrial regions of the English

---

[23] Cullum, 1993, 283.
[24] Sheilagh Ogilvie and Markus Cerman, 'The theories of proto-industrialization' in Sheilagh Ogilvie and Markus Cerman (eds), *European Proto-Industrialization*, Cambridge, 1996, 2-5.
[25] Maxine Berg, Pat Hudson and Michael Sonenscher, *Manufacture in Town and Country before the Factory*, Cambridge, 1983, 19.
[26] Berg, 1994, 100.
[27] Rowe, 1953, 42.

Midlands and North.[28] Furthermore, as we shall see, Cornwall's industrial society, if not its economy, continued to be strongly marked by proto-industrial forms through to the 1840s.

2) Growth

The legacy of the transitional period was felt throughout the period of growth, for example in continuing traditions of dual employment, along with customary attitudes that seemed conservative, in the context of industrialising Britain. However, the copper region created in the eighteenth century was qualitatively different from the earlier 'proto-industrial' tin region. The central motif for most narratives of Cornish history in the period 1740-1870 is the expansion of mining. John Rowe suggests that already, as early as the 1740s, a third of Cornwall's men were affected by the fortunes of its mines and a quarter of its population were directly dependent on the mining sector.[29] This estimate may be on the high side, but for Rowe, the 1740s marked the beginning of a 'revolutionary transformation'. Large scale organisation and an increasingly sophisticated division of labour in mining required larger injections of capital. Capitalist partnerships were now the norm, replacing the co-operation of the 'free' miners of earlier times. At the same time, a new intermediate managerial group of mine captains and engineers, a technical middle class, began to emerge.[30] This 'revolution' was associated with the newer exploitation of copper ore reserves, the search for which was vigorously reshaping the mining industry. Copper extraction was 'extremely volatile. It was exciting, stimulating and always changing and expanding'.[31] It was an industry moving to the rhythm of capitalist markets which, during the eighteenth century, were themselves transforming the world. Within a century, metal mining in Cornwall had 'formed the basis of one of the most advanced engineering centres in the world ... and of a complex industrial society exhibiting early development of banking and risk-sharing to deal with the particular needs of local industry'.[32]

---

[28] Charles More, *The Industrial Age: Economy and Society in Britain, 1750-1985*, London, 1989, 56.
[29] Rowe, 1953, 28 and 39.
[30] Rowe, 1953, 40.
[31] Allan Buckley, *The Cornish Mining Industry: A Brief History*, Penryn, 1992, 16.
[32] Sidney Pollard, *Peaceful Conquest: The Industrialisation of Europe 1760-1970*, Oxford, 1981, 14.

Burt has re-emphasised the discontinuity of the eighteenth century although placing its origin earlier. The 'truly revolutionary changes that began in the last decades of the seventeenth century ... culminated around the mid eighteenth century'.[33] Between the 1660s and the 1680s, Cornish mines doubled their output of tin. By the end of the seventeenth century, tin mining, according to James Whetter, was monopolising capital investment in west Cornwall.[34] The largest tin mines were already rivalling the collieries of north east England 'in scale, complexity, the numbers of people they employed and the size of the capital investment they represented'.[35] Despite that, the output of tin metal remained on a plateau in the early eighteenth century with no clear upward trend. During the eighteenth century, its production was overshadowed by the rise of copper, as the mining interest in Cornwall turned their attention to this more lucrative mineral. By the 1770s, the income from copper ore had overtaken that from tin.

William Borlase, writing in the 1750s, noted the novelty of copper mining in Cornwall; 'the richness of our copper-works is not a late discovery, but indeed the application of the Cornish to work them effectually, is not so old as the present generation'.[36] Demand from a booming brass industry had 'bump-started the copper industry'.[37] Copper ore extraction in Cornwall, virtually non-existent since brief efforts to mine it at the end of the sixteenth century, grew rapidly. Both Borlase and William Pryce were keenly attuned to the revolutionary impact of copper on Cornish mining. For Borlase copper mining was '... a happy addition made within these forty or fifty years to the employ and revenue of this county' while Pryce echoed this, two decades later, by claiming that the 'publick is manifestly enriched by the great trade and circulation of money, consequential to this particular business'.[38] Pryce pointed to the multiplier effects of copper mining. 'The expense of coal, candles, timber, leather, ropes, gunpowder, and various other materials, added to the labour of men, women, children, and horses, occasion such a vast monthly charge, as will not easily be credited by those who are unacquainted with mining'.[39] Table 6.1 illustrates this dynamic growth of

---

[33] Burt, 1991, 268. And see Burt, 1995, 43.
[34] Whetter, 1974, 172 and 69.
[35] C.G.A.Clay, *Economic Expansion and Social Change: England 1500-1700*, Cambridge, 1984, 59.
[36] William Borlase, *Natural History of Cornwall*, Oxford, 1758, 205.
[37] Burt, 1995, 40.
[38] Borlase, 1758, 207; William Pryce, *Mineralogia Cornubiensis*, London, 1778, xii.
[39] Pryce, 1778, ix.

copper ore production. Note that after the 1770s, the amount of metal extracted from the ore was declining, indicating the falling standard of ore mined as the more easily exploitable and shallow ore bodies became exhausted.

Table 6.1: Annual mean copper production, Cornwall and Devon, 1750s-1850s

years	copper ore (tons)	change (%)	copper metal (tons)	change (%)
1755-59	15,788		c.1,900	
1775-79	28,678	+81.6	3,443	+81.2
1795-99	47,488	+65.6	5,185	+50.6
1815-19	81,846	+72.4	6,675	+28.7
1835-39	147,518	+80.2	11,743	+75.9
1855-59	191,376	+29.7	12,390	+5.5

Source: Roger Burt et al, *Mining in Cornwall & Devon*, Exeter, 2014, 60, 80, 120-121.

As Figure 6.1 below illustrates, from the 1750s to the mid-1830s metallic copper production grew steadily with just two breaks. One of these occurred in the 1770s and early 1780s, a period when copper supplies outstripped demand, as a result of the discovery of the more easily exploited ore deposits of Parys Mountain in Anglesey in the late 1760s.[40] The difficulties of this period eventually led to the formation of the Cornish Metal Company in 1785, in an attempt to control the marketing and therefore the price of copper ore in agreement with Thomas Williams of Anglesey.[41] But, despite a sharp slump in 1788, ore production had already, by 1785, resumed its strong upward trend, and this continued until the second short break in growth in the years around 1810, occasioned by a sudden drop in the price of copper from its wartime peak in 1805.

---

[40] Rowe, 1953, 69-72.
[41] Rowe, 1953, 81-88; J.R.Harris and R.O.Roberts, 'Eighteenth century monopoly: the Cornish Metal Company agreements of 1785', *Business History* 5 (1962), 69-82.

Figure 6.1. Metallic Copper and tin output, Cornwall and Devon, 1750-1860.

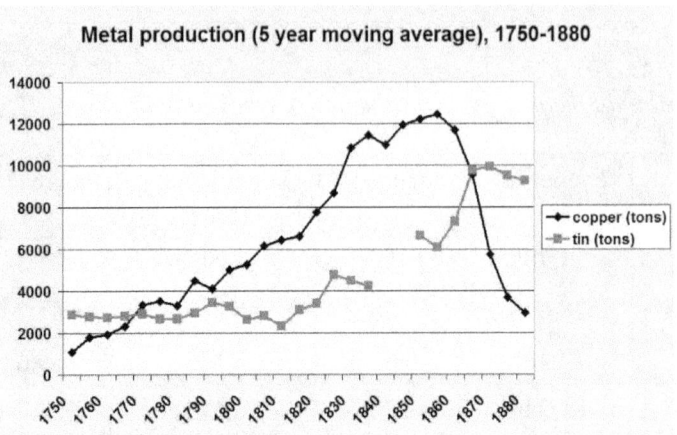

Apart from these two periods, however, copper production grew at more than two per cent per annum. Indeed, during the decades of the 1750s, 1760s, 1790s, 1800s and the 1820s, that rate exceeded four per cent per annum. After the mid-1830s production appeared to peak. Growth rates of copper metal usually lagged behind those of ore as the quality of ore generally declined with increasing depth of extraction. There was an exception in the mid-1840s, when production of metal rose at rates of three per cent a year (at a time when ore production was growing at less than one per cent). This temporary reversal of the norm reflected the opening of new, shallower and richer ore reserves in east Cornwall and at Devon Great Consols, just across the Tamar in Tavistock.

An expanding output of copper ore in the second half of the eighteenth century was no longer dependent on the multiplication of small production units. While it is possible that, in the eighteenth-century copper industry, 'there were great numbers of tiny concerns, most of which were abandoned as soon as ore above adit was exhausted, as the adventurers had not the desire or the capital to install adequate pumps',[42] the increasing scale of some mines also resulted in a growing concentration of copper output as compared with the more dispersed tin production. By 1838 Cornish mines were 'altogether larger affairs than contemporary coal mines'.[43] This greater capitalisation and scale of

---

[42] T.A.Morrison, *Cornwall's Central Mines: The Northern District 1810-1895*, Penzance, 1980, 9-10.

operations was typical of the development of metal mining regions as gradually deepening mining transformed the proto-industrial and small-scale organisation of the industry.[44] Before the end of the eighteenth century, the largest ten mines were producing over 75 per cent of the value of copper output and the largest five accounting for around half.[45]

Consolidation of the bulk of output on relatively few mines meant there was a parallel spatial concentration of the copper mining district. Rowe has noted that 'practically the entire copper mining region was within eight miles of the summit of Carn Brea', midway between the mining towns of Camborne and Redruth.[46] Figure 6.2 on the following page illustrates this geographical concentration of Cornish mining in 1795. The rise to dominance of copper mining during the eighteenth century had thus directed income into a relatively small part of Cornwall. As capital congregated in this small area this stimulated 'backward and forward linkages with advanced engineering supply and processing industries (creating) the "critical mass" necessary for sustained growth and the emergence of the region as a leading industrial centre'.[47] The first part of the general economic upswing of the later eighteenth century had thus produced, by 1815, in west Cornwall, a concentrated industrial district based on deep copper mining as opposed to the more dispersed geography of the tin mining proto-region.

As the growth in copper mining slowed after 1830, resources shifted back into tin production. The extraction of this metal was no higher in the early 1810s than it had been in the early 1750s. For tin, growth rates in excess of four per cent per annum marked a later 'take-off' in production over the period from 1815 to 1827. According to Rowe, this expansion after 1815 'marked the beginning of an era of mechanisation and speculation in Cornish tin mining'.[48] After a decline in the late 1820s and early 1830s tin production resumed a strong upward trend in the 1840s.

---

[43] Maxine Berg, 'Factories, workshops and industrial organisation', in Roderick Floud and Donald McCloskey (eds), *The Economic History of Britain since 1700, Volume 1, 1700-1860*, Cambridge, 1994, 140.
[44] Burt, 1998, 102-103.
[45] 'Report from the select committee adopted to enquire into the state of the copper mines and copper trade of the kingdom', *British Parliamentary Papers*, 1st series, X, 653, 1799, 152-158.
[46] Rowe, 1953, 66.
[47] Burt, 1998, 103.
[48] Rowe, 1953, 188.

Figure 6.2. Distribution of mining income, 1794-96.

Source: Calculated from BPP, 1799, 152-158.

How did this industrialisation compare with other industrial regions? Pat Hudson argues that regional sectoral specialisation and factor markets were features of the emerging nineteenth century industrial regions.[49] With this in mind, we can investigate three comparative aspects: the degree of sectoral specialisation in terms of output and employment; the role of Cornwall in technological change; and the existence of a regional capital market.

Sectoral specialisation
Copper mining in Cornwall grew as fast as did coal mining elsewhere in the period from 1750 to 1830, as Table 6.2 on the following page indicates.

---

[49] Pat Hudson, *The Industrial Revolution*, London, 1992, 102-106.

Table 6.2: Production of coal and copper metal, 1750 – 1830

year	coal (thousand tons)	change (%)	copper in Cornwall & Devon (tons)	change (%)
1750	5,230		c.1,100	
1775	8,850	+69	3,500	+218
1800	15,045	+70	5,250	+50
1815	22,265	+48	6,600	+26
1830	30,375	+36	10,860	+65

Source: Coal from Flinn, 1984, 26; copper as Table 6.1.

Cornish copper production grew faster than total coal output before 1775 and then again from 1815 to 1830. If coal output is broken down into its component mining regions we find that only south Wales (Monmouthshire and Glamorganshire) showed a faster growth from 1750 to 1775 and only north Wales grew faster from 1815 to 1830. Over the whole period only Lancashire, south Wales and the east Midlands saw a faster overall rate of growth in mining output.[50]

Table 6.3: Growth of real output in selected industrial sectors (% per annum)

	cotton	wool	iron	coal	Cornish copper
1700-60	1.4	1.0	0.6	0.6	2.7
1760-70	4.6	1.3	1.7	2.2	6.9
1770-80	6.2		4.5	2.5	-2.3
1780-90	12.8	0.5	3.8	2.4	3.4
1790-01	6.7		6.5	3.2	2.5
1801-11	4.5	1.6	7.5	2.5	1.6
1811-21	5.6		-0.3	2.8	3.3
1821-31	6.8	2.0	6.5	3.7	3.5

Source: Hudson, 1992, 43. Cornish copper calculated from Burt et al, 2014.

---

[50] M.W.Flinn, *The History of the British Coal Industry, Volume II, 1700-1830: The Industrial Revolution*, Oxford, 1984, 26.

Indeed, as Table 6.3 above shows, the annual compound rate of growth of copper output was faster than the main industrial sectors before the 1770s and comparable with most in the 1780s and again in the 1810s. Before 1770 copper output had even grown faster than cotton. Copper production in Cornwall was one of the fastest growing sectors of the British economy in the second third of the eighteenth century. Moreover, its rate of growth remained well above the average rate of growth of industrial production to the 1800s. Although still continuing to grow at about the same rate after 1800, growth then became no faster than industrial production in general.[51]

Copper exploitation provided Cornwall with its specialised export product, the base of an emerging industrial region in its growth phase. The role of mining in the local economy was further boosted in the nineteenth century by expanding tin production and the briefer emergence of lead mining. However, in the absence of estimates for the total income of the nineteenth century Cornish economy, the only way to assess the degree of sectoral specialisation is to identify the proportion of the population directly employed in mining.

Reliable figures for the labour force in mining did not appear until the late 1830s. Sir Charles Lemon calculated the total numbers employed in Cornish mines as at around 28,000 in 1836, obtaining his total by aggregating the numbers employed in each mine.[52] The 28,000 was then around 8.7 per cent of the total population. After 1841 the published census provides totals for the whole mining and quarrying sector. Comparing the 1841 totals with Lemon's estimates, we might suggest that the Census underestimated slightly the total numbers involved in mining, perhaps failing to enumerate some part-time workers.

This suggests that, at its peak, the mining sector employed almost a quarter of the working population. But these totals include those working in the china clay pits and in granite and slate quarrying. However, the 1881 census figure can be checked against the detailed employment returns in the Mineral Statistics, available on an annual basis after 1878, which distinguishes those working in metal mines. This latter source indicates that metal mining still employed 15,241 people in Cornwall in 1881.[53] This implies that the mines at their peak employed at least 35,000 in 1861, around 10 per cent of the total population and 22 per cent of the labour force. The 22 per cent or so of men employed in mining in the

---

[51] R.V.Jackson, 'Rates of industrial growth during the industrial revolution', *Economic History Review* 45 (1992), 2 and 19.

[52] Charles Lemon, 'The statistics of the copper mines of Cornwall', *Journal of the Statistical Society of London* 1 (1838), 65-84.

[53] Calculated from returns in Burt et al, 2014.

Table 6.4: Numbers employed in mining and quarrying

	number	% of population	% of employed
1841	27,560	8.1	23.8
1851	36,149	10.2	24.4
1861	38,553	10.4	24.1
1871	29,868	8.2	19.6
1881	18,348	5.5	13.9

Source: based on C.H.Lee, *British Regional Employment Statistics, 1841*-1971, Cambridge, 1979.

1850s meant that the Cornish economy had similar rates of specialisation as those found in south Wales for coal mining (26 per cent of men in 1851) or the North West of England for textiles (27 per cent).[54] At a different spatial level of comparison, of the 200 or so English and Welsh Registration Districts with the highest proportion of men employed in mining in 1861, four were found in Cornwall. In Redruth RD, (covering the area known to contemporaries in Cornwall as the 'central mining district'), over 52 per cent of men were employed directly in mining, second only to the much smaller Reeth RD in North Yorkshire.[55] Even at this relatively late stage Cornwall was still home to almost one in ten of all the miners and quarriers of Great Britain and almost half (46 per cent) of the copper, lead, tin and iron miners.[56] No doubt, those proportions would have been higher in the late eighteenth century before the rate of growth of employment in the coal mines began to increase.

Specialisation, it is argued, gave rise to regional fragmentation; and regions became less like one another as early industrialisation proceeded. One way of quantifying this is by using a simple Index of Dissimilarity, comparing the differences in the occupational structures of various areas. (The Index of Dissimilarity (ID) is calculated by the formula ID = (X_i - Y_i)/2 where X_i is the percentage of the workforce in place X in each occupational group and Y_i is the percentage of the workforce in place Y in each occupational group).

---

[54] C.H.Lee, *British Regional Employment Statistics, 1841*-1971, Cambridge, 1979
[55] David Gatley, *Census Vital Registration Data Base*, Stafford, 1996.
[56] Lee, 1979; Roger Burt, *The British Lead Mining* Industry, Redruth, 1984, 200.

Figure 6.3. Index of dissimilarity, occupational structure: base Great Britain and Cornwall, 1851.

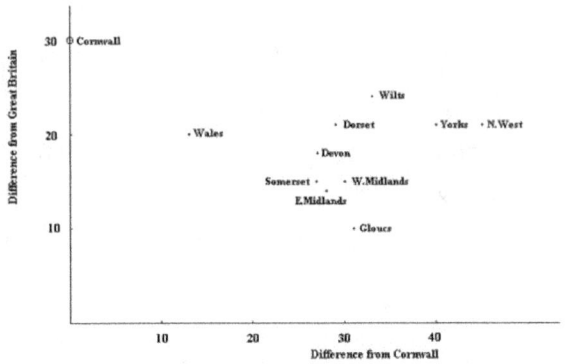

Calculated from Lee, 1979.1994, 199-200.

Figure 6.3 represents the distance between Cornwall and Great Britain, the neighbouring English counties and other selected industrial regions. Of all these areas, Cornwall's occupational structure differed the most from the British average, and Gloucestershire the least (shown on the vertical axis). When compared with Cornwall the greatest difference was the North West and the smallest was Wales (shown on the horizontal axis). This rather blunt measure does nevertheless suggest that the occupational structure of Cornwall was markedly different both from counties in south west England and industrial regions of the north and Midlands.

Technology
According to Hudson 'successfully expanding regions often came to influence the methods of an entire sector'.[57] In one area of technology – the steam engine – Cornwall played a leading role. Von Tunzelmann concludes that 'one half of the fuel savings on reciprocating engines and one third of the savings over all, were accounted for by just one county – Cornwall. The significance of the Cornish copper and tin mines in the spread of best-practice technology in the eighteenth century cannot be

---

[57] Pat Hudson, 'The regional perspective', in Pat Hudson (ed.), *Regions and Industries: A Perspective on the Industrial Revolution in Britain*, Cambridge,1989, 23.

exaggerated'.[58] Maintaining levels of labour productivity at the same time as mines were being deepened meant reducing the costs of draining those mines and hauling the ore to surface. Water power and drainage projects such as the Great County Adit had sufficed in the early years of copper mining.[59] But by the 1770s deep mines were becoming dependent on steam power for drainage and hauling. Given Cornwall's lack of coal reserves, attempts to reduce costs had, of necessity, to centre on the efficiency of the steam engine. It was here that striking technological advances took place.

Emphasis has moved to the distinction between the classical inventions of the industrial revolution and the small scale mechanical development and improvement that followed. Joel Mokyr has proposed that a cluster of 'macro-inventions' in the period from 1765 to 1800 was followed by a series of micro-adaptations in which the initial breakthrough was applied and consolidated.[60] Berg re-interprets this to suggest that the second stage, of 'learning by doing', was more crucial in the process of technical change.[61] Burt has already pointed to the importance of this secondary 'sub-invention' stage in changes in metal mining techniques in the early modern period, but this was also the situation in the late eighteenth and early nineteenth centuries.[62]

The original breakthroughs of Newcomen, Smeaton and Watt in the eighteenth century only paved the way for even more rapid technical advance and increases of efficiency in the early nineteenth century. By 1840, steam engines in Cornwall were 'three to four times as efficient thermodynamically speaking as Watt's own engines'. As a result, 'most authorities regarded the Cornish engine as the highest level of technological accomplishment in its field between, say 1815 and 1840'.[63] This had occurred, argues von Tunzelmann, through a series of on-the-job 'disembodied' developments, needing no major changes to the engine but improving the way it was operated. Such small-scale changes were then rapidly diffused through what was a geographically tightly bounded industrial region.

---

[58] G.N.von Tunzelmann, *Steam Power and British Industrialization to 1860*, Oxford, 1978, 252.
[59] See Allen Buckley, 'The Great County Adit', M.Phil thesis, University of Exeter, 1992.
[60] Joel Mokyr, 'Technological change, 1700-1830' in Floud and McCloskey (eds), 1994, 12-43 and *The Enlightened Economy: An Economic History of Britain 1700-1850*, London, 2009, 57-60.
[61] Berg, *Age of Manufactures*, 1994, 29.
[62] Burt, 1991, 253.
[63] von Tunzelmann, 1978, 256 and 263.

Empirical tinkering on such a successful scale was, by the 1810s, embedded in a culture which had experienced two generations of technological change. In the 1780s and 1790s William Murdoch, James Watt's agent, was experimenting with steam locomotives and first used gas for lighting purposes at Redruth. Murdoch was just one of a number of engineers and inventors active in Cornwall in those years, men such as Jonathan Hornblower and his brothers, Edward Bull, Richard Trevithick and the young Arthur Woolf.[64] Rivalries and competition between these men and the mines that employed them helped to establish a critical mass of ingenuity that in turn enabled the culture of empirical tinkering to flourish after the 1810s.

The central symbolic role of the steam engine in Cornish culture by this date is well illustrated by the publication of the *Engine Reporter* by the Lean family from 1811. This listed the performance of pumping engines at Cornish mines, including the 'duty', or weight of water raised per unit of coal consumed. Described as a 'symptom of and a stimulus to the competitive spirit prevailing between rival engineers over duty',[65] the publication also helped to establish a wider interest in steam engine performance among shareholders and educated opinion locally, reinforcing the iconic status of the steam engine as a measure of the prosperity and progress of the Cornish economy. By the 1830s the cultural place of the steam engine was thus firmly established and Cornwall's role in its development was seen as a cause for much local pride. An anonymous writer in the *Quarterly Mining Review* summed this up in words, which, when read from a vantage point that encompasses the wreckage and desolation of de-industrialisation, are both prophetic and deeply poignant:

> It is farther (sic) the boast of this district, that the steam engine, a machine which has influenced the destinies of nations, and will probably continue to do so beyond the power of the human mind to foresee, was here first encouraged, and has been matured to its present highest power and greatest perfection; a circumstance which will attract the attention of future generations, when, perhaps, after a lapse of centuries, the mines of Cornwall shall have become exhausted, the population dispersed, and the surface more barren and desolate than ever.[66]

However, in 1832 such intimations of doom were mere journalistic insight. For most contemporaries, looking to the recent past rather than an unpredictable future, what was most impressive was Cornwall's role

---

[64] See Rowe, 1953, 96-113.
[65] von Tunzelmann, 1978, 254.
[66] 'On the mining district of Redruth', *Quarterly Mining Review* 2 (1832), 225.

in steam engine technology. The relatively early growth of copper mining and its growing drainage requirements had resulted in Cornwall becoming, by the 1780s, one of the main locations for the new steam engine. In the period 1734-80 only the north-eastern coalfield saw more engines erected.[67] In terms of absolute numbers Cornwall was surpassed in the last two decades of the eighteenth century by the spread of steam engines to general manufacturing processes elsewhere. Although if horsepower is compared, rather than the number of engines, Cornwall probably came first as late as 1800.[68]

Factor markets

Another element in the industrial regions model is the emergence of regional labour and capital markets. I will focus here on the capital market. Did Cornwall have a coherent and independent capital market of its own or was capital for the mining industry imported from elsewhere?

Banks appeared relatively early in Cornwall.[69] It is significant that the emerging Cornish merchant-bourgeoisie, together with some of the landed class, were very closely involved in the first and most important banks.[70] These same groups were central to the financing of metal mining. Here, the organisational breakthrough in the eighteenth century was the institutionalisation and formalisation of the cost book system of financing and its application to the new copper mining ventures. This was no innovation. Indeed, John Hatcher suggests that cost book financing can be found as early as the fourteenth century.[71] In the cost book system a number of investors (known in Cornwall as 'adventurers') would share the start-up costs of a mine. If it proved a success, then the profits made were divided among the adventurers at regular intervals. If not profitable, then calls for extra capital would be made to those same shareholders. Burt explains how cost-book companies (a cross between extended partnerships and joint stock companies) were designed to give shareholders, all with little capital, the stability, consistency and regular organisation of the more opulent coal mining companies. He goes on to argue convincingly that, whatever their long-term disadvantages, such a

---

[67] Calculated from John Kanefsky and John Robey, 'Steam engines in 18th century Britain', *Technology and Culture* 21 (1980), 176-177.
[68] G.N.von Tunzelmann, 'Coal and steam power', in John Langton and R.J.Morris (eds), *Atlas of Industrializing Britain*, London, 1986, 76.
[69] Compare Larry Neal, 'The finance of business during the industrial revolution', in Floud and McCloskey (eds), 1994, 165-169.
[70] J.A.Shearme, *Cornish Banks and Bankers*, Looe, n.d.
[71] John Hatcher, *English Tin Production and Trade before 1550*, Oxford, 1973, 60-61.

form of financial organisation, with its 'qualified form of limited liability' encouraged the investment required by the increasingly capitalised mines.[72] This judgement is echoed by John Rule who points to the success of the cost-book system in mobilising capital for an 'expanding but speculative industry'.[73] Capital from a host of small shareholders could be raised, these supplementing the larger, core holdings of the merchant-bourgeoisie and landowners.[74]

In 1799, it was estimated that around a third or a quarter of adventurers had a direct interest in supplying the mines that received their investment.[75] John Taylor, the mines manager and owner, was critical of this practice, writing in 1814 that 'the concerns are often supplied by a part of the adventurers who are dealers in the articles required and who therefore have a consuming interest in allowing exorbitant prices and an unlimited consumption'.[76] As Edmund Newell points out, the role of merchants in mines investment 'demonstrates how closely mining was related to merchanting, transport, ancillary industries and landownership in the county'.[77] This reminds us of the strategic role the mining industry played within a web of networks and economic relationships by the early nineteenth century. Even before this, sufficient profits had certainly been generated, whether from within mining itself, from supplying the mines, from advancing money to the mines or from smelting and exporting the products of the mines, for the local merchant-bourgeoisie and landowners to find the capital to finance the Cornish Metal Company in 1785, 'one of the most heavily capitalised enterprises in the whole of the eighteenth-century economy'.[78]

The above implies that little capital was needed or sought from outside the region in the later eighteenth century. This is what we might expect from the industrial regions model which proposes that, because labour

---

[72] Burt, 1984, 72 and 79. See also Roger Burt and Narikazu Kudo, 'The adaptability of the Cornish cost book system', *Business History* 25 (1983), 30-41.

[73] John Rule, *The Vital Century: England's Developing Economy, 1714-1815*, London, 1992, 172.

[74] Rowe, 1953, 65 estimates there were approximately 500 to 1,000 shareholders in copper mines by 1775

[75] BPP, 1799.

[76] Roger Burt (ed.), *Cornish Mining: Essays on the Organisation of Cornish Mines and the Cornish Mining Economy*, Newton Abbot, 1969, 26.

[77] Edmund Newell, 'The British copper ore market in the nineteenth century, with particular reference to Cornwall and Swansea', D.Phil thesis, Oxford University, 1988, 56.

[78] Rule, 1992, 178. See also Pollard, 1981, 14.

and capital markets were not yet fully 'national', specialised industrial regions possessed, for a period, largely internally integrated intra-regional flows of labour and capital. This remained the case, according to Hudson, at least as late as the 1830s and 1840s.[79]

Most writers on Cornish mining present a relatively simple picture of initial local financing of mining followed by a gradually increased involvement of outside capital. The implication in the literature is that Cornwall was progressively drawn into a wider capital market. Thus, Morrison argues that the 'need for heavier investment and the rising commercial power of London and the Midlands made them vital sources of capital'.[80] Others broadly follow suit and differ only in their timing of this process.

Burt, who suggests that metal mining in Britain went through three phases, provides the most comprehensive descriptive model of this process. In the first phase, in the early eighteenth century, metal mines were small scale and locally financed. In the second phase, from the mid-eighteenth to the early nineteenth century, mines were regionally financed and in the third phase metal mining was financed by a state-wide capital market.[81] Applying this to Cornwall, he argues that for most of the second half of the eighteenth century, Cornish mines were 'clearly in the second stage of development', part of a regional capital market, with the leading adventurers being 'smelters, local landowners ... tradesmen, professional classes and farmers'. While there was some investment by outside adventurers like Boulton and Watt in the late eighteenth century, in 1800 most Cornish mines still derived most of their capital from within Cornwall.[82] According to Burt, the change to a wider capital market in metal mining was pioneered by the Cornish mines and began in the 1820s, when 'large scale, nationally financed mining began to develop'. By the 1850s Cornish mining was attracting 'large quantities of outside capital, particularly from the London area' and had moved towards a dependence on 'anonymous and speculative capital'.[83]

This model, however, requires some qualification both in its chronology and in its assumptions of a progressive, stage process from local to regional to national capital markets. To begin with, it appears that distant adventurers had been active in tin mining as early as the seventeenth century.[84] Yet it seems that this outside investment declined

---

[79] Hudson, 1989, 15.
[80] Morrison, 1980, 16.
[81] Burt, 1984, 57.
[82] For investment by Boulton and Watt after 1785 see Rowe, 1953, 82.
[83] Burt, 1984, 70 and 82-83.

in importance as the end of that century neared. Whetter points out how local merchant capital supplanted the London pewterers in the later seventeenth century and Gill Burke reinforces this by arguing that Cornishmen were buying out the London tin dealers in the seventeenth century, so much so that by the eighteenth century a 'small all-Cornish group' tightly controlled the smelting, financing and purchasing of tin.[85] This was formalised by 1780 in meetings of the Association of the Proprietors of Tin, which met regularly to fix the price of that metal until 1818.[86]

Whereas tin mining was increasingly financed regionally, the early investment in deep copper mines again drew on adventurers from outside Cornwall - this time from Bristol industrialists and businessmen with interests in the brass industry. Outsiders became prominent shareholders in a few mines in the early eighteenth century, in Gwinear and Illogan for example.[87] Yet, again, the early involvement of outside capitalists soon ended. Cornish capital seems to have supplanted it and became dominant in the development of copper mining in the second and third quarters of the eighteenth century. Despite the involvement of Boulton and Watt in Cornish mining from the early 1770s no fundamental change occurred in the regionally capitalised industry in that century.

John Vivian's evidence to the parliamentary committee enquiring into the state of the copper trade of 1799 allows us to identify the major shareholders in nine copper mines in that year. These included five of the fifteen most productive mines. Just over 100 separate adventurers were noted, but as Table 6.5 on the next page indicates, a quarter (25.8 per cent) of the shares were in the hands of just five individuals and companies and almost 42 per cent were held by just ten individuals and companies. Merchants, bankers and smelters held over a quarter of the shares, with landowners and the clerical gentry possessing about another fifth. These two groups combined owned over 40 per cent of the shares in these major copper mines. Boulton and Watt were the only major non-Cornish investors.

---

[84] Buckley, *Cornish Mining Industry*, 1992, 11.
[85] Whetter, 1974, 172; Gill Burke, 'The Cornish miner and Cornish mining industry 1870-1921', PhD thesis, University of London, 1981, 37.
[86] Rowe, 1953, 166.
[87] Buckley, *Cornish Mining Industry*, 1992, 14.

Table 6.5: Principal shareholders in nine Cornish copper mines, 1799

adventurer	Number of mines in which shares held	Share of total ownership (%)
Merchants, bankers, smelters		
G.C.Fox & sons	5	6.8
John Williams & sons	4	5.3
John and M.C Vivian	5	4.3
Philip Richards	2	4.3
Thos Reed and Wm Carne	3	4.1
Ralph Daniell	1	1.9
John Edwards	2	1.4
total		**28.2**
Landowners and clergy		
Francis Rodd	3	5.0
Reverend John Vivian	3	3.4
Reverend Henry Hawkins	3	3.0
John Rogers	1	1.8
Basset family	1	1.4
Reverend Mr Walker	1	1.4
Robert Gwatkin	1	1.4
total		**17.5**
Others and unidentified		
Mr Hole	4	3.1
Mr Wallis, solicitor	2	2.3
Boulton & Watt	2	2.1
Thos and James Kevill	2	1.8
total		**9.3**

Source: BPP, 1799, 160-163; Boase and Courtney, 1890.

Allen Buckley suggests that it was only after 1805, when copper mining expanded, that outside capital was drawn in.[88] Jim Lewis also identifies an influx of London capital after 1809, resulting in the reopening of several previously abandoned mines. Another wave of outside investment occurred in the 1820s.[89] The most active non-local adventurer was John Taylor, originally from Norwich, who launched the Consolidated Mines at Gwennap in 1818, with a capital of £15,000 provided by himself and 'other investors, mainly from the London area'. John Taylor himself suggested in 1814 that 'shares in these undertakings are now frequently bought and sold at a distance from the districts in which they are situate'.[90] By the 1840s and 1850s, there is more evidence for the involvement of outside capital. Thus, Stephen Bartlett points out how London investors were active in the new lead mines of Menheniot in east Cornwall in the 1840s.[91] Further east, the phenomenally rich copper mine of Devon Great Consols was initially financed in 1844 with the help of five London stockbrokers as a joint stock company, divided into 1024 £1 shares.[92] A few years later, in 1850, it was being reported that 'a gentleman from Manchester, who is a large holder in (Phoenix mine, in the Caradon district) has been the means of keeping the mine going to the present time'.[93]

However, it is significant that the weight of this evidence for growing involvement relates to mining districts in east Cornwall and west Devon in the 1840s and later. Further west, the Taylor family's involvement in at least thirty mines in the 40 years after 1818 seems to be the exception rather than a new rule.[94] In an important contribution Lewis proposed that the role of London capital was notable in kickstarting the growth of mining after the difficult years of the Napoleonic wars. However, a combination of mistrust, lack of understanding of Cornish mining and distance from the mines, together with a number of fraudulent schemes, meant that the enthusiasm of London-based investors waned. By the

---

[88] Buckley, *Cornish Mining Industry*, 1992, 14.
[89] Jim Lewis, 'Cornish copper mining 1795-1830: economy, structure and change', in Philip Payton (ed.), *Cornish Studies Fourteen*, Exeter, 2006, 164-186.
[90] Burt, 1969, 28.
[91] Stephen Bartlett, *The Mines and Mining Men of Menheniot*, Truro, 1994, 4 and 24.
[92] J.B.Richardson, *Metal Mining*, London, 1974, 98.
[93] *Mining Journal*, 6 July 1850, 316.
[94] Roger Burt et al, *Cornish Mines: Metalliferous and Associated Minerals 1845-1913*, Exeter, 1987, xix.

mid-1830s London capital had 'ebbed away' and mining was firmly back in 'local hands'.[95]

Other evidence bears this out. While it is claimed that 'many' of the principal adventurers in Tresavean, Consolidated and other mines in 1835 had no Cornish connections, there is also ample evidence that other mines were solidly financed by local capital. For example, at Wheal Vor at least 74 per cent of the shareholders in 1820-22 were Cornish.[96] At around the same time, in 1815-16, Cornish capitalists still held at least 81 per cent of the shares in the Pembroke mine in the new copper mining district east of St Austell while local tin smelters had 75 per cent of the interest in Ding Dong tin mine near Penzance. Similarly, at least 72 per cent of the shares in Cooks Kitchen in 1808 and 66 per cent of those at East Crofty in 1835, both in Illogan, were held by Cornish adventurers.[97] Although London capital was active in the Menheniot district in the 1840s, in the same decade at the older lead mine of East Wheal Rose (then the richest lead mine in Cornwall or Devon) various Cornish merchant families held over 50 per cent of the shares.[98]

It is not difficult to find other examples. For instance, Dolcoath mine, one of Cornwall's richest and most productive, remained firmly in Cornish hands.[99] And as late as 1872 79 per cent of the adventurers in Levant mine lived in Cornwall.[100] Barton suggested that in the nineteenth century 'there was not a tin mine of any consequence ... in which smelters (who were predominantly Cornish) did not hold an important, and in many cases, a majority share'.[101] Evidence for local domination of tin mining seems clearer than for copper in the 1850s and more pronounced in west than in east Cornwall.

In fact, Cornish capital was being exported for use elsewhere by the first two decades of the nineteenth century. After the crisis of the 1780s had been overcome, Cornish capitalists had moved after 1800 to

> eradicate once and for all the dominance of outside (copper) smelters, be they Gloucestershire or Welsh. The great Cornish families took control of their own destinies during the early decades of the nineteenth century by moving their money into

---

[95] Lewis, 2006.
[96] Burt, 1984, 91, citing *Quarterly Mining Review* of 1835; Barton, 1967, 50.
[97] Calculated from cost books at CRO X362/2 (Pembroke Mine, 1815-16) and CRO TEM 156 (Various mine plans).
[98] Calculated from Leslie Douch, *East Wheal Rose*, Truro, 1964, 38-39.
[99] T.R.Harris, *Dolcoath, Queen of Cornish Mines*, Camborne, 1974.
[100] Burke, 1984, 48.
[101] Barton, 1967, 110.

Welsh smelting, of which they retained control for most of the century.[102]

The Fox family, too, had moved into Welsh coal and iron mines in the same period and Burt notes the important role of Cornish capital in the revival of the north and central Wales lead mining industry after 1815.[103] Meanwhile, the copper smelting firm of Williams, Foster and Co, financed mainly by Cornish capitalists, was by the 1830s beginning to invest on a large scale outside Cornwall.[104] It was not only mining and smelting that received the export of Cornish capital. William Praed, the Truro banker, was an important investor in the Grand Union Canal in the Midlands.[105]

This survey suggests there was no simple linear progression from local to national capital investment in Cornish mining. If anything, there seems to be an ebb and flow, with an early involvement of outside capital being replaced by a vigorous regional capital market, one boosted by the late eighteenth century development of banking in the west Cornish towns. Cornish mining was financed predominantly by a regional, Cornish capital market in the later eighteenth century and through to the 1810s. Thereafter, although there is evidence for a growing involvement of outside capital, the bulk of the capital required for mining continued to be raised from a regional, even local, network of adventurers or shareholders. Incidentally, this pattern – of initial outside investment replaced by the dominance of local capital – was also seen in the infant china clay industry.[106]

The second theme suggested by this overview is that, while some outside capitalists began to invest in Cornish mining from the 1810s, Cornish capitalists were themselves at the same time investing in other regions and overseas. What was happening was a generally more vigorous and wider circulation of capital. An economic region had emerged by the late eighteenth century, largely financed through its own regional capital market. As industrialisation proceeded that industrial region became part of a growing inter-regional capital market, rather than the endpoint of a flow of capital.

Two further points need to be made about this regional capital market. Even when the proportion of extra-regional capital grew this might not

---

[102] Buckley, *Cornish Mining Industry*, 1992, 24.

[103] Edmund Vale, *The Harveys of Hayle; Engine Builders, Shipwrights and Merchants of Cornwall*, Truro, 1966, 51; Burt, 1984, 82.

[104] G.C.Boase, *Collectanea Cornubiensis*, Truro, 1890, cols 1251-1254.

[105] Michael Freeman and Derek Aldcroft (eds), *Transport in the Industrial Revolution*, Manchester, 1983, xx.

[106] Rita Barton, *A History of the Cornish China Clay Industry*, Truro, 1966, 59.

necessarily entail a loss of local control. Thus, Burt concludes that, despite increased penetration by outside adventurers, 'most Cornish mines' in the 1850s were 'still dominated by local in-adventurers'.[107] Problems of distance meant that day to day management remained local. Furthermore, local investors were in a far better position in terms of quality of information. Barton claims that the failures of tin mining investment in the 1850s were predominantly 'London-owned ventures' and goes further, to argue that a 'considerable proportion of the mines at mid-century were run for (the merchants') prime benefit, unknown to the world at large'.[108] Ownership did not necessarily mean control and the evidence suggests that the balance of power (and information) in Cornish mining remained with local adventurers rather than outsiders throughout the industrial period.

The relationship between Cornish and non-Cornish investors was often a wary one, tinged with suspicion and hostility. Several commentators have noted how Cornish mining interests were quick to blame 'foreign' interests during short term crises in the later eighteenth century and before.[109] Indeed, it was the reaction of Cornish mining interests against the domination of foreign smelters and capitalists in copper refining that led to the creation of another 'unique' institution of Cornish mining in 1725, the practice of regular ticketing, which attempted (though largely unsuccessfully) to guarantee a free market in copper ores and reduce collusion by the buyers.[110] The brittle relations between Cornish adventurers and others in the period from the 1820s to the 1850s, with the occasional outright fraudulent practices designed to part 'foreign' investors from their money as quickly as possible, is further, later, evidence of conflicts between Cornish and 'foreign' interests. In 1840, letters in the *Mining Journal* illustrate the 'information deficit' felt by outside investors. A 'severe sufferer in Cornish mines' wrote from London that Cornish mines were 'ruinous to those who have been gulled by the insidious statements of some who ought long since to have been brought up at the Old Bailey'.[111] Clearly cultural factors were here interacting with more 'purely' economic factors in the generation of such frictions. In this sense the creation of a self-conscious economic region clarified interests that were perceived as being in opposition to those of other sectors and regions despite similar class positions. This, in turn,

---

[107] Burt, 1984, 91.
[108] Barton, 1967, 110 and 121. See also Burke, 1984, 48-49 and Burt, 1984, 80.
[109] See for example Rowe, 1953, 68.
[110] Buckley, *Cornish Mining Industry*, 1992, 15; Rowe, 1953, 21-22; Newell, 1988, 115-133.
[111] *Mining Journal*, 12 September 1840.

reinforced feelings of regional identity and echoes Langton's point about the fragmented regional economy of early nineteenth century Britain accompanying a rising consciousness of regional differences.[112]

Of course, while Cornwall can be viewed as an integrated capital market in the early nineteenth century, it was at the same time linked to other regions, particularly perhaps to London, by other inter-regional flows. Notable among these were circuits of political and market information, via the press.[113] Early nineteenth century Cornwall is thus perhaps best seen, not as having a peripheral relationship to a metropolitan centre at this time, but as a node in a more general regional circulation, a circulation that was both creating regions and reproducing them. The rise of copper mining had grafted newer links, for example to the coal mining region of south Wales, onto older ones with the metropolis.

But it had done more than create new inter-regional links and a new place for Cornwall as one of Britain's early industrial regions. It had also become the pole around which a new form of Cornish identity was cohering. As Hudson points out, the emergence of recognisable industrial regions was accompanied by a growing identification of 'all social groups with the economic, social and political interests of their region'.[114] As chapters 3 and 4 have suggested, by the 1820s the Cornish identity was crystallising around the icons and fortunes of the mining industry. For those in the heartlands of mining this was only to be expected. But in all spheres, there was a clearer articulation of a regional identity by the second quarter of the nineteenth century. This was an articulation that did not hesitate to unite the artefacts of an industrial age with the local sense of place. For example, the first railway locomotive built by the Sandys, Carne and Vivian works at Hayle in 1838 was promptly named the 'Cornishman'.[115]

3. Modernisation

Growth continued into the 1850s. We have already seen how copper provided the basis for the eighteenth-century expansion of the mining industry. After 1815 it was joined by a rapid rise in tin production. These were not, however, despite the impression portrayed by local mining

---

[112] Langton, 1984.
[113] See Derek Gregory, 'The friction of distance: information circulation and the mails in early nineteenth century England', *Journal of Historical Geography* 13 (1987), 130-154.
[114] Hudson, 1989.
[115] Rowe, 1953, 149.

historiography, separate industries. Many mines, such as Dolcoath, shifted from one metal to another during their working lives while other mines produced both copper and tin together over long periods. Morrison, in a percipient comment, has stated that he finds it 'impossible to view separately metals which were hoisted through the same shafts' and Burt and Timbrell agree that 'it clearly makes little sense to try to write separate histories of copper and tin mining'.[116] Therefore, in order to gain a more holistic picture of the fortunes of the whole Cornish mining industry the value of its total output must be assessed. The sources available allow us to do this for copper and tin from 1770 with the only gaps for copper production occurring in the early 1790s and in tin production in the late 1830s. (Using Stannary Court records and ticketing sales, some of the gaps in the data have now been plugged since this was first written. The statistics below use the updated figures in Burt et al, 2016.)

The value of lead mining cannot be calculated before the 1840s when there was an expansion of the major lead producing mine of East Wheal Rose and a new lead mining district near Menheniot opened. Less than ten years before this Henry de la Beche had found that 'at present little (lead) is produced'.[117] He claimed that manganese was at that time a more important mineral, contributing around £40,000 a year to the value of mining. Yet even this amount was only around 11 per cent of the value of tin output and a mere four per cent of that of copper.

Prices fluctuated considerably over this period: that of copper went from a low of £40 a ton at the mine in 1788 to a wartime high of £138 in 1805 and was only £60 a ton again in 1849. Tin prices also rose from a low of £52/10 for a ton of metal in 1774 to £157 at their peak in 1810. They had drifted back to £72 by 1842, only to rise again to just over £136 in 1860.[118] To allow for this the real value of mining has been calculated, based on 1851 prices, and related to the cost of living indices of Lindert and Williamson and Bowley.[119] From the graph on the next page we can see that the total real income of Cornish mining rose from the 1780s to peak in 1805. There was then a sharp fall to a low in 1812.

---

[116] Morrison, 1980, 17; Roger Burt and Martin Timbrell, 'Diversification as a response to decline in the mining industry: arsenic and south-western metal production', *Journal of Interdisciplinary Economics* 2 (1987), 53.

[117] Henry de la Beche, *Report on the Geology of Cornwall, Devon and West Somerset*, London, 1839, 610.

[118] J.B.Hill and D.A.MacAlister, *Memoirs of the Geological Survey: The Geology of Falmouth and Truro and the Mining District of Camborne and Redruth*, Southampton, 1906, 311-312.

[119] B.R.Mitchell, *British Historical Statistics*, Cambridge, 1988, 737-738.

Growth then resumed to reach a plateau in the 1850s, with the periods 1815-1835 and 1848-58 being ones of particularly strong growth.

Figure 6.4. Real value of Cornish mining, 1775-1895.

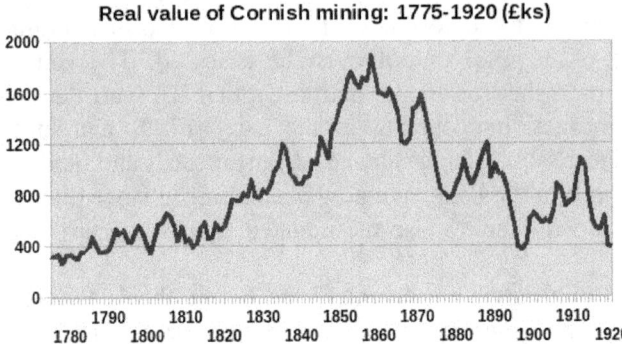

Calculated from Burt et al., 2016 and cost of living index from Mitchell, 1988, 737-738.

The production plateau of the 1850s has long been noted by other writers. But these statistics of the real income of Cornish mining suggest something insufficiently emphasised previously: the total income of mining rose at a rapid rate from the late 1840s to the late 1850s, with growth rates as high as any achieved in its previous history. The regional economy, by this time dominated by mining, thus remained remarkably buoyant into the 1850s. This late growth has often been over-shadowed in the literature by portents of decline, as historians, focusing on copper production and the beginnings of mass emigration, tend to view these years with a hindsight dominated by the disastrous crises and long-term restructuring of the years after the mid-1860s. For example, Goodridge, in his descriptive study of the historical geography of the industry, includes a section entitled 'Decline: actual and potential' when discussing the period from 1830-56.[120] Rowe also saw the 1850s as 'but the brief and illusory Indian Summer of the Cornish copper mining industry'.[121] However, contemporaries still saw prospects of continued profits in metal mining as late as the mid-1860s.[122]

---

[120] J.C.Goodridge, 'The historical geography of the copper mining industry in Devon and Cornwall from 1800 to 1900', PhD thesis, University of London, 1967, 94.

[121] Rowe, 1953, 164.

Nevertheless, structural shifts were clearly visible by the 1840s. New mining districts were being developed near Liskeard and Tavistock in east Cornwall and west Devon, extending the boundaries of the industrial region eastwards. In transport, early railway developments in and after the 1810s had replaced the traditional reliance on mules for carrying ore and coal between the ports and the mines. New foundries were being established in the 1840s, as at St Austell and Charlestown. These met the needs of the small clay works that mushroomed after the 1830s, to cope with a rising demand from the pottery, textile and paper industries. Moreover, the granite quarrying industry was growing fast in the 1840s in the Penryn and Caradon districts and Cornish firms were beginning their domination of the market for safety fuse. More generally, the 1840s appear to have marked shifts in both the source of capital and in the intensity of information flows. The *West Briton* remarked of 1846 that 'a new era began in the magnitude of mining operations, in investment, and especially in the spread of information'.[123]

Moreover, consolidation was occurring in cultural terms. The small town middle classes were gaining in confidence and beginning to assert themselves after the political reforms of the 1830s freed their boroughs (or at least some of them), from the deferential ties of landlordism. In these places by mid-century a vigorous Liberalism was emerging to challenge the older political establishment. At the same time the religious practice of these Cornish towns was becoming markedly more respectable, deliberately distancing itself from rural small chapel Methodism. These socio-cultural changes will be considered below but at this stage we can note that the urbanisation of the central mining district was proceeding apace, despite a slow-down in population growth generally in Cornwall from the late 1830s. In the two decades from 1841, while the population of Cornwall only grew at eight per cent, that of the urbanising parishes of Camborne, Redruth and Illogan grew by almost 30 per cent. By 1861 the population of these three parishes was over 35,000. The central mining district appeared to be on the way to creating an unambiguous central place for Cornwall, as the newer industrial towns moved into a position of parity with long established marketing and merchant centres.

---

[122] See Thomas Spargo, *The Mines of Cornwall and Devon: Statistics and Observations*, London, 1865.
[123] *West Briton*, 15 January 1847.

4) De-industrialisation
But this was not to be. The partial diversification, geographical spread and urbanisation of the industrial region was halted. Camborne and Redruth remained embryonic regional centres, lacking a full range of central place functions. As the world economy entered a downswing, Cornwall was one of those regional economies that became 'easy prey to the acute backwash effects of downswing'.[124] Indeed, in Cornwall the proportion of men employed in agriculture and fishing rose from 29.5 per cent in 1861 to 34.5 per cent in 1881, indicating de-industrialisation from the 1860s to the 1880s, with the 1870s, when the proportion rose from 30.1 per cent to 34.5 per cent, being the decade in which change was most abrupt.[125]

The proponents of the industrial regions perspective have pointed to the importance of interdependent diversity and critical mass in enabling regions to establish a base for sustaining their economic leadership.[126] Interdependent diversity involved the growth of backward and forward integration, linking service trades to the manufacturing specialisation and markets to suppliers. As this diversity emerges and grows, 'economics of conglomeration' take effect and a critical mass of industrial activity is reached.[127] Successful regions can then be host to a sequence of industries as one takes over the reins of regional leadership from another, as in the north east of England, where coal gave way to glass and chemicals, then iron and steel, shipbuilding and engineering. Regions that failed to reach this elusive 'critical mass' fell by the wayside.

One reason why Cornwall's economy declined so rapidly after the 1860s was already foreshadowed in its demographic history after the 1830s. From 1801 to 1841 Cornwall's population growth was broadly in line with that of England and Wales. However, a marked slowdown set in from 1841, the population growing just 8 per cent in the following 20 years, compared with a 26.4 per cent growth in England and 21.9 per cent in Wales. Despite the continued absolute and relative expansion of the mining industry in the period of modernisation, Cornwall's population growth was slower even than that of Devon from 1841 to 1861, reversing the situation of the earlier four decades. The gap in terms of population size between Cornwall, already smaller than the other industrial regions, then began to widen even more rapidly, as Table 6.6 shows.

---

[124] Hudson, 1989, 35.
[125] Calculated from Lee, 1979.
[126] Hudson, 1989, 28-29.
[127] Berg, *Age of Manufactures*, 1994, 114.

Table 6.6: Cornwall's population in context, 1801-61 ('000s)

	Population			% of England/Wales		
	1801	1841	1861	1801	1841	1861
Cornwall	192	342	369	2.15	2.15	1.84
Lancs & Cheshire	866	2,063	2,935	9.73	12.96	14.63
West Riding	572	1,164	1,508	6.43	7.31	7.52
North East	317	574	852	3.56	3.61	4.25
South Wales	116	306	492	1.30	1.92	2.45
Devon	340	533	584	3.82	3.35	2.91
England/Wales	8,896	15,914	20,066			

Source: calculated from 1861 Census; Summary Tables, xiv.

In addition, the growing population of the eighteenth and first third of the nineteenth century had not been associated with major urbanisation. If we adopt a crude measure of urbanisation as the proportion of the total population living in parishes with more than two persons to the acre then, as Table 6.7 shows, numbers living in 'urban' parishes grew only slightly faster than those in rural ones. Indeed, before the 1840s the rural population grew faster in terms of absolute numbers.

Table 6.7: Proportions of Cornish population in urban and rural parishes, 1801-1831

	urban	rural
1801	10.5%	89.5%
1831	14.4%	85.6%

Source: calculated from published Census Reports, 1801 and 1831.

Furthermore, the impact of urbanisation was effectively diluted across a number of small towns, rather than being concentrated in one or two central places. The largest town in Cornwall by 1861, Truro, only had a population of just over 11,000. Two other places, Penzance and Falmouth, had populations between 9 and 10,000 whilst the twin mining centres of Redruth and Camborne each had populations between 7 and 8,000. If we apply a log-normal model to this, one that tests the degree of centralisation by ranking settlements and then seeing how far they conform to a log-normal distribution (i.e. the sequence 1, 1/2, 1/3, 1/4,

1/5 etc) we can see that Cornish settlements were clearly below any log-normal line. Truro, the largest town, was only marginally larger than the next two, and the fifth largest, Camborne, was still 64 per cent the size of Truro, instead of the expected 20 per cent.

What this means is that Cornwall's settlement network had a notably decentralised pattern. This was in marked contrast to the larger industrial regions with their dominating cities. It also contrasted with Devon, where Plymouth, with around 127,000 people in 1861 was almost four times the size of the next largest town, Exeter, which, at 34,000, was almost three times as big as the next towns, Torquay and Tiverton. While mid-nineteenth century Cornwall displayed a decentralised settlement pattern, Devon possessed the strongly centralised settlement structure much more typical of England, both industrial and agricultural.

Cornwall's slowdown in population growth after the 1830s and its dispersed settlement pattern might be connected. Dudley Baines suggests that, in nineteenth century Europe, emigration rates from areas surrounding small towns would be higher than those near large towns.[128] Cornwall's lack of the latter may have been one factor making emigration a more attractive opportunity for the rural population. It was, of course, the growing propensity to emigrate that explains the slowdown of population growth after the 1830s. (The process of emigration is analysed further in the next chapter). Emigration and slowing population growth in turn helped to guarantee that local markets for consumer goods remained small and fragmented. In consequence, the industrial towns of Camborne, Redruth and St Austell competed with the older market towns of Penzance, Falmouth and Truro, but never became dominant. The result was not just a dispersed population geography but a tendency to cultural and political fragmentation and localism that existed in tension with the notions of Cornwall that were crystallising at the same time.

Critical mass had clearly not been attained, in that no central place had emerged comparable in functional status to those great provincial cities such as Manchester, Leeds or Birmingham, which all provided a leadership role for their respective hinterlands. Such cities were also a reservoir for the specialised demands and skills required for further industrial diversification. While Cornwall had achieved sufficient critical mass in eighteenth-century conditions to enable the emergence of a concentrated industrial region based on metal mining, its scale of development was insufficient to enable the region to take the next step, towards diversification. The lack of a major urban centre and the small

---

[128] Dudley Baines, 'European emigration, 1815-1930: looking at the emigration decision again', *Economic History Review* 47 (1994), 538.

absolute size of the region meant that such diversification was unlikely to occur in Cornwall and it was here that the region differed most profoundly from other major industrial regions in the mid-nineteenth century.

Conclusion

Cornwall's industrial history was important in two ways. It supplied the symbols for the territory's 'symbolic shape' and the parameters for its 'space of possibilities'. Early industrialisation produced some unique institutions, for instance cost book financing. The intensely concentrated industrial region produced by copper mining in the eighteenth century led to both a regional pride in the achievements of mining and a culture of empirical tinkering. Among other things, these established an iconic status for the steam engine in local representations of place. Yet the way the mining industry had become intertwined with the territorial identity by the 1850s may itself have been a factor in the de-industrialisation that followed the 1860s.

Hudson suggests that the long term economic survival of regions was related to a variety of factors, which were cultural and political as much as economic. She suggests that 'flexible, cheap labour', which had 'little strong institutionalised attachment to earlier methods of working', may be one of these factors.[129] From this perspective we might propose that the centrality of the mining industry in Cornish people's representations of themselves by the 1860s had itself become counter-productive, closing off alternative representations and making the option of emigration in order to continue to work within the mining industry more rational than that of staying put and taking up or creating other opportunities.[130]

Cornwall's industrial experience, despite its ultimate restrictions, was therefore a central element in the history of Cornish communities in the century from 1750. But this was an experience that was not shared equally in all parts of Cornwall. To restore a sense of heterogeneity we now need to delve into some intra-Cornish differences to see if they shed light on the form and intensity of the Cornish sense of place at different locations within Cornwall.

---

[129] Hudson, 1992, 60 and 1989, 30-33.

[130] For a neoclassical take on this see Roger Burt and Sandra Kippen, 'Rational choice and a lifetime in metal mining: employment decisions by nineteenth century Cornish miners', *International Review of Social History* 46 (2001), 45-75.

Chapter Seven
People on the move

Places are not just spaces with names and meanings. They are also spaces across which people and material flows. The previous chapter discussed the movement of capital. This one moves on to encompass the movement of people. Meanings and representations of place cannot exist independently of human agency. People reproduced regional identities but people also, in their life courses, were constantly on the move. By focusing on the changing population distribution of people within Cornwall and on the flows of people both within and beyond Cornwall we are reminded of the dynamic aspect of territorial identities. People carry representations of place and construct new representations, simultaneously of the new places and the old places left behind. Their movement, therefore, tells us something of the shifting geography of the Cornish identity in our period, providing a framework for the changing representations of Cornwall and the Cornish identified above. I argue, specifically, that flows of people to new occupational communities carried ideas of 'Cornwall', ideas the heartland of which lay in the mining districts of the west, to new places in Cornwall in the first half of the nineteenth century. This expanded the popular sense of identity based on the mining region so that it more nearly matched the historic territory of Cornwall that underpinned the literary and antiquarian output of the local intelligentsia. In addition, flows of people beyond the boundaries of the region also bore ideas of Cornwall to places many thousands of miles distant from their origin. These places served as 'reservoirs' of Cornishness, later replenishing images of the region at a time when social changes were making those same images less relevant.

Intra-regional flows
The demand for labour for the booming eighteenth-century copper mines 'could not be recruited from the immediate vicinity of the mines'.[1] Thus, the central mining district between Camborne and Gwennap had to draw in labour from agricultural parishes as well as from the older tin mining

---

[1] Norman Pounds, 'Population movement in Cornwall, and the rise of mining in the eighteenth century', *Geography* 28 (1943), 41.

districts. Even before 1750 there was a stark contrast between west and east Cornwall. From 1660, the western (mining) hundreds showed a strong population growth at a time when eastern hundreds were losing population. This may be evidence of east-west migration although Jonathan Barry concludes that natural growth could account for the changing distribution.[2] Norman Pounds originally suggested that the growing demand for labour from 1750 onwards involved migration from as far away as Devon.[3] However, this seems unlikely as the rate of growth could easily be accommodated by local rises in fertility and short distance migration from other parts of west and mid Cornwall. John Rule, in a later study, firmly concluded that 'it would not appear that at any time there was any significant movement into the county from outside'.[4] Comparison of surname distribution changes between the seventeenth and nineteenth centuries using the Protestation Returns and the Census enumerators' books appear to confirm this. For example, analysis of the surname Jago, almost entirely restricted to east Cornwall in 1641, suggests little movement to the west by 1881. If there was not much movement from east Cornwall, then we must assume even less from west Devon.

After 1810 the direction of movement reversed and began to flow from west to east. As mining spread into east Cornwall, it took with it a significant proportion of its early labour force. The new mines in the Liskeard district for example attracted only a minority of their labour force from places to the east, the dominant flow being from west to east. As a result, in both 1841 and 1861, Cornwall had a higher proportion of native-born among its resident population than any county did in England, despite the expansion of mining near its eastern border. The existence of strongly localised labour markets is indicated by the higher wages paid to farm labourers near the mining districts of Cornwall at mid-century. E.H.Hunt estimates that wages in the mining districts were almost 50 per cent higher than in rural Devon.[5] Furthermore, as in industrial northern England, money wages for Cornish agricultural labourers remained stable from 1833 to the 1850s. This was in stark contrast to the experience of southern England where such wages fell by 21 per cent.[6] So, we might expect a process whereby the core economic

---

[2] Jonathan Barry, 'Population distribution and growth in the early modern period', in Roger Kain and William Ravenhill (eds), *Historical Atlas of South-West England*, Exeter, 1999, 116-117.

[3] Pounds, 1943, 43.

[4] John Rule, 'Some social aspects of the Cornish industrial revolution', in Roger Burt (ed.) *Industry and Society in the South West*, Exeter, 1971, 76.

[5] E.H.Hunt, *Regional Wage Variations in Britain, 1850-1914*, Oxford, 1973, 14.

area in west Cornwall established links, via migration flows, with a network of parishes for the most part situated entirely within Cornwall.

Before the 1851 Census, when details of the place of birth of individuals become available, it is impossible to identify the parameters of this regional migration network with any degree of confidence. However, sex ratios can be used as a surrogate indicator of out and in-migration. It might be expected that mining districts, with their demand for male labour, would contain more men than women. Conversely, market towns, where demand for domestic servants was high, would produce a female surplus. For different reasons, linked to the unavailability of work for women, purely farming districts might also show a surplus of men. Figure 7.1 shows the districts in Cornwall where the sex ratio differed from the overall English/Welsh ratio by more than two standard deviations in 1801, during a period of rapid population growth. (The territorial units of analysis are based on registration sub-districts.)

Figure 7.1. Sex ratios, 1801

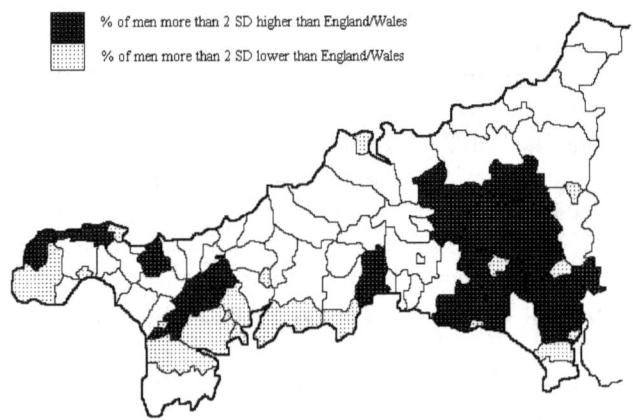

Source: Calculated from 1801 Census

This figure indicates a block of districts in east Cornwall in 1801 with a surplus of men and some scattered districts in the west with a similar

---

[6] Keith Snell, *Annals of the Labouring Poor: Social Change and Agrarian England 1660-1900*, Cambridge, 1985, 130.

surplus. It is likely that the reasons for these differ. In this period mining activity was extremely limited in the east so the surplus of men is likely to be the result of the exodus of women to the towns in search of work. This is clearly indicated on the map by the sex ratios in the small towns of east Cornwall. And just across the border were the fast-growing towns of Plymouth and Devonport. However, in mid and west Cornwall the male surplus in districts such as St Austell, Wendron, Hayle, St Just in Penwith and Towednack may well be the result of mining activity in these areas drawing in men. What is clear is that there was no large-scale gender bias in migration to west Cornish industrial districts in the late eighteenth century. Nevertheless, the female surplus in a belt of rural parishes between Mevagissey in the east to St.Buryan in the west may indicate an out-migration of men either to nearby mining districts or to maritime occupations (or their absence at sea). As Figure 7.2 indicates, agricultural east Cornwall also experienced a slower population growth after 1801. Those districts with the highest population growth correlate closely with the mining industry.

Figure 7.2 Population change 1801-1841

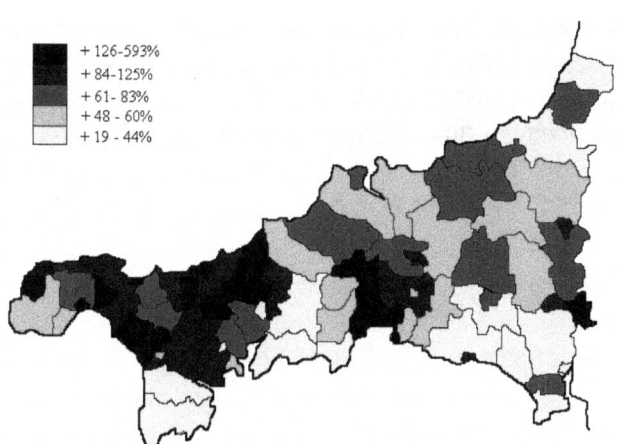

Source: Based on published Census Reports, 1801-1841.

For a clearer picture of the migration system in the second quarter of the nineteenth century we can turn to the census enumerators' books. The method adopted here is based on that used by W.T.R.Pryce in his work on the migration matrix in North East Wales in the mid-nineteenth century.[7] Pryce's work remains the prototype for this kind of research as a literature search rather surprisingly reveals no other major studies of regional migration networks using the CEBs. This is partly because of the large numbers involved and the time required to extract the data and partly because of the difficulties involved in identifying relevant boundaries for the migration network in advance. The second of these difficulties is largely overcome in the Cornish case, as Cornwall is surrounded on three sides by the sea and there are relatively few 'leakages' outside the regional system.[8] To some extent, the first problem can be reduced through adopting a systematic sampling method, using the household as the sampling unit and registration sub-districts as the basic sampling frame. This method has been adopted here with the added refinement that sub-district boundaries were redrawn to allow for the analysis of some of the towns and parishes of more than 3,000 population separately from larger sub-districts. This results in 76 sampling districts within Cornwall. To maintain confidence in the sample and reduce sampling error, variable sample proportions were adopted, from one household in two in the less densely populated rural sub-districts of the far north to one in nine in Camborne. These proportions guaranteed total sample numbers in excess of 800 for the vast majority of sub-districts, which meant that 95 per cent confidence intervals for point estimates are mostly within the range $\pm\ 4$ per cent. The main difference from Pryce's method is that only those aged 14 or over have been included in the sample in order to focus on voluntary migration.

Pryce constructed maps of estimated gross and net migration flows between neighbouring districts based on lifetime migration. Gross flows show the migration process and net flows provide a measure of the outcome. Adopting the same procedure in Cornwall results in the net flows shown in Figure 7.3.

---

[7] W.T.R.Pryce, 'Migration and the evolution of culture areas: cultural and linguistic frontiers in north-east Wales, 1750 and 1851', *Transactions of the institute of British Geographers* 65 (1975), 79-107.

[8] The obvious leakage is Plymouth. For information on Cornish migration to Plymouth before 1851 see Mark Brayshay and Vivien Pointon, 'Migration and the social geography of mid-nineteenth century Plymouth', *The Devon Historian* 28 (1984), 3-14.

Figure 7.3. Estimated net migration flows between adjacent districts 1851

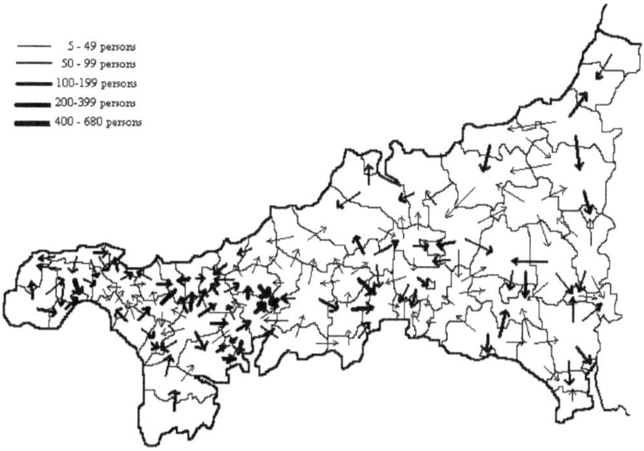

Source: Based on sample from Census enumerators' books.

This figure indicates a complex interchange of population with a less obvious directional bias than the clear west-east stream towards the coalfield areas around Wrexham and the south-north movement towards the coast that Pryce discovered in north east Wales. The greater volume of migration west of Truro reflects the larger population in the industrial west. Within this area, the attraction of the towns of Penzance, Falmouth and Truro is clear, whereas Camborne and Illogan are also the foci of moves to the central mining district. Certain remoter or upland rural areas appear to act as a reservoir of migrants, notably St Buryan in the far west, Towednack in the north of Penwith, the Meneage peninsula and Wendron/Stithians, a sub-district on the Carnmenellis upland. Similarly, in mid-Cornwall St Stephen in Brannel was also a net supplier of migrants to surrounding districts. Here, the mining area of St Austell, St Blazey and Tywardreath is a secondary focus of migration separated from the Truro area by a zone where gross migration flows resulted in a balance of movements in both directions. Further east there is some suggestion of a north-south flow, with the newer mining districts of St Cleer and Menheniot exerting a noticeable, though hardly spectacular, pull on surrounding areas.

However, Figure 7.3 obscures the situation somewhat. If the overall flows are disaggregated by gender two rather different maps result. Figure 7.4 shows the major gross moves of men at this point in the mid-nineteenth century. It also shows all major flows, not just those between neighbouring districts. This can be compared with Figure 7.5 showing the major female gross moves.

Figure 7.4. Gross moves of men, 1851

Figure 7.5. Gross moves of women, 1851.

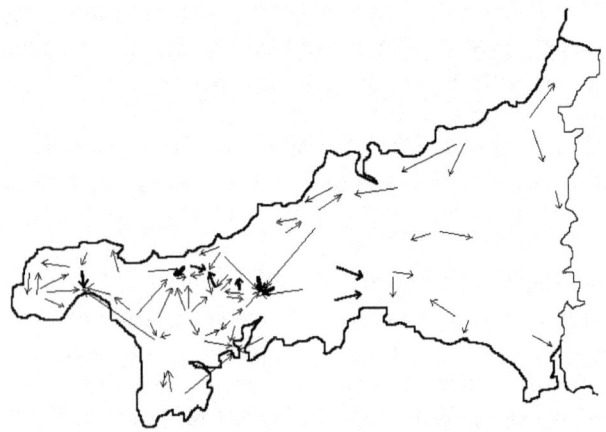

There are two obvious contrasts. First, women seem to be generally far more mobile. Second, the influence of the towns of Truro, Camborne, Redruth, Penzance and Falmouth on female migration patterns is marked. Rural-urban moves are even clearer when estimated net migration flows of women are mapped (Figure 7.6). There were four major foci for female migrants - Penzance, Camborne, Falmouth and Truro. These towns exerted a pull over a wide area of West Cornwall, with net migration flows to Truro from as far east as St Columb, to Penzance from the Scilly Isles and to Camborne, Penzance and Falmouth from the St Keverne district. There were, in addition, net inter-urban flows from places like Redruth and Helston to Falmouth and Falmouth/Penzance respectively. To the east there are no equally strong rural-urban flows, the moves into St Austell parish from the west being part of a more general shift towards the booming parish of St Blazey to its east.

Figure 7.6. Net moves of women, 1851

Turning to the net migration flows of men (Figure 7.7) the role of Truro, Penzance and Falmouth is reduced but the attraction of Camborne and the mining heartland becomes more distinct. Camborne received estimated net flows in excess of 50 migrants from eight other districts and there is a particularly strong south-north migration flow from the agricultural Meneage peninsula towards Camborne and Illogan. Furthermore, welded onto this movement to the central mining district and to the towns of Penzance, Falmouth and Truro there is some evidence of net long-distance movement from west to east as miners and others responded in the 1830s and 1840s to the expansion of mining in east Cornwall. Net flows from Gwennap to Calstock and from Breage to

Menheniot show up on this map, as does the movement from St Austell in mid-Cornwall to Liskeard and St Cleer

Figure 7.7. Net moves of men, 1851

Overall, these maps based on the 1851 CEBs portray a labour market for industrial west Cornwall restricted to the western half of the region. However, the long-distance moves from west to east parallel the extension of the industrial region eastwards after the mid-1830s. Although in quantitative terms this migration did not match short-distance flows in the west, it indicates how the newer mining districts drew from the older heartlands of Cornish mining. This was certainly what was most striking for contemporaries like John Allen who, writing in Liskeard in the early 1850s, noted how 'the dialect of the people grew more provincial and Cornish than before'.[9] In this observation Allen both re-emphasised the cultural hegemony within Cornwall of the west, as the dialect of natives of the east could just as easily be described as 'Cornish', and revealed how the operation of the local labour market was extending the cultural patterns most associated with the west to other parts of Cornwall as they too industrialised. It is likely that similar west-east movements accompanied the earlier development of mining in the St Austell district in the first quarter of the nineteenth century. This is borne out by the fact that many of the apparent long-distance moves to east

---

[9] John Allen, *History of the Borough of Liskeard*, London, 1856, 398.

Cornwall at mid-century were step-migration moves via the St Austell district.

We might conclude, therefore, that the historical geography of the Cornish mining industry helped to disseminate both representations of Cornwall and Cornishness and the discourses of differentiation that had originally emerged most strongly in the towns and villages of industrialising west Cornwall. Thus, a view of the Cornish as 'paragons of industrialisation' fitted the historic territory of Cornwall more neatly by the 1850s than it had done in the 1790s. And the migration flows themselves reinforced both local myths of 'industrial civilisation' and the role of mining as an icon of Cornish culture. Indeed, migration had, by the 1850s, spilled over the administrative border into Devon. As copper mining rapidly expanded in that district from 1844, the industrial proto-region, showing no respect for historic boundaries, was extending its influence into the mining parishes around Tavistock in west Devon.

Some have seen this as pushing 'the frontier of Greater Cornwall' across the Tamar.[10] Yet, the interesting contrast here is with the contemporaneous, and quantitatively far greater, movement to Plymouth, also in west Devon. Nobody makes similar claims for this movement. The reasons are clear. Although important in absolute numbers the relative influence of the Cornish in Plymouth was less marked, being around 10-12 per cent of the city's population in 1851.[11] But much more important, the gender and status components of this migration stream differed markedly from that to the Tavistock district. Women were far more prominent in the city-ward movement. In addition, those women heading for Plymouth tended to be young single, uneducated and untrained, attracted to Plymouth by the possibility of domestic service.[12] Overall, migration to Plymouth seems to have been the option for the very poor and dispossessed, migrants outside networks of strong kin support and lacking the resources to go further afield. The Cornish identity was, by the 1840s, clearly a male gendered identity, resting on symbols of industrial civilisation and the mining industry. The migrants to Plymouth do not sit happily with the notion of the prototype 'Cornish' skilled mine worker. Meanwhile, in the 1840s, other migration flows were adding to this movement to east Cornwall and west Devon.

---

[10] Philip Payton, *The Cornish Overseas*, Fowey, 1999, 16.
[11] Brayshay and Pointon, 1984.
[12] Judith Walkowitz, *Prostitution and Victorian Society: Women. Class and the State*, Cambridge, 1980, 154.

Extra-regional flows

The 1851 CEBs, with their suggestion of complex short-distance moves between adjacent mining parishes do not support Roger Burt's contention that in Cornwall 'extreme parochialism restricted such short-distance movements, with many miners preferring to emigrate to distant villages rather than the next village'.[13] The original informant for Burt's comment, L.L.Price, was writing towards the end of the century and was imbued by a romanticism (as the title of his work *West Barbary* suggests) that preferred to view widespread overseas emigration as an example of parochialism.[14] But what is important here is the reminder that, in the 1840s and afterwards, internal migration in Cornwall co-existed with major emigration flows. It is the volume of these latter that made Cornwall distinctive in comparison with most other industrial regions. However, it was not 'parochialism' that caused this emigration. Rather, it was the location of the Cornish miner in a wider labour market, one that, by the 1830s, should be seen in global terms, resulting in the observation by Robert Louis Stevenson in 1857 that the Cornish were 'the most locomotive of mankind'.[15]

First, we need to put these patterns of emigration in context. As already noted in chapter 6, the population of Cornwall rose at a similar rate to the English and Welsh norm in the first decades of the nineteenth century. In the 1820s and 1830s that growth rate fell slightly below the English level but if Cornwall is compared with other regions it can be seen from Table 7.1 below that its population was still growing considerably faster than neighbouring agricultural counties to the east. Nevertheless, Cornwall's rate of population growth after the 1820s did not keep up with the larger industrial regions. Before 1821 Cornwall's population grew faster than that in north east England and only a little slower than the West Riding but these latter regions surpassed Cornwall during the third decade of the century. And after the 1830s, Cornwall's growth rate was not much different from the levels in agrarian regions like south west England.

Overall, the growth rate in Cornwall, 18.4 per cent in the 1810s and 13.6 per cent in the 1830s, fell more quickly than the English rate. After 1841 this divergence became much more marked, as Table 7.2 shows.

---

[13] Roger Burt, *The British Lead Mining Industry*, Redruth, 1984, 197.
[14] L.L.Price, *'West Barbary', or Notes on the System of Work and Wages in the Cornish Mines*, London, 1891.
[15] John Rowe, *Cornish Methodists and Emigrants*, Redruth, 1967

Table 7.1: Population growth rates in selected areas, 1801-1861 (%)

	1801-21	1821-41	1841-61
England & Wales	+34.9	+32.6	+26.1
Cornwall	+35.8	+31.1	+8.0
Devon	+28.8	+21.6	+9.6
Somerset & Dorset	+28.4	+21.6	+4.9
Northumberland & Durham	+27.9	+41.3	+48.4
Lancashire & Cheshire	+52.8	+55.9	+42.3
West Riding	+41.5	+43.8	+29.6
Glamorgan & Monmouthshire	+52.8	+71.9	+61.1

Source: Census 1861: Summary tables, xiv

Table 7.2: Decadal Population change, England/Wales and Cornwall, 1801-1861 (%)

	England/Wales	Cornwall	% difference
1801-11	+14.6	+14.7	+0.1
1811-21	+18.1	+18.4	+0.3
1821-31	+15.8	+15.4	-0.4
1831-41	+14.5	+13.6	-0.9
1841-51	+12.7	+3.9	-8.8
1851-61	+11.9	+3.9	-8.0

Source: Census 1861: Summary tables, xiv

The decades of the 1840s and 1850s, decades during which the output and income of Cornish mining continued to rise at least until the mid-1850s, was a period when Cornish population growth slowed dramatically. This relative slowdown prefigured an absolute fall in numbers after the mid-1860s as the mining sector began to contract.

Behind this changing demographic pattern lay growing numbers choosing to leave Cornwall after the late 1830s. Dudley Baines has demonstrated how Cornwall after 1861 was the major emigration region of the UK outside Ireland (and, presumably, the Scottish Highlands) with migration rates for both men and women that were three times the mean for England and Wales.[16]

> Cornwall alone lost 118,500 people (overseas), the equivalent of over 40% of its young adult males and over 25% of its young adult females ... Assuming that the rate of return to Cornwall was about the same as to England and Wales as a whole, gross emigration must have been about 20% of the male Cornish-born population in each decade and about 10% of the female. This is not as high as from the famous regions of Italy, some of which achieved emigration rates of 30% or more per decade, but it must be remembered that mass emigration from Italy lasted for not much more than twenty years.[17]

In a footnote Baines further points out that, as the numbers returning to Italy were far higher, the difference was narrower than this. Cornwall lost about eight per cent of its population per decade over a period of 40 years, compared with a loss of 15 per cent per decade from southern Italy in a period of less than 20 years.

But this emigration was not triggered by the economic crises heralding the beginnings of de-industrialisation in the later 1860s. It was the continuation of an earlier process that can be dated back at least to the end of the 1830s.[18] Some of the earliest emigrants went to South America, but the two principal destinations were North America and Australia. A.L.Rowse suggested that the USA was the place 'to which the Cornish have emigrated in larger numbers than anywhere else'.[19] Other work suggests that, while North America was the most popular destination in the 1840s, it was temporarily overshadowed in the 1850s by a buoyant emigration stream to Australia.[20]

However, the total number of emigrants cannot easily be aggregated from the fragmentary evidence of the various individual migration streams. An alternative method is to estimate flow volumes from the published Census figures. The results are shown in Table 7.3 below. This

---

[16] Dudley Baines, *Migration in a Mature Economy: Emigration and Internal Migration in England and Wales, 1861-1900*, Cambridge, 1985, 152-153.

[17] Baines, 1985, 157.

[18] Philip Payton, '"Reforming Thirties" and "Hungry Forties": the genesis of Cornwall's emigration trade', in Philip Payton (ed.), *Cornish Studies Four*, Exeter, 1996, 107-127.

[19] A.L.Rowse, *The Cornish in America*, London, 1969, ii.

[20] Philip Payton, *The Cornish Farmer in Australia*, Redruth, 1987, 114-115; Patricia Lay, *Cornish Immigrants: Assisted Arrivals in New South Wales 1837-1877*, Queanbeyan, 1995.

indicates that overseas emigration was more significant than migration to England and Wales before the 1870s. Allowing for return migration as many as 110-120,000 people left Cornwall directly or indirectly for overseas destinations from the 1840s to the 1860s. It was only with the onset of economic crises that migration to England and Wales (temporarily) exceeded emigration.[21]

Table 7.3: Migration from Cornwall, 1841-1901

	Net Cornish-born migration to England and Wales (%)	Net Cornish-born emigration direct from Cornwall (%)	Net Cornish-born emigration from England and Wales	Total net Cornish-born out-migration
1841-51	16,300 (4.8)	21,300 (6.2)		37,600
1851-61	18,400 (5.2)	25,100 (7.1)		43,500
1861-71	26,200 (7.1)	27,800 (7.5)	10,300	64,300
1871-81	40,800 (11.3)	32,400 (8.9)	3,300	76,500
1881-91	18,100 (5.5)	18,900 (5.7)	11,100	48,100
1891-1901	24,000 (7.4)	13,000 (4.0)	1,800	38,800

Source: Deacon, 2007; Baines, 1985, 289; 1851-61 calculated from published Census (BPP 1852-53 [1631] LXXXV; 1863 [3221] LIII) and Registrar General's Annual Reports, BPP 1852-1862.

Somewhat paradoxically, more is known of the destinations of emigrants than of their precise origins within Cornwall. The 1841 Emigration Census suggests that the bulk of Cornish emigrants in that year were miners from the Camborne-Redruth district or farmers from the Lizard. The location of applicants for free passage to South Australia in 1836-40 also suggests that those districts in Cornwall that saw the

---

[21] For details of the Cornish migration to England and Wales see Bernard Deacon, 'A forgotten migration stream: the Cornish movement to England and Wales in the nineteenth century', in Philip Payton (ed.), *Cornish Studies Six*, 1998, 96-117. For an overview of Cornish emigration patterns see Bernard Deacon, '"We don't travel much, only to South Africa", reconstructing nineteenth-century Cornish migration patterns', in Philip Payton (ed.), *Cornish Studies Fifteen*, Exeter, 2007, 90-116.

greatest relative demand either were urban (Launceston, Penryn) or mining (St Blazey, St Agnes, Gwennap) or both (Redruth). The main exception to this pattern was a group of rural districts to the north and east of Bodmin Moor: Altarnun, Linkinhorne and Stokeclimsland. The sub-districts where applicants for free passage amounted to more than 0.5 per cent of the 1831 population are shown here.

Figure 7.8. Origins of applicants for free passage to South Australia, 1836-40

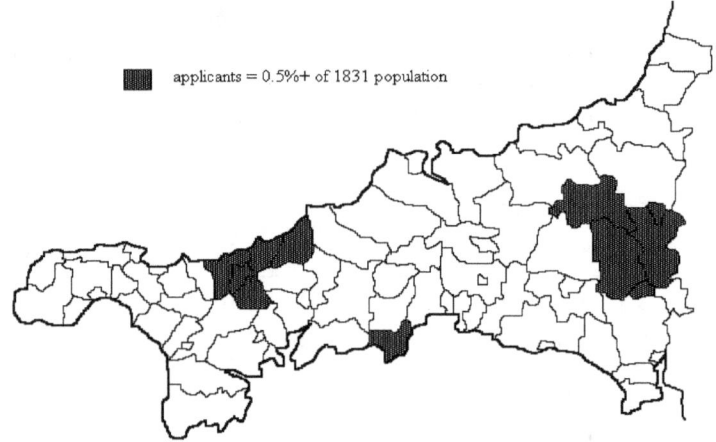

Source: calculated from Payton, 1987.

However, if we look at another migration stream to Australia, over a longer and later period, then we find a rather different picture. Assisted emigration to New South Wales over the period 1837-60 (with the bulk of arrivals during the 1850s) was much less dominated by miners, who accounted for a mere 15 per cent of male emigrants in this period.[22] The origins of those immigrants who provided details of parish of origin for the official records in New South Wales indicate that urban places such as Penryn, Truro and Helston were still prominent, as were mining districts such as Kenwyn/Chacewater, Gwennap and Perranzabuloe. But rural, agricultural districts more peripheral to the industrial region also figured in this emigration stream, notably St Keverne and St Buryan, districts we have already identified as sources of net internal migration within Cornwall in this period.

---

[22] Lay, 1995.

Having outlined the major patterns of emigration before the 1860s how might these trends be explained? Historians have explained overseas emigration in two main ways. First, they have adopted what Baines calls 'determination of migration models', attempting to relate changes in emigration rates to changes in economic conditions either in the country of origin or the country of destination or both.[23] This emphasis on relative economic conditions (whether wages or employment opportunities as the main driving force has remained a subject of some debate) clearly has affinities with earlier push/pull models of emigration. Although these are regarded as problematic because of the difficulty of differentiating between push and pull effects and because of the undynamic view of migration that it implies, push/pull classifications were still until recently the main explanatory device used by writers on Cornish emigration.

For example, Payton sees rural poverty in the 1830s and the 'hungry forties' combining with the discovery of mineral reserves in Australia and the United States.[24] Less specifically, Edmund Newell uses a simple explanatory framework of the push factors of depression in the Cornish economy interacting with the pull of attractive employment opportunities overseas.[25] While in a broad sense this was no doubt the case, it cannot explain the strength and the continuity of the Cornish emigration process in the 1850s when the Cornish economy was hardly depressed and when Cornish mining reached new production peaks. As Baines suggests, such 'economic' frameworks may to some extent explain the timing of migration,[26] particularly the onset of mass emigration streams in the 1830s and 1840s, but cultural factors and emigration networks (implying feedback of information and chain migration) were probably more important factors by the 1850s. Indeed, because of its costs, overseas migration peaked not at times of crisis but in good times and among the relatively socially privileged. Certainly, after the 1860s emigration was strongest not in the worst years of recession but in years after severe recessions or in the intermittent boom periods.

---

[23] Dudley Baines, 'European emigration, 1815-1930: looking at the emigration decision again', *Economic History Review* 47 (1994), 525-544.

[24] Philip Payton, 'Cornish emigration in response to changes in the international copper market in the 1860s', in Philip Payton (ed.), *Cornish Studies Three*, Exeter, 1995, 61-62.

[25] Edmund Newell, 'The British copper ore market in the nineteenth century, with particular reference to Cornwall and Swansea', D.Phil thesis, Oxford University, 1988, 61.

[26] Baines, 1994, 528.

What relative income models do not explain is why some people emigrate and others do not and why, given similar economic circumstances, some regions had higher emigration rates than others. Because of these problems historians have become more attracted to the ideas implied in a 'chain migration model' that focuses on the flows of information between origins and destinations. Put simply, this suggests that once a migration route is established the information conveyed back to the originating region by letters and by return migrants stimulates a continuing chain of migrants. Therefore, differences in levels of migration are explained to a large extent by differences in previous levels of migration. Such an approach emphasises the dynamic nature of the migration process and the continuities and networks involved in this process. It also directs attention to the family as the key social institution in which migration decisions were taken and suggests that perceptions of conditions overseas may have been more important in the migration decision than some 'objective' economic reality.

Locally, a variety of emigration routes from Cornwall had already been established before mass emigration set in after 1830. For example, as early as 1819 passages on boats from Cornwall to Quebec were being advertised in local newspapers. In 1817 Richard Trevithick was in South America erecting pumping engines and in 1826 returned emigrants from Central America astonished the natives (at Redruth) by appearing in the street in the dress usually worn by Mexican miners.[27] These early pioneers were establishing the networks that enabled others to follow in much larger numbers during the 1840s and 1850s. Nonetheless, the chain migration/flow of information model is not without its own problems. What is difficult to explain, given the model's prediction of continuity (as migration flows grow so information grows and so further migration is stimulated) is how migration streams end and how one chain replaces another. To make this more concrete what made someone in Cornwall emigrate to South Australia rather than North America? Was this just a matter of local fashion or were there different chains for different families or communities? The answers to such questions await more detailed data, particularly about migration streams to North America.

Cornish historians have, until recently, failed to put the Cornish experience of emigration in its proper context. There has been little comparison with other groups or with the broader literature on overseas emigration. However, in the 1990s there was a move towards a more holistic approach to Cornish emigration, one that prioritises synthesis and

---

[27] Frank Michell, *Annals of an Ancient Cornish Town, being Notes on the History of Redruth*, Redruth, 1978, 94.

the drawing together of hitherto compartmentalised strands. Philip Payton was among the first to call for this and followed it up by his overview monograph on the Cornish overseas, which deals with most of the major emigration streams.[28] Until this point there had been several studies of individual overseas flows and, while Payton claims they have 'by and large, avoided the worst of the filio-pietistic, antiquarian and parochial approaches that have sometimes marked (and marred) the study of other emigrant ethnic groups in new lands', they remained resolutely idiographic in their methodology, giving pride of place to movements of miners and to conditions in the countries of destination.[29] Texts on Cornish emigration, sometimes referred to as the 'Great Migration', find it difficult to escape the influence of a heroic tradition that viewed 'emigration (as) the crown of Cornish accomplishment', a symptom of Cornish energy and enterprise.[30] As a result the hitherto considerable stress on the life histories of individual permanent colonists can still leave a demand for a 'piecing together of a general picture of Cornish emigration, a picture which can then be juxtaposed with other emigrant groups'.[31]

One such attempt to put Cornish emigration in its broader context was made by Gill Burke. She argued that the Cornish mineworker played 'a crucial part in the expansion of world metal production during the nineteenth century', being 'a segment of the labour force which could be flexibly deployed wherever there was a need for labour to enable commodity production to expand'.[32] Burke's view, in her own words, 'poses a challenge to individualist perspectives' on labour migration and 'to those who interpret labour migration in terms of betterment'.[33] Eschewing push and pull factors, Burke insisted that Cornish emigration

---

[28] Payton, 1999.

[29] Payton, 1999, 27; Philip Payton, *The Cornish Miner in Australia: Cousin Jack Down Under*, Redruth, 1984; A.L.Rowse, *The Cornish in America*, London, 1969; A.C.Todd, *The Search for Silver: Cornish Miners in Mexico, 1824-1947*, Padstow, 1977; John Rowe, *The Hard-Rock Men: Cornish Immigrants and the North American Mining Frontier*, Liverpool, 1974; Graham Dickason, *Cornish Immigrants to South Africa*, Cape Town, 1978. For a self-proclaimed 'revisionist' approach to Cornish emigration see Sharron Schwartz, *The Cornish in Latin America: Cousin Jack and the New World*, Dublin, 2016.

[30] John Pearce, *The Wesleys in Cornwall*, Truro, 1964, 27.

[31] Margaret James-Korany, '"Blue books" as sources for Cornish emigration history', in Philip Payton (ed.), *Cornish Studies One*, Exeter, 1993, 44.

[32] Gill Burke, 'The Cornish miner and Cornish mining industry 1870-1921', PhD thesis, University of London, 1981, 65.

[33] Burke, 1981, 74-75.

was 'determined by international development and investment with concomitant shifts in international demand for labour'.[34] It was the particular location of Cornwall's economy in the activity space of metal mining that opened it up relatively early to globalising influences. Within these arenas Cornish labour moved overseas, apparently freely, but within a structure determined by Cornwall's place in the international mining economy. Nevertheless, Burke's neo-marxist approach, while having strengths in locating Cornish emigration within the territorial expansion of capitalism, is over-reliant on economic factors and ignores the role of culture as an independent variable. Migrants were not forced to emigrate. They still made choices about whether to go, where to go and, once gone, whether to stay.

To pursue the role of human agency in this process, it is helpful to try to put this Cornish experience into its European context. The older view that emigrants to North America in the first half of the century were those on the margins of industrial society, fleeing bad times and rural poverty, has now been largely undermined. Charlotte Erikson has found that, in 1841, immigrants to the USA were more likely to have been farmers than agricultural labourers while, in proportion to their strength in the whole English labour force, industrial workers were over-represented.[35] With the significant exception of post-famine Ireland, the new explanatory orthodoxy stresses that 'the majority of emigrants must have come from places that were in the mainstream of economic change, not, for example, from the remote rural areas'.[36]

The well documented wave of emigration from the remoter agricultural districts of North Cornwall and the Lizard in the early years of mass emigration may go some way towards suggesting that, in contrast, in Cornwall rural areas peripheral to the major centres of economic change were involved in early emigration.[37] However, this emigration was soon swamped by the mass emigration of miners and town dwellers.

It has been suggested that industrial emigrants might have been more likely to originate from sectors 'where growth was relatively fast but where technological change was threatening some occupations'.[38] Both in Britain and in Germany a large number of emigrants came from

---

[34] Burke, 1984, 75.
[35] Charlotte Erikson, 'Emigration to the USA from the British Isles, part II: who were the English emigrants?', *Population Studies* 44 (1990), 26 and 30.
[36] Baines, 1985, 281.
[37] John Rowe, *Cornwall in the Age of the Industrial Revolution*, Liverpool, 1953, 238-239 and 252. See also John Rowe, *Changing Times and Fortunes: A Cornish Farmer's Life 1828-1904*, St Austell, 1996; James-Korany, 1993.
[38] Baines, 1994, 537.

declining proto-industrial as opposed to either entirely agricultural areas or from areas of mechanised industry.[39] Hence it is speculated that population pressure may have been a major cause along with declining demand for particular skills. This is an intriguing suggestion which links back to Burt's speculation about the proto-industrial status of western districts of Cornwall in an earlier period.[40] However, there is no obvious case of de-skilling of sections of the mines labour force in the 1840s. Nevertheless, the role of population pressure is perhaps one that requires further investigation.

Comparative work only belatedly homed in on this really striking demographic difference between Cornwall and other British industrial regions in the second quarter of the nineteenth century. As we have seen, here was a region where the dynamic sector was still growing yet which was beginning to experience mass emigration on a scale totally unknown in most other industrial regions. In the later nineteenth century when more reliable statistics are available, people were twice as likely to emigrate from Cornwall as from the other industrial regions most prone to emigration, north east England and south Wales. Emigration from the textile regions of Lancashire and Yorkshire and from the west and east Midlands was, in turn, much lower and ran at rates lower than the mean for England and Wales.[41]

Payton's work expands on this comparative perspective, contrasting the Cornish experience with emigration from other parts of 'so-called "Celtic Britain" and Ireland'.[42] In particular, he draws attention to the one other part of Britain where high levels of emigration co-existed with industrialisation. Tom Devine has argued that in nineteenth century Scotland emigrants were as likely to be from the industrial Lowlands as the rural Highlands and that Scottish emigration was 'professional and entrepreneurial' in nature, with a high proportion of skilled emigrants.[43] This 'distinctively Scottish' emigration experience had its roots in a culture of mobility, established well before the peak years of emigration in the later nineteenth century. Industrialisation combined with cultural expectations, relatively low wages and an open economy to produce an international labour market in Scotland and, unlike in England and Wales,

---

[39] Erikson, cited in Baines, 1994, 537.

[40] Roger Burt, 'Proto-industrialisation and "stages of growth" in the metal mining industries', *Journal of European Economic History* 27 (1998), 85-104.

[41] Baines, 1985, 152-153.

[42] Payton, 1999, 22.

[43] Tom Devine, 'The paradox of Scottish emigration', in Tom Devine (ed.), *Scottish Emigration and Scottish Society*, Edinburgh, 1992, 1-15.

served to stimulate emigration. There are certainly intriguing parallels between Lowland Scotland and Cornwall, although the considerable differences in industrial context and scale and the contrasts in the relative propensity to emigrate need further and more detailed exploration

The Scottish comparison might usefully raise questions about the homogeneity of the Cornish emigration experience. For example, Stephen Hornsby proposes that there were two distinct Scottish emigration streams to Canada. Emigration from the Highlands was concentrated in a few major channels whereas that from the Lowlands was diffuse. This he links to 'the community nature of Highland emigration, as compared with the more individualistic Lowland movement'.[44] Does this resemble the Cornish case? Was there one type of community-based migration, predominantly overseas or to industrial regions within the British Isles, originating from rural-industrial parishes and the mining towns, and another, more individualistic, emanating from market towns and coastal districts and supplying a more diffuse migration stream to England? Moreover, does this help to explain why the Cornish identity flourished in some overseas arenas, creating a myth of 'Cousin Jack' that rested on mining skills and culture, and yet not in others?

The openness of the Cornish economy and the global links of its leading sector, metal mining, laid down the necessary conditions for movements overseas. The exploitation of new mining districts during the eighteenth century and their demand for labour helped to foster a 'tradition' of mobility. As the mining frontier expanded with late eighteenth and early nineteenth-century colonialism, capital and labour became even more mobile. By the time this happened Cornwall was a major metal mining region. Therefore, it is unsurprising that the dominant mining region was the source of the relatively skilled labour that newer mining regions sought. In this way Cornish miners acted, in Marx's telling phrase, as the 'light infantry of capital'.[45]

Yet this 'light infantry' was also the advance guard for the massed ranks of emigrants, miners and non-miners who travelled the routes established by the expanding mining frontier. Therefore, Payton, in his writings on the Cornish emigration, is right to stress the role of an 'emigration culture' which, reinforced by an active 'emigration trade' had been established as early as the 1840s.[46] This 'emigration culture' was itself part of a broader regional popular culture, and should be seen

---

[44] Stephen Hornsby, 'Patterns of Scottish emigration to Canada, 1750-1870', *Journal of Historical Geography* 18 (1992), 387.
[45] Cited in Burke, 1984, 65
[46] Payton, 1995, 61-62.

as part of a complex of factors including systems of land tenure, employment relations, the role of Methodism and the absence of a large town to soak up potential emigrants. In this last respect it provided a marked contrast to urbanising Scotland. Other factors, too, acted to establish and perpetuate emigration as a popular strategy, as we shall see in chapters 8 and 9 below.

Conclusion
We can conclude this chapter by tracing the links between this Cornish 'culture of mobility' and the territorial identity.[47] Payton suggests that the Lowland Scots 'deployed [their] ethnic identity to assert their particular suitability to the rigours of life on the frontier, stressing thrift, hardiness, determination; their Protestant work ethic'.[48] Cornwall's predominantly Methodist culture, committed to self-help, improvement and individual salvation, was also especially suited to this self-image. The Cornish carried this aspect of their identity with them to their communities overseas. Self-help joined with mining prowess to form elements of the 'Cousin Jack' myth overseas. In this sense the narrative of Cornwall as 'industrial civilisation' produced in the late eighteenth and early nineteenth centuries was an important enabling factor in the culture of emigration that was established after the 1830s.

As emigrants carried representations of themselves and of Cornwall with them, the identity of industrial prowess seems to have become more assertive and more sharply delineated on the mining frontiers of South Australia and the United States. It also heightened the distinctiveness of the Cornish experience during the second quarter of the nineteenth century, creating new family and community links that were not bound by the parameters of the British nation-state or even the British Empire. These links established inter-connected reservoirs of Cornishness scattered across the globe, reservoirs that, after the 1860s, when de-industrialisation set in at home, acted to replenish myths of 'industrial civilisation' through the mechanism of return migration. Then, the existence of Cornish industrial communities overseas acted to conserve representations that were becoming increasingly inapplicable to a de-industrialising society.[49]

In terms of the definition of identity established in chapter 1 migration patterns are one aspect of the context of the formation of the Cornish

---

[47] Payton, 1999, 29-30.
[48] Payton, 1999, 26.
[49] For an analysis of the contrasts between the Cornish identity in Cornwall and overseas at the end of the nineteenth century see Payton, 1999, 374-378

identity. But movements of people did more than just provide a context. They added to integration, by drawing parts of east Cornwall and even west Devon into the mining region through incorporating new districts into the regional labour market after 1830. They produced new elements of distinction, by creating an emigration pattern markedly different from most other industrial regions in Britain. They also carried narratives of Cornishness and Cornwall to other places, and especially overseas, where such narratives fed back via return migration to a later Cornwall in the stages of de-industrialisation. Finally, because of different propensities to emigrate, they alert us to micro-geographical and intra-Cornwall variations. Significantly, localised economic difficulties in the mining industry in the 1840s combined with a noticeable rural-urban tendency in short-distance migration patterns. This conjuncture meant that those rural-industrial districts where, as we shall see, the distinct 'proto-industrial' society of eighteenth century Cornwall had most deeply embedded itself were exactly the places that tended to experience the greatest degree of out-migration after the 1830s.

Returning to Paasi's model, internal migration patterns reinforced the territorial shape of the region in the second quarter of the nineteenth century, aligning the informal institutions of the industrial region with the more formal institutions of the administrative county. At the same time mass emigration flows produced new elements for the symbolic shape of the region, elements that established themselves as part of Cornish identity and that, indeed, continue to resonate in the early twenty-first century.

The next chapter turns to another element in the context of Cornish identity. In doing this we return to interrogate in more detail the concept of a proto-industrial society in the early nineteenth century Cornish 'region'. The parameters of this society will be ascertained and the pressures leading to structural change from the 1840s identified.

Chapter Eight
A society of dispersed paternalism

The argument of the previous chapter was that patterns of mobility provided part of the context for identity formation in Cornwall. This chapter explores this further by reviewing aspects of the social relations of Cornwall in its industrial period. In doing this, moreover, the discussion cannot confine itself solely to context. For, in pursuing the context of identity in Cornwall, we inevitably return to issues of process and narrative.

The social history of Cornwall, the relations between social groups and the patterns of authority and dependence that held social relations together added to that 'space of possibilities' within which the Cornish identity was transformed during industrialisation. This chapter looks at three readings of Cornish social relations in this period. First, and most briefly, it revisits a dominant contemporary reading of social relations in early nineteenth-century Cornwall. Second, it assesses an influential academic reading of social relations in nineteenth century Cornwall, one firmly established in the mainstream of post-1960s British social history. Finally, it suggests a third reading of some features of the Cornish industrial experience. Elements, individually present in other places, were combined in Cornwall in a unique social compromise, constructed during the eighteenth century and lasting through to the 1840s. By utilising the concept of 'discourse' at this point we can explain more comprehensively certain unique aspects of Cornish social relations in the early nineteenth century. Furthermore, in reconceptualising the history of class relations in Cornwall we can introduce a sense of process into the constraints of material and narrative structures and contexts.

As we have seen, mining was the dynamic sector of Cornwall's economy and, by the early nineteenth century, miners were the largest occupational group in Cornwall. The dominant outside reading of the miners was that of well-ordered and civilised paragons of the progressive spirit permeating the industrial regions of Britain. By the 1840s, J.D. Tuckett, comparing the Cornish miners with other labouring groups, concluded that they presented 'the brightest picture we have met with, of the condition of any considerable body of the labouring class in England at the present day'.[1]

Although described by Tuckett as a 'class', Cornish miners steadfastly – admirably in the opinion of a succession of bourgeois commentators – refused to act like other sections of this 'working class'. As Rule has pointed out, the representation of Cornish mining as 'strike-free' and the Cornish miner as unsullied by the trade unionism and Chartism convulsing other industrial regions in the 1830s and 40s became a 'cliché as one writer picked up from the account of another'.[2] 'No one has heard of disagreements between the Cornish miners and their employers – no combinations or unions on the one side or the other exist' wrote the mine manager John Taylor in 1834.[3] On his trip to Cornwall, Wilkie Collins found 'few grumblers'.[4] Strikes were 'unheard of in the Cornish mines' and the miners supposedly remained 'comparatively indifferent to political agitation' well into the 1850s.[5]

Because of this reputation, in traditional historical readings the Cornish working class has been a void or absent group. Without the characteristics traditionally associated with a class or labour consciousness the Cornish rarely feature in work produced by British social and labour historians since the 1960s.[6]

An absent working class? British historians and social class
Social class and class identities were at the forefront of the social history written by British historians from the 1960s to the 1990s. For marxist and non-marxist alike, class became the central organising concept applied to understanding nineteenth century society.[7] By far the most influential voice amongst this body of work was that of E.P.Thompson, in his path-breaking *The Making of the English Working Class*. For Thompson, people produced classes in a dialectical process during which

---

[1] J.D.Tuckett, *A History of the Past and Present State of the Labouring Population, volume 2*, London, 1846, 536-537.

[2] John Rule, 'A "configuration of quietism"? Attitudes towards trade unionism and Chartism among the Cornish miners', *Tijdschrift voor Sociale Geschiedenis* 2/3 (1992), 250.

[3] Cited in Roger Burt (ed.), *Cornish Mining: Essays on the Organisation of Cornish Mines and the Cornish Mining Economy*, Newton Abbot, 1969, 38-39.

[4] Wilkie Collins, *Rambles Beyond Railways*, London, 1852, 78.

[5] J.R.Leifchild, *Cornwall: Its Mines and Miners*, London, 1857, 146; Herman Merivale, 'Cornwall', *The Quarterly Review* 102 (1857), 312.

[6] For a rare mention see Eric Hobsbawm, *Labouring Men*, London, 1964, 30.

[7] Harold Perkin, *The Origins of Modern English Society, 1780-1880*, London, 1969; E.P.Thompson, *The Making of the English Working Class*, London, 1963.

their agency operated within the limits and parameters set by economic structures. As a result, classes were historical relationships produced by the acts and thoughts of real people in real places but people who were, nevertheless, anchored to an economic context, their experience moulded and contained by that context. Thus, underlying Thompson's cultural marxism, there remained an ultimately materialist account of class formation. For twenty years, most British social historians accepted the broad model of class proposed by Thompson.

Furthermore, there was a distinct tendency to assume a teleological process of class and labour formation. From this viewpoint groups and times that diverged from a 'naturally driven path' became problems in methodological terms.[8] This explains why so much has been written about the 'problem' of working class reformism in Britain in the mid-Victorian period, after Chartism. In a similar way, in Cornwall the 'problem' as to why the miners were not more involved in early unionism and in the Chartist movement has taken centre stage. But, just as the earlier focus on the 'working class quietism' of mid-Victorian politics has been described as an 'old chestnut',[9] so it might be proposed that the absence of an expected class identity amongst the Cornish miners deflects our attention from a fuller understanding of the context of their actual lived identities in the early nineteenth century.

In the 1980s, the pendulum swung away from 'materialist' accounts. Gareth Stedman Jones suggested that more attention be given to 'languages of class' rather than the economic structures underlying class formation. Seeking the languages of class in the early nineteenth century, Jones and, later, Patrick Joyce were unable to find them.[10] People in the nineteenth century, argued these revisionists, adopted languages of populism or of democracy but only rarely saw themselves as class subjects. Writers influenced by post-structuralism echoed these conclusions. Class had no fixed meanings at all; instead nineteenth-century languages of class were 'complicated, heterogeneous and variable'.[11] Materialist accounts of class as the dominant identity of

---

[8] Richard Price, 'The future of British labour history', *International Review of Social History* 36 (1991), 251.

[9] Dror Wahrman, 'The new political history: a review essay', *Social History* 21 (1996), 346.

[10] Gareth Stedman Jones, *Languages of Class: Studies in English Working Class History 1832-1982*, Cambridge, 1984; Patrick Joyce, *Visions of the People: Industrial England and the Question of Class 1840-1914*, Cambridge, 1991.

[11] Joan Scott, 'On language, gender and working-class history', in Leonard Berlanstein (ed.), *The Industrial Revolution and Work in Nineteenth Century Europe*, London, 1992, 174.

industrialising Britain were thus challenged by idealist accounts that viewed class as just one identity among many, if that.

The debate over class and the 'linguistic turn' in social and labour history was waged with some heat for a decade from the late 1980s. While idealists accused materialists of an economic reductionism, materialists counter-charged idealists with linguistic reductionism. To some extent both positions are guilty of caricature. Social historians working within the 'Thompsonian' tradition had been alert to language and culture, while most historians adopting the linguistic turn have, in their published work, not denied the existence of reality. The debate quickly cooled. Joyce called for a 'return to history' while others pointed to common ground between Thompson's work and post-structuralist concerns.[12] Later in this chapter I will propose one way in which material and idealist accounts of class formation may be combined. But first, just how exceptional were Cornish mining communities in the early nineteenth century?

Cornish exceptionalism

By 1851, as Figure 8.1 on the next page indicates, miners were the dominant occupational group in many districts of Cornwall, especially the west. In this and other ways, they manifested some of the structural preconditions cited as necessary for group identity. (Fishermen would be another group with an obvious occupational identity.) But, not all isolated and self-enclosed communities with dense social ties facilitated political mobilisation; just as many displayed political passivity.

For example, in the literature on British social history, Chartism plays a pivotal role in narratives of class formation. This movement, expressing political demands in a language of class opposition, if not class conflict, and linking up dispersed local communities into a national movement directed at the centre of political power, has been viewed as a moment of crystallisation of consciousness, although the debate continues about the class nature of that consciousness. In Cornwall, however, the relative absence of widespread Chartist activity among the miners was taken as indicating the absence of class consciousness, a position bolstered both by contemporary accounts of a consensual and strike free society and by later historical readings.[13] Yet, when removed

---

[12] Patrick Joyce, 'Refabricating social history; or, from labour history to the history of labour', *Labour History Review* 62 (1997), 147-152 and 'The return of history: postmodernism and the politics of academic history in Britain', *Past and Present* 158 (1998), 207-235.

[13] For a re-assessment of Cornish Chartism see Bernard Deacon, *From a*

geographically from Cornwall, Cornish miners were just as likely to organise and unionise as any other group, as their role in the Burra Burra strike in South Australia in 1848/49 would suggest.

Figure 8.1: Proportion of miners and quarrymen, 1851

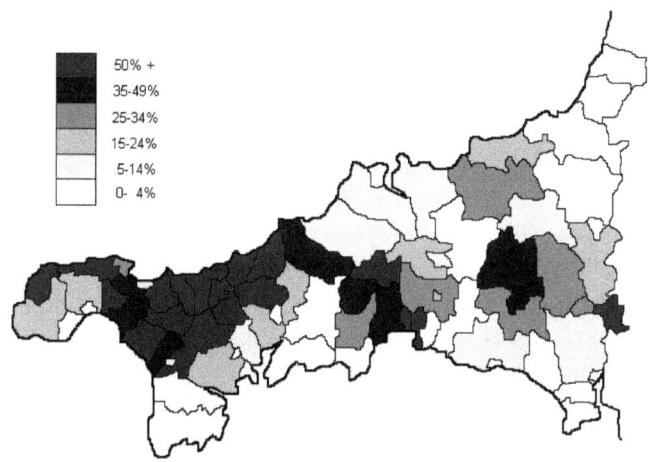

Therefore, to explain the relative absence of Chartist, union and strike activity, attention must be directed towards local social relations. In a series of articles John Rule advanced the proposition that, as individual variables also occurred in regions where unionisation and strikes were widespread, we must explain Cornish miners' exceptionalism through a combination of factors, a 'configuration of quietism', the 'combined or cumulative effect [of which] could be the outcome of an environment impropitious for the growth of trade unionism and popular political radicalism of the kind exemplified by Chartism'.[14] Principal among these cumulative factors was the tributing method of wage payment. This involved competitive and individual wage bargaining between groups of miners. Tributing combined with another factor, Methodism, which siphoned off potential activism through its popular revivalism. Methodist

---

Cornish Study, Redruth, 2017, 123-154.

[14] Rule, 1992, 248/249. This restates his argument in 'The labouring miner in Cornwall c1740-1870', PhD thesis, Warwick University, 1971 and is re-affirmed in turn in *Cornish Cases: Essays in Eighteenth and Nineteenth Century Social History*, Southampton, 2006, 202-221.

opposition was compounded by landlords' paternalism, producing a 'web of dependence and deference', the cost book system of financing the mines, which had led to 'the practical disappearance of the employer', and distance and isolation from other industrial regions. Rule's work indeed takes us a considerable way towards explaining the lack of industrial organisation among Cornish miners before the 1860s. However, extending this to a model of Cornish 'working class quietism' more generally is less convincing. In particular, it implies an overly narrow definition of collective activity and insufficiently contextualises the miners' non-work experience. For, as we shall see below, there is considerable evidence that Cornish communities were not over-determined by work and the social relations of the workplace.

'Quietism' assessed
An absence of explicit and formal combinations does not mean there was no collective organisation. Rule himself drew attention to the established custom among the miners of not bidding at the regular auction of tribute pitches against the pare (group) of miners who were already working that pitch.[15] This, together with evidence for widespread 'kitting' or cheating on tribute bargains, implies a level of collusion among groups of miners and the existence of 'tacit combinations'.[16] These co-existed in early nineteenth century Cornwall with other examples of collective organisation.

Rule has claimed that 'miners lacked the experience of the independent mutual funds which played a clear role in the development of artisan trade unions'.[17] But the evidence appears to contradict this. In 1839 there were five miners' Friendly Societies in Cornwall, one in mid-Cornwall and the other four in the west. That in mid-Cornwall and one of those in the west had been formed before 1825. This was at a time when there was only one similar society in the south Wales coalfield.[18] Friendly Society membership in Cornwall was relatively high early in the century. In 1815 the number of members of Friendly Societies in Cornwall was

---

[15] John Rule, *The Vital Century: England's Developing Economy, 1714-1815*, London, 1992, 253.

[16] John Rule, 'Cheating on tribute in the Cornish tin mines 1775-1850', *Bulletin of the Society for the Study of Labour History* 52 (1987), 2-43 and John Rule and Roger Wells, *Crime, Protest and Popular Politics in Southern England 1740-1850*, London, 1997, 53-66.

[17] Rule and Wells, 1997, 59.

[18] Humphrey Southall, 'Towards a geography of unionization: the spatial organisation and distribution of early British trade unions', *Transactions of the Institute of British Geographers*, NS13 (1988), 471.

equal to 10.4 per cent of the 1811 population.[19] Only the industrial counties of northern England, plus Monmouthshire and neighbouring Devon, had higher rates of Friendly Society membership. As many as 29-33 per cent of the adult male population of Cornwall or 42-48 per cent of families were supported to some extent by Friendly Society funds in 1815.[20] Martin Gorsky's detailed analysis of membership at parish level also indicates that the mining parish of Illogan had one of the highest densities of Friendly Society membership.[21] It seems that membership of independent mutual societies co-existed with the insecure and dependent support of the employer-run sick clubs for miners. Significantly, in 1841, Seymour Tremenheere noted, in relation to independent benefit clubs, that people in the mining districts 'are strongly inclined to their formation'. Moreover, 'the population is strongly adverse to the interference of gentlemen in their concerns'.[22] This indicates a hitherto unstressed but important role for benefit societies in the self-identification of mining communities.

Furthermore, extending a description of 'quietism' from the political consciousness of Cornish miners to the outlook of the broader community stretches the concept too far. In 1772 the meaning of 'quietism' is first documented as 'a state of calmness and passivity ... repose, quietness, tranquillity'. Yet, less than a year later, in January and February 1773 Cornish miners and others engaged in one of their periodic collective actions, descending in large crowds on local markets and towns, demanding and obtaining lower prices for grain.[23] The role of 'food riots' in Cornwall suggests we should reject the concept of 'quietism' as a general description for Cornish labouring communities.

Rule has shown that major instances of food rioting occurred regularly in Cornwall from 1729 to 1847.[24] Thompson noted that 'notoriously the Cornish tinners [sic] had an irascible consumer consciousness, and a readiness to turn out in force'.[25] John Bohstedt, quantifying the numbers

---

[19] Calculated from P.H.J.H.Gosden, *The Friendly Societies in England, 1815-1875*, Manchester, 1961, 22.
[20] Martin Gorsky, 'The growth and distribution of English friendly societies in the early nineteenth century', *Economic History Review* 51 (1998), 493.
[21] Gorsky, 1998, 495.
[22] Seymour Tremenheere, 'On the state of education in the mining districts', *British Parliamentary Papers* 1841 (317) XX.97, 92-93.
[23] *Sherborne Mercury*, 1 February 1773 and 22 February 1773.
[24] John Rule, 'Some social aspects of the Cornish industrial revolution', in Roger Burt (ed.), *Industry and Society in the South West*, Exeter, 1970, 71-106; Rule, 1971, 146ff.
[25] E.P.Thompson, *Customs in Common*, London, 1993, 213.

of riots in the crisis decades of the 1790s and 1800s, found that the number of riots per 10,000 persons in Cornwall in this period was almost three times higher than in the most riot-prone parts of England – London, Nottinghamshire and Devon.[26] Yet Rule insisted that such examples of collective action be clearly bracketed off from 'industrial disputes *per se*'.[27] Food riots merely 'revealed the miners' conservatism and commitment to a prior political economy, rather than their potential for political radicalism'.[28]

Yet Rule's mentor, E.P.Thompson, in establishing his classic case for food rioting to be seen as a part of the 'moral economy of the crowd', pointed out how, 'while their moral economy cannot be described as "political" in any advanced sense, nevertheless, it cannot be described as unpolitical either, since it supposed definite and passionately held notions of the common weal'.[29] Indeed, the crowd, bent on establishing their 'moral economy', undertook actions that look remarkably similar to contemporary bodies of striking workers elsewhere. In Cornwall the miners, at the core of the majority of rioting crowds, could 'ensure that all males effectively struck work and then mobilised to secure moral economic conditions'.[30] For example, miners from Charlestown United went from mine to mine in mid-Cornwall in 1847 calling out workers, preparatory to descending on the market at St Austell.[31] Such tactics, and the mutual purpose behind them, suggest that the ends may have differed but the means were very similar to much early nineteenth century strike action in industrial northern England.

If crowd action in Cornwall to control the food market involved many of the same features as strikes and political mobilisation, then continuing to ignore these when studying the collective behaviour of working people would seem untenable. Indeed, Neville Kirk does not distinguish food riots from trade unions, attacks on machines, cooperatives, Friendly Societies and political organisations. For him, these were all ways in which workers could act collectively.[32] If we accept this approach, then the notion of 'quietist' Cornish mining communities dissolves.

---

[26] John Bohstedt, *Riots and Community Politics in England and Wales, 1790-1810*, Cambridge MA, 1983, 239.
[27] Rule and Wells, 1997, 6.
[28] Rule and Wells, 1997, 80.
[29] Thompson, 1993, 188.
[30] Rule and Wells, 1997, 5.
[31] *West Briton*, 18 June 1847.
[32] Neville Kirk, *Labour and Society in Britain and the USA. Volume 1: Capitalism, Custom and Protest, 1780-1850*, Aldershot, 1994, 7.

Adopting a comparative perspective also poses questions about the relative 'quietism' of mining communities in Cornwall. Roger Burt, in a comparative study of the coal and metal mining sectors, concludes that there was no great gulf between them. While 'the causes and chronology of the development of strikes in both sectors were similar ... only the outcomes [permanent trade unions] were significantly different'. He explains this largely through the differing conditions the two groups of workers faced. Metal miners found themselves coping with declining prices in a shrinking sector after the 1860s, whereas coal mining boomed. He also bluntly concludes that 'there was no Cornish exceptionalism'; in all metal mining regions industrial relations were relatively tranquil until the mid-nineteenth century.[33]

The concept of 'quietism' therefore rests on too narrow a definition of collective agency. Instead of merely viewing the Cornish working class as a community with an absence of labour history we need to reconstruct the social relations of Cornwall. In moving to the preferred reading of this chapter I will first clarify the context for the emergent identities of the period before the mid-nineteenth century. In this way, incidentally, we can also begin to link the economic and political spheres of people's lives with the social and the cultural.

Merchant capitalism and independent communities
As we saw in chapter 5, two groups dominated Cornish society in the late eighteenth and early nineteenth centuries. Landlords owned the land and mineral rights and sometimes invested directly in mines adventuring and other industrial activities. Over the eighteenth century, merchant capitalists joined them, diversifying their trading interests into smelting and the advance of credit. This produced a social matrix in west Cornwall that resembled a form of merchant capitalism. Merchant capitalism rests on the exchange and distribution of finished goods; merchant capitalists act as commercial agents and assume banking functions. In industrial capitalism, the focus moves from accumulation through exchange to accumulation from production and control over labour processes. Merchant capitalism tends to accompany an exchange-based critique, of monopolies, speculators and bankers, and attention moves beyond the workplace. In contrast, in industrial capitalism the flash point becomes the workplace and the social relations embedded in it.[34]

---

[33] Roger Burt, 'Industrial relations in the British non-ferrous mining industry in the nineteenth century', *Labour History Review* 71 (2006), 57-79.
[34] Kirk, 1994, 22.

Moreover, merchant capitalism produces a particular relationship between capital and community. Gerald Sider, studying Newfoundland, has explained how 'tradition' emerges in the context of merchant capitalism, when production of commodities occurs alongside the relatively autonomous reproduction of communities. Merchant capitalism produces a space for 'independent' communities and, in this space, 'traditions' are created, involving an increased 'local or regional particularity'.[35] Cornwall was not merchant capitalist in the same sense as Newfoundland. Nonetheless, this comparison resonates across the Atlantic. Both places contained communities that, on the one hand, experienced tightening bonds because of their shared occupational culture but, on the other, were becoming 'hollowed out' and increasingly powerless. In mining communities there was an increased density of interactions within a distinct occupational culture, one in which new eighteenth century 'traditions' such as tributing retained an echo of the early-modern free miners. But these traditions had themselves been consolidated 'as a result of the needs of the capitalised industry to develop a sophisticated method of payment' that 'would ensure the largest degree of application possible from unsupervised labour'.[36] At the same time the tentacle-like spread of market relations and a global market for tin and copper was, by the end of the eighteenth century, exacerbating the vulnerability of these same communities.

Sider's insights connect the materialist logic of accumulation with an idealist logic of tradition and allow us, to some extent, to explain the paradoxical combination of 'new' recognisably capitalist forms and 'traditional' institutions and forms of behaviour in eighteenth century Cornwall. Within such a merchant capitalist milieu folk culture itself became part of the battleground. Collective self-assertion was a struggle against appropriation and an assertion of the relative continuity of community. Tight bonds of kinship and dense networks of community gave rise to a community consciousness. As their propensity for food rioting shows, communities dominated by mining were sufficiently cohesive to deploy important shows of strength in defence of a moral economy after the 1720s.

But were the communities created by merchant capitalism really independent? The literature veers confusingly between narratives of independence and dependence. Rule, for example, has pointed to the weaker hold of paternalism and deference among mining communities in

---

[35] Gerald Sider, *Culture and Class in Anthropology and History: A Newfoundland Illustration*, Cambridge, 1986, 86.

[36] John Rule, *The Experience of Labour in Eighteenth-Century Industry*, London, 1981, 67.

the eighteenth century, with their 'special sense of being "communities apart"'.[37] But he has also argued that a 'web of dependence' existed, whereby charity and patronage from the landed class guaranteed deference and order from the poor.[38] It is not difficult to find examples of such patronage. William Jenkin, the steward at Redruth for the Hon. Charles Agar of Lanhydrock, in 1795 gave £1.11s.6d. to a 'poor woman whose husband was killed a few days ago in Tincroft mine' and made an 'advance [of £12] to purchase corn and flower [sic] for the labourers in Tincroft mine in conjunction with their adventurers'.[39] But it is significant that this landlord influence was mediated through stewards. With the notable exception of the Basset family, who lived at the heart of the central mining district at Tehidy, between Camborne and Redruth, most mineral lords resided at some distance from their mining properties. Furthermore, the estates of Cornish landowners were not concentrated, being dispersed over a wide reach of Cornish countryside.[40] There were, it is true, other factors producing dependence. One such was the system of subsist in the mines, an advance of pay on expected earnings, which combined with widespread use of credit at the shops to produce dependence on mine captains and shopkeepers.[41] This was a dependence that may have been felt more keenly on a day-to-day basis than the indirect impact of the more remote landlord effected through his steward.

Moreover, considerable counter-evidence exists for independent 'manners' alongside such webs of dependence. Miners, like early nineteenth century artisans, were described as possessing 'that independence of feeling, and the reluctance to have recourse to the poor-rate, which characterise the class to which they belong'.[42] For one local middle-class contemporary, the miner was a:

> man of frank and independent manners. He is not often insolent, but he is usually blunt. Something beyond this must be said of many, of the younger men especially. Indeed, rudeness – a want of civilization – is the most unfavourable feature of the mining as compared with the urban or agricultural classes. [There was a] character of independence – something American – to this population.[43]

---

[37] Rule, 1981, 18 and 208.
[38] Rule, 'Quietism', 1992, 255-257.
[39] 'Estate accounts, Lanhydrock 18th and early 19th centuries', CRO CL317.
[40] Edwin Jaggard, *Cornwall Politics in the Age of Reform*, Woodbridge, 1999, 152.
[41] Tremenheere, 1841, 89.
[42] Tremenheere, 1841, 93.
[43] Charles Barham, 'Report on the employment of children and young persons in

Charles Barham went on to pinpoint the causes: a lack of social contact with the adventuring classes, the system of wage payment for underground miners, with its impression of independence, combined with the ever-present chance of limited social mobility through a good period of earnings. The tributer, especially, could hope to join those 'wealthier individuals near him, who have for the most part, at no remote period, occupied some of the lower steps of the ladder on which he himself now stands'.[44]

Charity and patronage from stewards and the gentry may, indeed, be evidence as much for the presence of independent as dependent communities. The steady drip of charity was a necessary ransom on property provided in the face of a potentially turbulent crowd. In a letter to the Home Office, Thomas Cummins of Bodmin, clerk to the Tywardreath division of the Powder Bench, reported in 1830 that 'it requires the greatest attention, care and caution on the parts of the Magistrates to keep such a body of men [the miners] in order'.[45] At this time, when the Swing riots were convulsing southern England, magistrates were unwilling to provoke the population: 'we deem it inadvisable' wrote the magistrates of the western division of Penwith, 'in the present quiet and orderly state of this part of the Kingdom, by a public act of our own to create alarm, or to show an unmerited distrust of the peacableness and loyalty of the neighbourhood'.[46] Local magistrates were wary of communities that were not fully tied into the restrictive threads of patronage.

Class and space

We need, finally, to reinsert space into this account. Workplace and place of residence had long been separate in the mining districts, with the development of large mines since at least the mid-eighteenth century. This facilitated the appearance of a distinct culture, outside traditional social ties. Geographically dispersed mining communities and an absence of contact with the middling classes, plus the relatively short hours of work of underground miners had, in the eighteenth century, already produced a society where, as one St Just respondent to the Children's Employment Commission in 1841 later reported, the miners

---

the mines of Cornwall and Devonshire', *British Parliamentary Papers* 1842 (380) XV.1, 759.

[44] Barham, 1842, 759.
[45] Letter from Thomas Cummins to Home Office, 17 August, 1830, PRO HO 52.
[46] Letter from magistrates of the Western Division of Penwith, 16 December 1830, PRO HO 52.

were 'less subject to a master's control'.[47] The miner was part of a crowd, regularly meeting in large numbers. This was noted with some trepidation by the propertied classes. In 1842, there were several reports of the miners' habit of meeting together on a Saturday, the 'crowds of idle youths', the 'congregating in large numbers on market days' and the tendency to 'congregate in large masses, without efficient discipline'.[48] Earlier, in 1796, three Cornish JPs had gone so far as to write to the Home Secretary expressing their concern that, in relation to mining communities, 'no Magistrate can attend in Person ... for the Civil Power to venture amongst them, unattended by the Military, would ... be unsafe, dangerous and thoroughly ineffectual'.[49]

Such evidence of the independent temper of local communities dominated by mining can be related to an important contribution to the literature on class formation and space developed by Michael Savage. He suggests that territory is important in terms of class formation in two ways.[50] First, particular places become habitats for certain social groups and thus become the bases for collective identity. But, in building on this, Savage proposes, secondly, that 'class formation can take place as social classes stretch across space by building networks which link members of that class together'. He then introduces a significant insight.

On the one hand the density of some networks allows the construction of solidaristic and communal ties on an intra-locality and segmental basis. On the other, the construction of social networks of a wide range, linking members across many different sites, creates an extensive inter-locality basis for solidarity. The latter is clearly necessary for class formation on anything more than a limited, community level. However, the two networks, those with a high density and those with a wide range, may in practice compete. Thus, the involvement of individuals 'in wide-ranging networks may preclude them from the dense local world of the neighbourhood'.[51] At the same time dense ties may produce a cultural self-containment that inhibits wider links. Savage concludes that 'dense ties do not in themselves appear to be enough to sustain class formation at the level of political mobilisation'. Instead, 'political mobilisation depends upon the creation of links between specific places'.[52] What

---

[47] Barham, 1842, 761.
[48] Barham, 1842, 761.
[49] Cited in Roger Wells, *Insurrection: The British Experience 1795-1803*, Gloucester, 1983, 258.
[50] Michael Savage, 'Space, networks and class formation', in Neville Kirk (ed.), *Social Class and Marxism; Defences and Challenges*, Aldershot, 1996, 59.
[51] Savage, 1996, 69.
[52] Savage, 1996, 74-75.

Savage is saying here is that local networks may give rise to group identities but it was only with the construction of territorially more extensive networks that these identities could be amalgamated within broader, more explicitly class conscious forms of identity.

Savage's network model takes us some way towards explaining the historical geography of early nineteenth century Cornwall. Here were communities dominated by the mining industry, culturally differentiated and collectively integrated, exhibiting the dense network ties conducive for a solidaristic community identity. Yet these were apparent class communities without a language or a consciousness of class. This was because the dense ties of the local crowd did not exhibit a great range.

Andrew Charlesworth has observed that, in contrast to food riots in Devonshire and counties to the east, riots in 1795 and 1801 in Cornwall were sporadic and confined to market days, suggesting a reaction primarily reflecting the rhythm of the market place.[53] To the east he detects clear waves of protests in both those years, centred on Exeter and Plymouth, implying an active communication of protest. This he ascribes to the presence of a 'trade unionist organisational network', which facilitated mobilisation across a range of different localities. Such contacts did not exist in Cornwall where, following Savage, the dense community solidarities of lightly supervised Cornish rural-industrial communities were in tension with extended inter-community networks.

Dispersed paternalism

Independent communities in the eighteenth century were not, moreover, restricted to the mining districts. In the 1760s Thomas Carlyon was experiencing considerable aggravation from the fishing communities at Mounts Bay. In 1766 'the ungrateful behaviour of the masons in leaving the work' at Mousehole quay was upsetting him, as were the 'exorbitant demands of the Newlyn [fish] cellar women'.[54] In February 1768 the Newlyn women were demanding the maintenance of a customary right to 'druggs' (dregs of the catch) and 'skimming the washing troughs'. Viewing this as a 'cloak for embezzling things', Carlyon determined to abolish the custom. In May the women were still holding out despite threats to import women from nearby villages 'in order to break the back of all those wicked combinations'.[55] Some fishing communities, also enmeshed in smuggling activities, were, it appears, not easy to control.

---

[53] Andrew Charlesworth, 'The spatial diffusion of riots: popular disturbances in England and Wales, 1750-1850', *Rural History* 5 (1994), 10.

[54] Letter, Thomas Carlyon to William Veale, 1766, CRO ML 781.

[55] Letters of 3 February 1768 and 26 May 1768, CRO ML 791 and 793.

Yet they were not out of control. In Cornwall, as in other regions, a balance was reached, a 'negotiated compromise ... between the economic and social pressures of dependence and independence'.[56] In coal mining areas coal owners in the 1840s turned to 'strategies of paternal social control' that produced a structure of autonomy at work and dependence above ground. In Cornwall the compromise differed in subtle ways. There was no visible class of mine owners, exerting influence in both workplace and community. On the other hand, there was no single major landlord, such as Lord Penrhyn, who dominated mid-nineteenth century Welsh slate quarrying communities.[57] Paternalism was present but in different forms, exercised by the agents of the adventurers, the captains in the mines, and by the agents of the landlords, the land stewards in the community. The pattern of dispersed paternalism that had emerged in eighteenth century Cornwall was a local version of compromise. In addition, what further qualified the pressures of merchant capitalist accumulation and stripped away some of the consequences of paternalism was the ambiguous position of a proportion of the mining community in relation to wage dependence.

Partial proletarianisation
Various writers on early nineteenth century Cornwall have viewed the Cornish labouring household as 'semi-proletarian', citing the 'commonly held image' of the miner as a 'worker-peasant', partly engaged in mining, partly in subsistence and family farming and partly in seasonal work such as fishing.[58] Metaphors of 'archaism' regularly surface, implying a group not fully engaged in capitalist commodity relations. Indeed, Alf Jenkin made an intriguing link between such archaism and Cornwall's status as a 'pioneer industrial area'.[59] We can build on this insight by proposing that the relatively early negotiated compromise of 'dispersed paternalism' reached in industrialising eighteenth century Cornwall both crystallised some apparently pre-capitalist non-market forms of commodity production and proved sufficiently durable to persist largely

---

[56] Richard Price, *Labour in British Society: An Interpretative History*, London, 1986, 83.
[57] Merfyn Jones, *The North Wales Quarrymen: 1874-1922*, Cardiff, 1981.
[58] Damaris Rose, 'Home ownership, subsistence and historical change: the mining district of west Cornwall in the late nineteenth century', in Nigel Thrift and Peter Williams (eds), *Class and Space: The Making of an Urban Society*, London, 1987, 110 and 120.
[59] Alf Jenkin, in discussion of John Rule, 'Methodism and Chartism among the Cornish miners', *Bulletin of the Society for the Study of Labour History* 22 (1971), 10.

unchanged into the 1840s. As we now realise from comparative work on areas outside Europe, the history of labour relations is not a simple linear one of the movement from unfree to 'free' wage labour. There are various intermediary forms of partial proletarianisation. Cornwall offers a historically and geographically specific variant of this.

Cornish underground miners' relative work autonomy did not differ significantly from other mining regions. What was more different - at least in comparison with coal mining districts - was the extent of access to non-commoditised production of housing and food. This can be seen in turn as part of a well-developed 'economy of makeshifts', mixing earned income with charity, savings, access to customary rights, help from neighbours and kin and other sources of income.

Self-built houses with a low ground rent and some land on which food could be grown provided many families with a subsistence 'safety-net' that supplemented earnings from mines employment. In 1841 Stephen Davey, a Redruth magistrate, reported how he and his brother 'have been in the practice of granting leases on three lives to the miners, especially in the St Agnes district, of one, two or three acres of coarse land, on which they are bound to build a house of a certain description'.[60] The Daveys were continuing a well-established practice, one attested on marginal land on Basset's Tehidy estate in Illogan in the second half of the eighteenth century.[61] The annual rent on these leases was around five shillings an acre in 1841, with a fine of £30 to £50 to set up a new life. The cost of building the house was £35-50.[62] The ability of the potential leaseholder to meet these capital costs was enhanced by the tribute payment system which resulted in great variability of earnings. Contract bonanzas enabled the purchase of a three-life lease and the building of a cottage. In the Redruth Poor Law Union it was suggested in the mid-nineteenth century that 'thousands of cottages have been built by miners. They occasionally get a "sturt", that is, they come upon a body of ore suddenly, and that gives them a sum varying from £50 to £200 or £300. The first thing they do with it is to build a cottage'.[63]

In evidence to the Children's Employment Commission in 1841 William Petherick, manager at Dolcoath, Camborne, stated that 'a great many of our miners get houses and little plots of their own', while Edward Carthew, agent at Balleswidden, echoed this; 'a great portion ...

---

[60] Barham, 1842, 830.
[61] Rowe, 1953, 225-226.
[62] Tremenheere, 1841, 84.
[63] 'Report from the Select Committee appointed to inquire into the law and practice with respect to the rating of mines', *British Parliamentary Papers* 1856 (346) XVI.1, 17.

live on little plots of their own'.[64] Barham summed the situation up as 'a very great number of miners are now located on leaseholds of an acre or two'.[65] Such access to land could make a considerable difference to the living standards of a mining family. Damaris Rose estimated that a three-acre smallholding might contribute half the cash value of the average family's food budget in the later nineteenth century.[66] However, contemporary accounts rarely quantify the number of families with access to such smallholdings. In his survey of the mining population in 1841 Tremenheere found that 23.5 per cent of 685 miners in the Redruth, St Just and St Blazey districts owned their own cottages.[67] But it is unclear how much land was attached to these cottages.

Perhaps because of this uncertainty there is disagreement over the economic importance of smallholdings. Some writers have tended to romanticise the significance of the level of access to land. Rose states that 'at least until the mid-nineteenth century, it was the norm for the Cornish miner and family to have some access to land for subsistence production' and that miners' cottages were 'typically surrounded' by plots of a half to three acres'.[68] In contrast, Rule noted that the dual occupation of tinner-husbandman of the early eighteenth century became less frequent with the rise of a more specialised workforce in the more heavily capitalised copper mines.[69] He suggested that, by the 1820s, the increase of population must have restricted opportunities for the renting of smallholdings.[70]

Evidence from the tithe apportionment surveys of 1839-43 suggests that the incidence of smallholdings varied considerably from parish to parish in the early 1840s.

---

[64] Barham, 1842, 838 and 847.
[65] Barham, 1842, 753.
[66] Rose, 1987, 119.
[67] Tremenheere, 1841, 84.
[68] Rose, 1987, 113.
[69] Rule, 1970, 73.
[70] Rule, 'Labouring miner', 1971, 57.

Table 8.1: Smallholdings, c.1840 (% of total occupiers)

Parish	1-5 acres	5-20 acres	Total
St Agnes	34.1	13.0	47.1
Redruth	17.7	8.2	25.9
Carnmenellis, Wendron	12.9	43.9	56.8
St Erth	11.8	5.6	17.4
St Hilary	12.5	8.0	20.5
Ludgvan	5.7	6.6	12.3
Pendeen, St Just	5.4	5.4	10.8

Source: Tithe apportionments, CRO TA 2, TA 197, TA 249, TA 59, TA 87, TA 129, TA 95

In upland Carnmenellis 71 per cent of the 93 families headed by copper miners and 81 per cent of the 16 families of tin miners held land in 1843.[71] In St Agnes, where over 70 per cent of the male workforce was employed in mining in 1851, access to smallholdings was also common; involving perhaps as many as a half of mining families, more if holdings of less than an acre are included. Significantly, in view of Rule's comments about population growth, even in the more urbanised parish of Redruth, almost a quarter of all households occupied at least an acre of land as late as 1840. However, to the west access to smallholdings of over one acre decreased and at Pendeen, a community like St Agnes dominated by mining, they were much less common.

Barham pinpointed the factors that lay behind differential access to land. There were two, 'the disposition of the lords to grant such leases' and the 'relative denseness of the population to the quantity of unoccupied land'.[72] Rose confirms the latter point: in urban areas 'even small allotments were out of reach of miners' by the 1840s.[73] Yet the relevant point here is that, in 1841, well over half the miners still lived outside towns. As late as 1851, on a generous definition of urban that includes the parishes of Camborne and Redruth, where at least half the people in 1851 lived outside the built-up areas, 78 per cent of male miners lived in rural parishes. In areas where smallholdings were less available, such as in the newer mining districts of east Cornwall in the

---

[71] Census enumerators' books for Wendron, 1841 and CRO TA 249.
[72] Barham, 1842, 754-755.
[73] Rose, 1987, 123.

1840s, wages were higher by as much as ten shillings a month, a fact put down by the *Morning Chronicle* reporters in 1849 to lack of cheap housing and allotments.[74] So, access to cheap housing and food was still clearly an important factor as late as the 1840s. It remained the experience of a considerable minority of mining families, especially those where the heads were engaged in more skilled, higher status tribute contracts.

Moreover, access to the means of subsistence was not restricted to leases of land. Smallholdings made up just one part of a wider system of what Barham termed 'collateral aid', a system, moreover, that had changed and developed over the previous half century. It is suggestive that, by 1840, collateral aids were 'most concentrated' in the far west, in St Just parish where, as we have seen, larger smallholdings were less commonplace. Here, joint ownership of cows and shares in fishing boats provided opportunities for labouring families.[75] But the most widespread collateral aid was the practice of farmers giving potato allotments to labouring families. This occurred widely in the early nineteenth century across western England, but it had become particularly common in Cornwall by the 1830s.[76] Tremenheere described how the system worked:

> The miner obtains a stock of potatoes, without, in general, any money-payment; the farmer in that case allotting a perch of land for each load of household manure furnished by the miner. The latter plants and draws the crop, the farmer preparing the land and carting the manure, of which he has the benefit for the corn crop of the following year. The number of perches which a miner can thus secure depends usually upon the quantity of manure he can collect; and this again greatly depends on his facilities for cutting turf or furze for fuel, of which the ashes form the staple of the manure. Those who are most careful will endeavour to cultivate from 30 to 60 perches, which, in ordinary years, at two Winchester bushels to a perch, will supply their families for some months; enabling them also to feed a pig, perhaps two, and to reserve seed for the year following.[77]

This practice was 'a common and growing one' in 1841 and appears to have emerged over the previous 30 or 40 years.[78] The growth in

---

[74] P.E.Razzell and R.W.Wainwright (eds), *The Victorian Working Class: Selections from letters to the Morning Chronicle*, London, 1973, 26.

[75] Barham, 1842, 754.

[76] Razzell and Wainwright, 1973, 28; 'Report on the Poor Laws', *British Parliamentary Papers*, 1834 (44) XXVII,1, 445-447; evidence of Joseph Vivian and Stephen Davey in Barham, 1842, 830 and 839. For the existence of the practice outside the mining districts see Rowe, 1996

[77] Tremenheere, 1841, 88.

cultivation of the potato has been dated to the 1790s, and by 1801 the proportion of the arable area in St Just under potato crops was already 25 per cent, although in the rest of Cornwall it was much lower.[79] It would appear that potato cultivation extended rapidly as population rose into the 1830s.

In addition, the evolving system of collateral aids in west Cornwall had implications that went beyond the economic sphere. An important element in this system was customary access to common land, providing a source of fuel. Regular excursions to collect furze from the commons involved the whole community in the early nineteenth century, a practice that Gill Burke viewed as indicating the lack of a clear sexual division of labour.[80] Employment of girls and young women at the surface works of mines had given women a taste of economic and social freedom and independence, an independence that was symbolised through conspicuous spending on clothes and accompanied, Burke suggests, by a lack of deference towards men. For women, an early experience of 'free' wage labour and continuing participation in community activities outside the home and, for men, the centrality of the smallholding and its cottage in their leisure time, meant that 'boundaries between the world of work and the world of home were less rigidly drawn'.[81] Smallholdings, collateral aids and access to subsistence goods outside the market combined with notions of domesticity and patriarchal ideas shared with wider eighteenth century artisan culture.[82] What emerged was a community of 'patriarchal sexual cooperation' rather than the patriarchal hierarchy pure and simple that was establishing itself in the better paid sections of the British working class by mid-century.

It is likely that these relations of 'patriarchal sexual cooperation', along with women's experience of mines surface labour, had their own geography and one that differed from the overall geography of mining communities. Female surface workers were much more likely to be concentrated in the four parishes of the central mining district (Camborne, Illogan, Redruth and Gwennap) in 1851 than were male miners (surface and underground). This district accounted for 46 per cent of female mine

---

[78] Barham, 1842, 754.
[79] Mark Overton, *Agricultural Revolution in England: The Transformation of the Agrarian Economy 1500-1850*, Cambridge, 1996, 102.
[80] Gill Burke, 'The decline of the independent bal maiden: the impact of change in the Cornish mining industry', in Angela John (ed.) *Unequal Opportunities: Women's Employment in England 1800-1918*, Oxford, 1986, 194.
[81] Burke, 1986, 194.
[82] Sonya Rose, *Limited Livelihoods: Gender and Class in Nineteenth Century England*, Berkeley CA, 1992.

workers but only 28 per cent of male miners.[83] Significantly, in 1847, during the corn riots of that year, women played a prominent role in the central mining district. At Pool, between Camborne and Redruth, it was the women who 'commenced beating the door of the (corn and flour) store house with large stones' before one of them 'ran across the road to a smith's shop, and seized a sledge hammer, with which she gave such determined blows at the door that it soon yielded and the mob rushed in'.[84]

Cornish society in the early years of the 1800s, with its merchant capitalist elite, its dispersed paternalism and its partially proletarianized workers, many of whom exercised a degree of autonomy in the work process and who, outside work, lived in 'traditional' households, resembled the industrialising Bradford described by Theodore Koditschek. There, before 1815, there was a 'world of few social distinctions, minimal division of labour above the level of the household, and little centralised knowledge or political authority', a society defined by Koditschek as 'proto-industrial'.[85] Proto-industrialisation was shattered around Bradford by rapid urbanisation after 1815, an urbanisation that was incompatible with 'traditional cultural forms and institutions'. But in Cornwall no similar levels of urbanisation occurred. An 'independent' and 'traditional' community, one retaining a consumer rather than producer consciousness of exploitation, remained in place for another generation, although the core processes were continually undergoing change. The 'collateral aids' described here were, moreover, part of a rich 'economy of makeshifts' in west Cornwall. This can in turn be located within a broader picture of a culture of welfare which, in its emphasis on making-do rather than dependency, possessed features in common with those in the north-west of England.[86]

From context to narrative

A context of independent communities and partial proletarianization is not all the story if we are seeking to explain the group identity of the Cornish labourer. Even the materialist social historian hints at the role of narrative. Thus, Neville Kirk proposes three criteria of class feeling, constituency, the size and character of bodies of workers with common identities, joined by independence, a separate set of ideas, institutions

---

[83] 1851 Census sample.
[84] *West Briton*, 11 June, 1847.
[85] Theodore Koditschek, *Class Formation and Urban-Industrial Society: Bradford 1750-1850*, Cambridge, 1990, 53.
[86] Steven King, *Poverty and Welfare in England 1700-1850: A Regional Perspective*, Manchester, 2000, 259-264.

and value systems and hostility, the level of commitment to a world uncontrolled by other classes.[87] The second and third of these criteria move from the objective to the subjective, although consciousness remains, in his view, a reflection, albeit indirect, of social conditions.

Others look upon self-awareness and self-consciousness differently. In an important article synthesising the ideas of the 'linguistic turn' among historians, Miguel Cabrera argued that reality only takes on meaning through concepts and categories. Consciousness does not arise directly from social conditions. Instead, social conditions acquire a certain meaning 'within a particular framework'.[88] Therefore, consciousness is seen as a 'linguistic mediation between individuals and their social contexts', something achieved rhetorically, through and by language. Thus, groups may be subordinate and lacking resources. But this will only be read as 'oppression' if an appropriate language is available. Cabrera rejects the charge of linguistic reductionism by emphasising both that the 'real' exists – the subordination – and that patterns of meaning are transformed and changed within social practice and through social agency.

These patterns of meaning or conceptual networks are usually termed 'discourses', a 'coherent set of categories which, in a given historical situation, works as a basic organiser of social relations'.[89] People articulate the meaning of the world and their experience within it through such discourses. Changes in historical conditions work to destabilise discourses, which are subject to constant rhetorical adjustments and a process of differentiation (combining and contrasting existing meanings to make sense of new conditions). When a discourse loses efficacy and no longer operates as a 'minimum discursive consensus' it is replaced by other discourses or discursive frames, but these always possess some link, some 'intertextuality', with preceding discourses. In this way William Sewell reads the production of working class consciousness in the early nineteenth century as the transformation of the previously existing discourses of collectivism and radicalism.[90] This approach is clearly relevant to issues of identity. In this light, it is the rhetorical constructions of discourse that fix identity as a means of social action.

---

[87] Kirk, 1994, 11.
[88] Miguel Cabrera, 'Linguistic approach or return to subjectivism? In search of an alternative to social history', *Social History* 24 (1999), 80.
[89] Cabrera, 1999, 81.
[90] William Sewell, 'How classes are made: critical reflections on E.P.Thompson's theory of working-class formation', in Harvey Kaye and Keith McClelland (eds), *E.P.Thompson: Critical Perspectives*, Cambridge, 1990, 50-77.

Discourse therefore supplies the link between social conditions or material reality and the world of meanings.

If we argue back to the Cornish situation from this position we can achieve a fuller understanding of working class identities, or their absence, in early nineteenth century Cornwall. It was Chartism that was, for many historians 'a truly hegemonic force in many working class communities'.[91] But apparently not in Cornwall. Rule has pointed out how the Chartist mission to Cornwall of 1839, while making links with pre-existing Chartist artisans at Truro and Hayle, failed to touch the mining population.[92] In comparison with the near contemporaneous teetotal agitation, Chartism was to be a damp squib among the miners, whose involvement was only tentative and sporadic.

What is striking in the comments of the Chartist missionaries in Cornwall are the regular references to the absence of a language of exploitation among the people. One of the missionaries, Abraham Duncan, wrote in 1839 of the 'ignorance of the people upon general politics', whereas his partner Robert Lowery reported that 'the People have never heard of the agitation, and know nothing of Political principles'.[93] A third missionary, William Cardo, who was sent to Devon, briefly visited Cornwall and he, too, remarked that 'the people were in the greatest ignorance concerning politics'.[94] Yet this cannot be read as a generalised unawareness of political issues in Cornwall. During the 1820s, a vigorous alliance had emerged to bring together farmers, small town professionals and other middle classes in the cause of political reform.[95] Moreover, there is evidence both that groups in the mining districts had liaised with the London Corresponding Society in the 1790s and that some, at least, of the language of the French Revolution had percolated local culture.[96] William Jenkin was told in 1795 that St. Just miners had planted 'the tree of liberty ... I am sorry to hear several cant words amongst the tinners much in use amongst the French'.[97] But the

---

[91] Neville Kirk, *Change, Continuity and Class: Labour in British Society 1850-1920*, Manchester, 1998, 76.

[92] Rule, 2006.

[93] Alf Jenkin, 'The Cornish Chartists', *Journal of the Royal Institution of Cornwall* NS9 (1982), 58.

[94] Jenkin, 1982, 61.

[95] Ed Jaggard, *Cornwall Politics in the Age of Reform*, Woodbridge, 1999.

[96] Roger Wells, *Wretched Faces: Famine in Wartime England 1763-1803*, Gloucester, 1988, 153-154.

[97] In A.K.Hamilton Jenkin, *News from Cornwall*, London, 1951, 33. See also Charles Gilbert, *An Historical Survey of the County of Cornwall*, London, 1817, 98 for an account of a Redruth man toasting Tom Paine

language of constitutional reform had not been transformed, during the 1810s, 1820s and 1830s, into a language of class exploitation which could make sense of the more 'economistic' message of the Chartists in 1839.

How might we explain this absence of a language of exploitation? Negatively, we might point to the absence of a strong artisanal tradition in Cornwall. The marginal role of domestic out-working in the eighteenth century Cornish economy meant that there was no entrenched artisan class that, under increasing pressure from the 1800s onwards, would become the 'radical reactionaries' at the core of new critiques of the emerging industrial capitalist economy. With this factor we can also associate that lack of range of local networks noted earlier. The unique compromise of dispersed paternalism created in and around the copper mining industry in the eighteenth century produced independent occupational communities with dense, local network ties but weak ties with other communities, even within Cornwall.

On the positive side we might cite a number of factors. First, the discourse of the moral economy of labour still seemed to work in Cornwall. Food riots could achieve their desired outcome as late as 1830. Reciprocity retained a continuing influence amongst the landed and merchant capitalist classes. Furthermore, on a day to day basis, as we have seen, an influential proportion of labouring families in the rural-industrial districts were protected from the more unpredictable repercussions of the market by their access to three life leases and housing, customary rights and subsistence food production.

These in turn linked to memories of the free and independent tinner-husbandman of the eighteenth century and earlier. E.P.Thompson noted that the tradition of the free miner 'coloured responses' among 'Cornish tin miners' into the nineteenth century.[98] More to the point, it persisted in colouring responses even among the now greatly expanded copper mines workforce.[99] Although the genuinely dual occupation tin streamer/miner-farmer was restricted to a few upland areas by the 1840s (the 1851 Census only records such dual occupations in the Carnmenellis area and near Luxulyan in mid-Cornwall), access to subsistence production kept alive the image of the 'worker-peasant'.

---

[98] Thompson, 1963, 68.

[99] Andy Wood, ('Social conflict and change in the mining communities of north-west Derbyshire, c.1600-1700', *International Review of Social History* 38 (1993), 31-58) has also noted how memories of the independent free miner conditioned class consciousness in late eighteenth century Derbyshire mining communities

This imagination was not the only one militating against the discourse of an exploited wage labourer. Cornish mining communities had become home to a cottage religion that, by the 1790s, provided many of the rituals and symbols of everyday life. Wesleyan Methodism came to Cornwall early and implanted itself before working class political radicalism appeared. This offered another discourse which fixed another identity, as the repentant and saved sinner. It was not an identity that necessarily precluded class-based action or organisation, as can be seen in Methodist communities in the north-east of England during the nineteenth century. But the way it had permeated life in Cornish communities meant that it provided what Rule has termed 'competitive opposition' to class politics.[100] Indeed, it is such an important element in the historical geography of the Cornish identity that it will receive special attention in the next chapter.

Finally, another competitive subject position available to the labourer in Cornwall was that of a 'Cornish man' or 'Cornish woman'. In the eighteenth century the crowd in many parts of England and Wales used the slogan 'one and all' to indicate their solidarity and determination at times of action over corn prices.[101] Food riots in Cornwall, too, echoed to the cry of 'one and all' and, by the 1790s, the slogan was being regularly invoked. A handbill at St Just in that year, calling on the people to 'muster and be independent' ended 'So one and all ... so one and all'.[102] However, with the decline of food rioting as a collective response in other parts of Britain after 1810 and the continuing predilection of Cornish communities for this form of protest, 'one and all' became seen as a particularly Cornish slogan. In 1839 the Truro radical and Chartist, John Spurr was using it at a meeting about the Corn Laws. 'I will have no compromise ... The Cornish motto is "one and all", and let us all go together on this occasion. Let us either have our rights, or let us be content till we get them'.[103] By this time 'one and all' had become more than the cry of the hungry and angry: it was the 'Cornish motto'.

However, it was a motto that could be made use of in ambiguous ways. For Spurr, a man with a sense of class consciousness, it was a slogan for the oppressed, but for others it had different meanings. Thus, Tremenheere referred to it as 'in any matter which recommends itself to the general opinion of the county, a unity of action among all classes

---

[100] Rule, 'Quietism', 1992, 258 and 1970, 82-83.
[101] For examples from Pembrokeshire and Berkshire in 1766 and 1795 see Thompson, 1993, 236 and 238.
[102] John Rule, 'Labouring miner', 1971, 158.
[103] John Rule, 'Richard Spurr of Truro – small town radical', *Cornish Studies* 4/5 (1976-77), 53.

appears still to be occasionally manifested. In such cases the Cornish motto, 'One and All' may be recognised as still possessing some degree of vitality'.[104] The discourse of Cornishness that had been popularised in the first quarter of the nineteenth century had adopted and adapted 'One and All' for its own purposes. In doing so it provided an alternative imagery for all classes in Cornwall, cutting across potential class-based identities. The Cornish crowd was, by 1847, being hailed in terms of their Cornishness and appealed to in a language that in this context emphasised social consensus. During the riots of that year a *West Briton* leader writer could pretend to be shocked at 'the use of threats which we are ashamed should proceed from the mouths of Cornishmen and Cornish women'.[105] By the 1830s this territorial identification was working against the formation of class identity in Cornwall. It could be used by some as a consensual veil for their own economic interests. Nevertheless, appeals to a common sense of Cornishness also demanded that those same interests maintained a certain degree of reciprocity and a web of charity that looked back in some respects to 'tradition' and, incidentally, acted to bolster the values of the moral economy of labour. A consensual identity of Cornishness thus worked to reinforce the traditional discourse.

Reconceptualising Cornish social history
By the 1840s that traditional discourse was fragmenting. Elements within the local middle classes were being drawn more to ideas of liberal rather than moral economy and the compromise of dispersed paternalism, established in eighteenth century conditions, was under pressure.[106] The 1847 riots were the last generalised crowd actions in nineteenth century Cornwall. Moreover, these riots were as much a response to change as a sign of continuity with past traditions.

Had not the potato blight appeared in 1846, it is unlikely that the rioting of 1847 would have taken place on the scale it did. Failure of the potato crop undermined the importance of the miner's potato patch and threw his family into a state of more overt dependence on the market. An editorial in the *Royal Cornwall Gazette* summed up the dilemma:

> In past seasons the industrious cottager or miner could rely on his potato crop in aid of this wages. With store of potatoes, the pig fed with the refuse of the crop, and a few hundreds of fish salted by in the Autumn, his winter comforts were secured; but his crops have

---

[104] Tremenheere, 1841, 100.
[105] *West Briton*, 18 June 1847.
[106] See *West Briton* editorial on Ireland, 15 January 1847.

failed, and he has nothing but his wages to rely on, with bread nearly double its usual price.[107]

As the reporters from the *Morning Chronicle* wrote two years later, the loss of the potato crops was 'a great blow' to mining families.[108] In the short term it led to the explosion of 1847 as communities resorted to understood ways of dealing with food shortages. In the medium term more men decided to emigrate as resources for an 'independent' life in Cornwall were squeezed. In the long run the potato blight heralded the breakdown of the traditional compromise. The social structures that had allowed a space for independence were dissolving. By the 1850s enclosure was more for commercial farming than for the creation of further smallholdings. The rising cost of leaseholds was making life increasingly difficult for new entrants. Non-market, subsistence production was still possible, but was becoming more difficult.[109]

At the same time new languages were appearing as the old discourse of the moral economy began to splinter and lose its effect. During the 1847 riots some of the crowd of quarrymen and miners who had descended on Wadebridge to stop the export of corn 'paraded the streets, one carrying a barley pasty on the point of his stick, and another a red flag'.[110] Here were two symbols of a 'new' Cornwall. First, the pasty was a symbol of a regional industrial community that was seeing itself through the lenses of an all-inclusive regional identity by the 1840s, an identity that helped to produce the mass audience for the dialect stories of the 1850s. Second, the red flag echoed the symbolism of blood that E.P.Thompson noted emerging elsewhere from the 1810s.[111] This may indicate a new openness on the part of the Cornish crowd to wider influences.

By the 1840s, too, there were at least some people in Cornwall speaking the language of Chartism. A consistent and under-reported level of Chartist activity was maintained in west Cornwall, especially in the towns of Penzance and Truro but also at Camborne and St Ives.[112] And, while still infrequent, strike action had begun to occur at local mines. Rule claims there were only seven strikes in the local mining industry between 1793 and 1859.[113] But most of these actually took place in the years after 1840.[114] While Rule is correct in stating that none of the

---

[107] *Royal Cornwall Gazette*, 22 January 1847.
[108] Razzell and Wainwright, 1973, 28.
[109] Rose, 1987, 123-125.
[110] *West Briton*, 21 May 1847.
[111] Thompson, 1993, 257.
[112] Deacon, 2017, 123-154.
[113] Rule, 'Quietism', 1992, 253.
[114] For examples see *Royal Cornwall Gazette*, 29 May 1840; *West Briton*, 1

strikes before 1859 were 'connected with the activities of a pre-existing trade union' there was, significantly, talk of forming a union during a strike at Consolidated Mines in 1842.[115] Other Cornish workers were also taking strike action in the 1840s and 1850s. These included granite quarriers (who had formed union branches in 1840), clay workers, building workers, pilchard seiners, shoemakers and even farm labourers. Cornish communities were actively involved in other new forms of collective activity. For example, Cornish working class communities took a full part in the first major surge of co-operative society formation outside Lancashire in 1857-63. By 1872 the geography of co-operation revealed more societies in Cornwall than in neighbouring (and larger) Devon.[116]

What this flickering of collective activity suggests is that Cornwall, after the 1840s, was converging with other industrial regions in terms of its working class-based institutions. By the 1850s, there was a discernibly increasing range of network contacts and even some unionisation. Older social relations were disintegrating, undermined by the rise of commercial farming, the greater confidence and self-identity of tenant farmers as a class, continuing processes of urbanisation and the improvement of long-distance communications. That said, the discourse of a moral economy and independent communities clung on, especially in the long established rural mining districts of west Cornwall. Here, early industrialisation had preceded the ideas of class, and Wesleyan Methodism, as we shall see in the next chapter, provided a cocoon of institutions that surrounded labouring families and communities. Nevertheless, this discourse was now in direct competition with others. Furthermore, as access to housing and other resources enabled the cost of emigration to be raised more easily within 'traditional' communities, mass emigration began to be felt most keenly after 1840 in exactly those places where 'tradition' was strongest. Cornish working class communities were beginning to disintegrate at just the time when permanent trade unions elsewhere were establishing themselves among semi and unskilled workers.

Conclusion
By the late 1700s Cornish labouring communities were living within the local compromise of dispersed paternalism, one created in conditions of

---

April 1842; 15 April 1853.
[115] Rule, 'Quietism', 1992, 253; *West Briton*, 1 April 1842.
[116] Martin Purvis, 'Popular institutions', in John Langton and R.J.Morris (eds), *Atlas of Industrializing Britain 1780-1914*, London, 195.

merchant capitalism and permitting considerable space for independence. A discourse of independence and of moral economy flourished within the networks of west Cornish communities. The durability of this compromise, with its partial proletarianization, guaranteed the effectiveness of this local identity into the early 1840s. This success also explains, in addition to the limited range of contacts with spatially extended networks, the difficulties that some competing discourses met with, for instance those of the Chartists in 1839. At the same time social relations in Cornwall, and the discourse of independence built around them in working class communities, could co-exist with other representational frameworks. Indeed, other meanings were central to the identity of the Cornish in the period before the 1840s. The rituals and imaginings that gave meaning to many Cornish people, and the symbolic repertoire they turned to was not political at all, but religious. It is to Methodism, which played such a central role in nurturing identities in Cornwall during its industrial period, that we must now turn.

Chapter Nine
Cultural formation: the role of Methodism

Because the secular and the sacred were intertwined in the eighteenth and nineteenth centuries the theme of 'national, regional and urban identities cannot be properly investigated without reference to religion'.[1] Therefore, unpacking the geography of religion and religious differences is necessary to reach an understanding of cultural institutions and distinctiveness across territorial space. Indeed, Michael Hechter went so far as to use religion, along with language, as one of his 'cultural differentiae'; as measures of the distinctiveness of the Celtic lands of the British Isles in the nineteenth-century.[2] Later, there was renewed interest in identifying the detailed denominational geography of England and Wales, as a basis for identifying 'cultural regions' and interpreting regional variations in culture.[3]

At the outset, we can note in the literature a broad two-way relationship between religion and identity. First, religion is viewed as expressing other identities in a surrogate fashion. In Britain, inevitably, religion was bound up with social class identity. Thus David Hempton suggests that the sectarian conflicts of new dissent from the 1820s to the 1850s were caused by a finely fragmented class society.[4] Conversely, Alan Everitt interprets the rise of dissent, old and new, as 'one of the many signs that local attachments, far from declining with the growth of national consciousness, were in many ways becoming stronger'.[5] Keith Robbins goes further: 'In the absence of devolved government, the churches have come to be perhaps the most significant institutional embodiments of regional or national identity'.[6] In relation to Celtic

---

[1] David Hempton, *Religion and Political Culture in Britain and Ireland: From the Glorious Revolution to the Decline of Empire*, Cambridge, 1996, 178.
[2] Michael Hechter, *Internal Colonialism: The Celtic Fringe in British National Development, 1536-1966*, London, 1975, 167.
[3] Keith Snell and Paul Ell, *Rival Jerusalems: The Geography of Victorian Religion*, Cambridge, 2000, 4-10.
[4] Hempton, 1996, 134.
[5] Alan Everitt, *The Pattern of Rural Dissent: The Nineteenth Century*, Leicester, 1972, 7.
[6] Keith Robbins, 'Religion and identity in modern British history', in Stuart

Britain religion has been granted a special role as giving rise to 'a form of surrogate nationalism in Scotland as well as Wales'.[7]

But, as well as giving expression to other, class and spatial, identities, religion may also be integrated into these identities. E.Wyn James has claimed that Christianity has been a 'key element in Welsh national identity'.[8] Similarly, in Ireland, the distinction between Celt and Catholic had already become blurred by the eighteenth-century. By then the tendency was to view 'all Irish as Catholics and all Catholics as Irish'.[9] In this light, religion is not merely a surrogate expression of other identities but takes its place as part of an identity matrix. Keith Snell and Paul Ell made the intriguing suggestion that religious allegiance was highest in areas 'where national and cultural identities were least ambivalent'. These were those places where 'the Welsh (or English), the Scottish, the Irish and perhaps (locally) … the Cornish' provided 'more far-reaching cultural and national options'.[10]

This chapter pursues the linkage between religious and territorial identity on a more micro-scale, seeking the reasons why 'Cornwall and Methodism are still inextricably linked'.[11] By 1801 Wesleyan Methodist membership, as a proportion of the total population, was higher in Cornwall than anywhere in England.[12] A few years later, in 1829, Richard Tyacke, Vicar of Sithney, gloomily wrote in his diary: 'Sunday – the Church was but thinly attended - the rain pattered down so thick and fast, though at evening I observed the roads that led to the Methodists' chapel were thronged in every direction'.[13] Methodist strength was reflected in the results of the 1851 Census of Religious Worship. Cornwall was the only region outside north Wales where attenders at Methodist chapels were in the majority. In his study of patterns of religious attendance in 1851 Bruce Coleman concluded that 'only Cornwall was remarkable for both the IA [Index of Attendance]

Mews (ed.), *Religion and National Identity*, Oxford, 1982, 468.

[7] David.Bebbington, 'Religion and national identity in nineteenth-century Wales and Scotland', in Mews (ed.), 1982, 503.

[8] E.Wyn James, '"The new birth of a people": Welsh language and identity and the Welsh Methodists, c.1740-1820', in Robert Pope (ed.), *Religion and National Identity: Wales and Scotland c.1700-2000*, Cardiff, 2001, 15.

[9] D.George Boyce, *Nationalism in Ireland*, London, 1982, 56.

[10] Snell and Ell, 2000, 417-418.

[11] John Gay, *The Geography of Religion in England*, London, 1971, 162.

[12] *Methodist Magazine* 3 (1824), 377-383. Membership density of Wesleyan Methodism in Cornwall was also, at this time, higher than that of Calvinist Methodism in Wales

[13] Diary of Richard Tyacke of Antron, CRO AD 715, entry for 5 April 1829.

and the PS [Percentage Share], and it is already apparent that, whatever regional homogeneity the rest of southern England might display, Cornwall has to be counted out ... Cornwall was *sui generis*'.[14]

The reasons for this spiritual hegemony of Methodism have been well rehearsed by historians of Cornish Methodism and will be briefly reviewed below.[15] But this chapter focuses on some less widely discussed issues. In 1981 Tom Shaw asked the interesting question 'Is there – or has there ever been – such a thing as Cornish Methodism?'[16] Was Methodism in Cornwall distinctive? And can it be characterised as 'Cornish' in anything more than simple geographical location? Later in this chapter this issue is pursued through focusing on the role of revivalism and lay control within Cornish Methodism. Asking the question 'How did Cornwall re-form Methodism?' contrasts with the traditional focus of native scholarship and local Methodist history on how Methodism reformed Cornwall.

This chapter also revisits three recurring themes: the elements of identity formation (distinction, integration, process, context and narrative), the issue of scale, and the institutionalization of regions over time. We start by looking at the reception and growth of Methodism in Cornwall, identifying the comparative patterns and briefly reviewing the reasons for its early spread. This links to the elements of context and process. As we shall see, the importance of an awareness of scalar differences join context when the micro-geography of the 1851 Religious Census is analysed in the following section. Distinction and integration then become the main foci as the claim is advanced that revivalism and issues of lay control helped to construct a distinctly 'Cornish' Methodism after the 1780s. This process, it is argued, played a key role in institutionalizing a Cornish identity in the early nineteenth-century. That institutionalization brings us, finally, back to narrative and the chapter ends by reflecting on the linkages between Methodism and private and public identities in nineteenth-century Cornwall.

---

[14] Bruce Coleman, 'Southern England in the Census of Religious Worship, 1851', *Southern History* 5 (1983), 157 and 172.

[15] See in particular Thomas Shaw, *A History of Cornish Methodism*, Truro, 1967; David Luker. 'Cornish Methodism, revivalism and popular belief, c.1780-1870', D.Phil thesis, Oxford University, 1987; John Rule, 'Explaining revivalism: the case of Cornish Methodism', *Southern History* 20/21 (1998-99), 168-188.

[16] Thomas Shaw, 'Thoughts on Cornish Methodism', *Journal of the Cornish Methodist Historical Association* 6 (1981), 39-44.

The reception of Methodism
Hempton has stated that an important historical question about Methodism was 'Why did it grow when and where it did?'[17] How and why did Methodism came to dominate early nineteenth century Cornwall? Charles and John Wesley's arrival in Cornwall in 1743 was part of a broader evangelical awakening that included widely separated 'revivals' in Wales and the North American littoral in the 1730s and in Scotland in the early 1740s, preceding the re-awakening of religious enthusiasm in Cornwall. In the Cornish part of this transatlantic Protestant community, Wesley's message was keenly received. By 1767, when reliable membership statistics begin, Cornwall supplied more than ten per cent of all British members of Wesleyan societies.

Three elements explain the early penetration of Methodism in Cornwall. These are structural factors; the way Methodism communicated its message; and the actual message it carried. John Walsh has pointed out how, generally, Methodism moved 'into some of the yawning gaps of the Anglican parochial system, providing pastoral care to communities where little was on offer previously'.[18] The weakness and indolence of the Church of England in Cornwall has long been cited as a major, sometimes the only, factor in Methodism's early growth; 'the combined effect of large parishes, remote churches, pluralism and absentee clergy had produced a virtually heathen population in Cornwall'.[19] Even more sober assessments reiterate factors such as churches remote from the population centre of parishes, a situation exacerbated as rural industrialization reinforced dispersed settlement patterns. As we saw in chapter 8 the Cornish settlement structure and local traditions, including an independent-minded tinning population, together with loose and friable bonds of landlord and customary influence, provided several of those criteria cited by Everitt as underpinning religious nonconformity: independent groups with a sense of freedom, rural industrial villages and new settlements near parochial boundaries at a distance from the parish church.[20]

David Luker has constructed the most sophisticated structural explanation of the growth of Methodism in Cornwall. He notes several

---

[17] David Hempton, *The Religion of the People: Methodism and Popular Religion c.1750-1900*, London, 1996, 1.

[18] John Walsh, 'Methodism and the origins of English-speaking evangelicalism', in Mark Noll, David Bebbington and George Rawlyk (eds), *Evangelicalism: Comparative Studies of Popular Protestantism in North America, the British Isles, and Beyond, 1700-1900*, Oxford, 1994, 30.

[19] Gay, 1971, 160.

[20] Everitt, 1972.

'external' structural factors - the size of parishes, the size of their populations, their economic and employment base and the absence of an effective, authoritative gentry - intersecting with internal factors such as the pastoral and administrative machinery of early Methodist societies and the degree of lay control within them.[21] Over time, the longer-term influence of social change accompanying industrialisation became an important issue. But at first 'environmental' factors were paramount in the rapid transformation of popular perceptions of Methodism. The structure of Cornish society more generally gave Methodism a popular accessibility. For example, Methodism's band and class meetings ideally complemented the small groups that were the backbone of metal mining.

But similar structural factors had not led to vigorous religious dissent in the seventeenth and early eighteenth-centuries. Indeed, dissent was extremely weak in early eighteenth-century Cornwall. Structural factors provided the preconditions but did not guarantee the emergence of religious pluralism. The second element in Methodism's reception was communication. Walsh has argued that the Protestant world of the early and mid-eighteenth century made up a 'highly effective communications network'; Methodism was built on the processes of connecting communities through the operation of itinerancy.[22] Preaching was able both to feed and to meet the volatile mood of eighteenth-century communities linked by networks of gossip and rumour. John Reed, the son of a yeoman farmer at Stithians, recalled in his memoir how

> in the year 1742 [sic], about the month of August, Mr Wesley and some of his preachers visited Cornwall. This soon occasioned a great rumour, and induced hundreds and thousands of people to assemble together, in various places, where notice was given for the new preachers to discourse to the people ... now there was no small stir among the people.[23]

The comment of the Anglican minister at Gwennap to the 1744 visitation queries also reflects the restless fluidity of early Methodism: 'there is a constant succession of teachers, that run up and down the country'.[24] Itinerant preaching and pastoral work enabled Methodists to connect communities in ways that the traditional Anglican clergyman could not, with his static ministry bound to the physical fabric of the church. Such dynamic methods were clearly well suited to the work of

---

[21] Luker, 1987, 85-105.
[22] Walsh, 1994, 29.
[23] Thomas Kelk, 'The life and death of Mr John Reed', *Methodist Magazine* 27 (1804), 193-200, 241-245 and 289-296.
[24] H.Miles Brown, *Episcopal Visitation Queries and Methodism*, Redruth, 1962, 7.

evangelising mining communities. This can be seen in the lack of popular opposition to early Methodism. Despite a later convenient (and common) narrative of persecution, opposition to Methodism was sporadic and short-lived, confined to towns such as Falmouth, with its more transient seafaring population. Even in 1745, when some of the local landed class resorted to the law to oppose John Wesley's preaching, they failed to use their powers to the full and, at many critical points in mining districts, were confronted by large crowds mobilised in support of the Methodist itinerants.[25] Wesley had introduced a new, itinerant ministry to Cornwall. Unlike Wales, no native dissenting tradition of itinerancy had prepared the people for this.

Yet structure and methods do not explain everything. The third factor explaining this religious change is the message itself. We need to restore the importance of the message that Wesley carried as well as the methods with which he disseminated it and the environment to which it was brought. The message of justification by faith and instant salvation was simple and attainable. It offered hope and security for labouring communities as the spread of market relations added to the already considerable uncertainties of life and death. It also helped to bridge the gap between formal church religion and popular spiritual beliefs. Taking their cue from James Obelkevich's work on Lincolnshire, historians of Cornish Methodism have pointed to the coalescence of belief systems involved in Methodism.[26] For example, John Rule argued that 'Methodism did not so much replace folk-beliefs as translate them into a religious idiom'.[27] In this respect it is also significant that Methodism in west Cornwall spoke in the dialect of the people. In explaining the popularity of the Methodist chapel in Sithney in 1829, Richard Tyacke wrote that 'the preachers of the persuasion are generally selected from their own sphere in life'.[28]

Together, structure, communication and message allow us to explain the early implantation of Methodism in Cornwall. But a distinctive aspect of eighteenth-century Methodism in Cornwall may lie in the way it was diffused. Walsh has proposed that the iconography of early Methodism is misleading. The 'characteristic image of the English movement is not that of John Wesley preaching to great crowds in the

---

[25] John Wesley, *Journal*, London, 1864, 475.
[26] James Obelkevich, *Religion and Rural Society; South Lindsey 1825-1875*, Oxford, 1976; Luker, 1987, 396.
[27] John Rule, 'Methodism, popular beliefs and village culture in Cornwall, 1800-50', in Robert Storch (ed.), *Popular Culture in Nineteenth Century England*, London, 1982, 63.
[28] Diary of Richard Tyacke, CRO AD 715.

sunken outdoor amphitheatre at Gwennap in Cornwall' but of him standing in 'a barn talking to a knot of people'.[29] 'Patient persistent Evangelism' marked the spread of eighteenth-century Methodism in England rather than periodic mass revivalism. There were too many social barriers for swift diffusion, unlike in 'more open and egalitarian societies like those of North America'. So, did the great outdoor Gwennap meetings indicate a pattern of diffusion in Cornwall more akin to America than to England? In 1764 it was reported from Wendron that 'the work of God greatly revived this year in almost every place in the circuit'.[30] This prefigured a pattern of diffusion in Cornwall marked by periodic surges of support rather than the 'patient evangelism' of English Methodism. To investigate this further we must establish the patterns of Methodist growth and set them in their comparative context.

Figure 9.1 Methodist growth, 1767-1840 (base 100=1800)

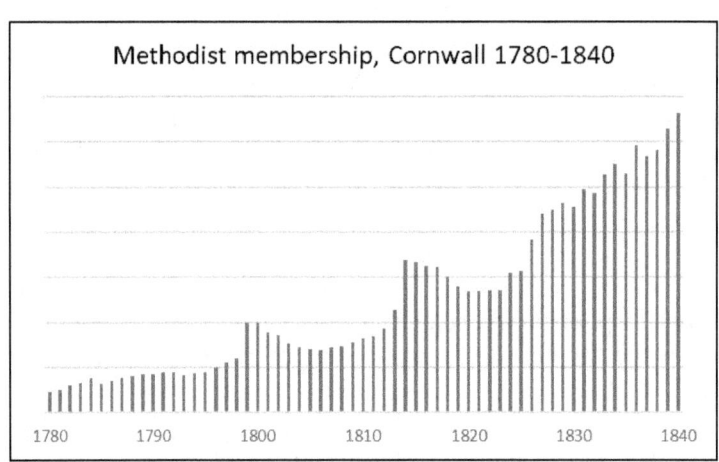

Source: Cornish membership statistics can be found in Rule, 1971, 217; Michael Edwards, *Cornish Methodism: A Study in Divisions 1814-1857*, Redruth, 1964, 246ff and Peter Hayden, 'Culture, creed and conflict: Methodism and politics in Cornwall, c.1832-1979', PhD thesis, Liverpool University, 1982, 427ff. I have also had access to John Probert's membership database. The British figures are from Robert Currie et.al., *Churches and Churchgoers: Patterns of Church Growth in the British Isles since 1700*, Oxford, 1977, 161-162.

---

[29] Walsh, 1994, 32-34.
[30] Kelk, 1804.

The chart above displays a pattern of growth in Cornwall marked by irregular surges. The actual number of members in Cornwall peaked during the revival of 1764/65 and then fell back. Membership data indicate another revival in 1770/71 (missing in the qualitative literature), which was followed by similar 'backsliding'. It was the revival of 1781-84, one that began in west Cornwall and spread to the east with a lag of a couple of years, that doubled membership within a few years. Membership then fell off again, until the spectacular gains of the 1798-1800 revival. A similar pattern, of a virtual doubling of membership and then a fall, can be seen after both major revivals of 1798-1800 and 1814. By 1805-06 the number of Methodist members in Cornwall was a full 30 per cent below the peak year of 1800; by 1820-21 membership was 20 per cent below the peak of 1814. But the same effect was much more muted after the later revivals of the mid-1820s and early 1830s. This suggests that the penetration of Methodism had reached certain limits in Cornwall by the 1820s and the steadier pattern of growth may reflect the putting in place of a more sophisticated pastoral and administrative machinery.

Table 9.1: Methodist membership as a proportion of the population, 1771-1901, Cornwall and England (%)

	Cornwall	England
1771	1.72	0.42
1791	2.85	0.75
1811	3.67	1.55
1831	7.89	2.29
1851	8.55	3.01
1871	9.37	2.78
1891	10.52	2.51

Source: Based on membership statistics from Currie et.al., 1977; Edwards, 1964; Hayden, 1982; John Probert's unpublished membership database and population estimates from E.A.Wrigley and R.S.Schofield, *The Population History of England 1541-1871: A Reconstruction*, Cambridge, 1989.

Methodism implanted itself in Cornwall relatively quickly. As Table 9.1 indicates, the density of Methodist membership in Cornwall, expressed as a proportion of the total population, peaked at just over ten per cent in the 1880s. This was over three times greater than the peak of Methodist density achieved in England. In terms of the diffusion of

Methodism, Cornwall led the English experience by at least half a century. By the later 1790s Methodist density in Cornwall had already reached the peak rates that were to be achieved in England in the 1840s. The 1798-1800 revival took Methodist membership in Cornwall to relative levels never to be seen in England. When comparing Cornwall with Wales it is noticeable that Wesleyan Methodism in Cornwall did not suffer the setbacks that Methodism did in Wales in the 1750s, resulting from personal and doctrinal disputes. While Welsh Methodism had pre-dated the Cornish 'awakening', the difficult years of the mid-century saw a haemorrhage of members to the dissenting churches. In Cornwall, relatively weak competition from dissent gave Wesleyan Methodism an effective monopoly of revivalist enthusiasm. As early as 1785 Methodist societies were present in 31 per cent of Cornish parishes, these including the largest and most populous. By the end of the thirty years of Methodist expansion following 1785, Methodist societies had been organised in 83 per cent of Cornish parishes. These years included the two great revivals of 1799 and 1814 and saw Methodism establish itself as the hegemonic religious institution of Cornwall.

The years of Methodist expansion generally from 1780 to 1830 have been linked to an outburst of itinerant preaching. In turn, this dynamic growth period has been explained as a part of 'wider structural changes'. Relevant factors cited have included population growth, subsistence crises, the commercialisation of agriculture, warfare and a sharpened class conflict accompanying the rise of a clerical gentry, who benefited from enclosures of land and tithe commutation.[31] Where social changes dislocated older hierarchies and communities, 'cottage based evangelicalism' spread rapidly.[32] Deborah Valenze has argued that cottage religion was a creative re-appropriation of religion by 'plebeian preachers', using the message of the gospel to legitimate the 'traditional' household economy of the labouring classes, one under increasing pressure from market relations.[33] As we saw in chapter 8 Cornwall's dispersed paternalist society of indirect landlord control and its discourse of moral economy would have made it particularly susceptible to cottage religion.

---

[31] See Hempton, *Religion and Political Culture*, 1996, 27.
[32] David Hempton, 'Evangelicalism in English and Irish society, 1780-1840', in Mark Noll et al. (eds), 1994, 156-176.
[33] Deborah Valenze, *Prophetic Sons and Daughters: Female Preaching and Popular Religion in Industrial England*, Princeton NJ, 1985 and 'Cottage religion and the politics of survival', in Jane Rendall (ed.), *Equal or Different: Women's Politics, 1800-1914*, Oxford, 1987, 32.

In Cornwall, as elsewhere, the spread and consolidation of Methodism after the revival of the early 1780s can be related to this broader process of cottage religion in turn connected to economic and social change. Luker argues that the 'early externalisation' of economic structures associated with the rise of mining, added to by changes in agriculture from the 1790s, fragmented 'traditional' society and produced a 'new found impotence and insecurity'.[34] This was fertile ground for planting the spiritual certainties of Methodism. But Methodism was aided also by the concomitant strength of custom, the access to smallholdings and the dispersed paternalism noted above in chapter 8. It was this combination of the new and the old which provided the space as well as the demand for Methodism.

Eighteenth-century cottage religion also had its own gender and territorial profiles. Unlike the Anglican version of evangelicalism, which tended to reinforce patriarchal authority within the family, nonconformity gave women the opportunity to move outside the home while re-affirming the idea of the household as a centre of labouring life. As a result, the role of women in the outburst of cottage religion from the 1780s to the 1830s is now generally accepted. Examples of informal, spontaneous, rural cottage Methodism and the involvement of women abound in Cornwall. In 1771, Ann Gilbert of Gwinear was 'going one day to preaching in the adjoining village, the preacher happened not to come'. She gave out the hymn, went to prayer and was then 'constrained to intreat and beseech them to repent, and turn to the Lord. The people were melted into tears, and many were convinced of sin'.[35] Ann, almost totally blind since the early 1750s, found in Methodism a role within the local community that granted her new respect and enhanced status. Clearly, Methodism appealed especially to women. In 1767 56.8 per cent of the members of the West Cornwall circuit were women, a proportion that approximates almost exactly to that in Macclesfield at the end of the 1700s.[36] It is also noticeable that societies in the mining districts had particularly high proportions of female members. The role of women in early, eighteenth century Methodism in Cornwall may, indeed, still be greatly understated in the historiography.

Cottage religion was, if anything, entrenched in Cornwall well before its appearance in rural parts of England. Luker alerts us to the

---

[34] Luker, 1987, 35-41.
[35] Joseph Taylor, 'The experience of Mrs Ann Gilbert, of Gwinear, Cornall', *Methodist Magazine* 18 (1795), 44.
[36] Book of Methodist Societies in Cornwall West Circuit, June and July 1767, CRO AD 350; David Hampton, *Methodism and Politics in British Society 1750-1850*, London, 1984, 13.

consequences of this early popular evangelicalism. Specifically, he points to an important distinction between west and east Cornwall. The larger numbers joining the Methodist societies in the 1780s in west Cornwall assisted 'the essential indigenisation of local Methodism' and established its character at a time when the organisational structures of Methodism were still fluid and evolving.[37] In contrast, in mid and east Cornwall, the later emergence of similar levels of Methodist support allowed connexional direction and circuit organisation to be more influential. This chronology produced a Methodism in west Cornwall at odds in many ways with the formal Methodism of the church authorities, something that continued well into the nineteenth-century and which helped to make local Methodism distinctively 'Cornish'. One outcome of this history was that 'cottage religion' in west Cornwall retained a clear Wesleyan strand. In contrast, beyond Cornwall non-Wesleyan Methodism, particularly the Primitives, after the 1810s became the 'dominant expression of cottage religion'.[38] Within Cornwall that role was taken by the Bible Christians.[39]

William Hockin, clergyman at Phillack, wrote in 1821 that 'of Westleian [sic] Methodists there are multitudes – this is indeed the predominating sect throughout the West of Cornwall which has nearly swallowed up all the others'.[40] In Cornwall, unlike in Wales, Wesleyanism and Methodism were synonymous before the 1820s. This, together with the weakness of old dissent, had helped to produce a homogenous religious culture that Ward describes as a 'Volkskirche'. Local lay leaders of Wesleyanism had established a popular church that 'did not bend easily to preachers' pressure'.[41] Methodism gave psychic reassurance for the individual in the face of economic and social change and created a framework for everyday life in the occupationally homogenous communities of west Cornwall. Such a 'cultural exchange between religion and the everyday life of working people' seems to have been a rare achievement.[42]

Thus, the appeal of Methodism in Cornwall was facilitated by the context of early industrialisation, together with the structural configuration of Cornish rural-industrial society. But it must be

---

[37] Luker, 1987, 281.
[38] Hempton, 1994, 314.
[39] Garry Tregidga (ed.), *Bible Christians*, Penryn, 2017.
[40] Miles Brown, 1962, 18.
[41] W.R.Ward, 'The religion of the people and the problem of control, 1790-1830', in G.J.Cuming and Derek Baker (eds), *Popular Belief and Practice*, Cambridge, 1972, 245-246.
[42] Hempton, 1994, 315.

emphasised that the growth of Methodism was not simply that of a new religion suiting new times; nor was it a functional response to industrial capitalism, two influential previous interpretations. In adopting the former explanation, John Rowe saw Methodism as the 'spiritual counterpart of the economic forces that, impatient of any and every restraint, blindly believing in infinite and unlimited progress, were driving forward'.[43] Rule, in proposing the latter interpretation, echoed a widespread view among historians in the 1960s. Methodism 'provided an inner discipline which aided in breaking in the labour force to the new disciplines of the machine age'.[44] Yet factors such as the role of cottage religion and the involvement of women in the early growth of Methodism suggest that Luker's more subtle interpretation of Methodism as a bridge between the old and the new, promoting individualist ideas but within structures of continuity and tradition, has more explanatory force.[45]

Distinction: the denominational geography of mid nineteenth-century Cornwall

By the later 1810s Methodism was providing the religious identity for most Cornish men and women. Moreover, it added a qualitative, cultural distinctiveness to the Cornish society we have sketched over the previous three chapters. But precisely how 'distinctive' was Cornwall's religious practice?

The 1851 Religious Census, because of its uniqueness, exercises an enduring fascination for historians of nineteenth-century religion in England and Wales. The quantitative data of this Census have been used as the basis for numerous accounts of Victorian religious practice.[46] Towards the end of the twentieth-century this quantitative approach to religious history was increasingly criticised for ignoring the actual religious experiences of men and women.[47] Yet, during this same period,

---

[43] John Rowe, *Cornwall in the Age of the Industrial Revolution*, St Austell, 1993, 261.20.

[44] John Rule, 'The labouring miner in Cornwall c.1740-1870', PhD thesis, Warwick University, 1971, 82-83.

[45] Luker, 1987, 408. See also Hempton, 1984, 28.

[46] The classic accounts are Gay, 1971; K.S.Inglis, 'Patterns of religious worship in 1851', *Journal of Ecclesiastical History* 11 (1960), 74-86; W.S.F.Pickering, 'The 1851 Religious Census: A useless experiment?', *British Journal of Sociology* 18 (1967), 382-407; D.M.Thompson, 'The 1851 religious census: problems and possibilities', *Victorian Studies* 11 (1967), 87-97.

[47] Hempton, *Religion of the People*, 1996, 28.

there were also renewed calls for a more rigorous analysis of the quantitative data contained in the Religious Census. Snell pointed out that there had been no detailed regional comparison using analytical quantitative methods such as explicit correlation coefficients. He had earlier argued that 'precise statistical descriptions of denominational regional strengths and complementary location' makes the variations more apparent and allows the conflicts (or lack of them) between denominations to be more fully understood.[48] Computerisation allowed the testing of earlier generalisations, the construction of a more detailed descriptive geography and comparison between religious and other socio-economic variables.[49]

This body of quantitative work rests on the central assumption that the 1851 Census of Religious Worship provides sufficiently robust data. When comparing reported attendances at registration district level with the provision of seating in the churches of the north Midlands, Snell found a 'reassuringly tight' fit and concluded that 'we can have considerable confidence in the internal consistency of the religious data of the 1851 Census.[50] His conclusions support those of earlier writers. Thus D.M.Thompson concluded that, 'although containing minor errors and omissions, there is no other collection of statistical material which is as complete for comparing varying [religious] practice from place to place and from denomination to denomination'.[51] Clive Field also concluded, in his comprehensive bibliographical essay relating to the 1851 Census, that it 'still remains a broadly accurate quantitative tool for examining the state of English and Welsh Methodism at mid-century, provided that the unit of geographical analysis is kept sufficiently large'.[52]

However, what is 'sufficiently large'? Both Snell and Ell and Slater conclude that county level data are 'clumsy' and 'inadequate' and prefer to use registration districts, adjusting to correct for missing data.[53] If the purpose is to draw broad regional distinctions and test regional denominational reciprocities then this level of analysis no doubt suffices.

---

[48] Keith Snell, *Church and Chapel in the North Midlands: Religious Observance in the Nineteenth Century*, Leicester, 1991, 54-55.
[49] Snell and Ell, 2000.
[50] Snell, 1991, 14.
[51] Thompson, 1967.
[52] Clive Field, 'The 1851 Religious Census of Great Britain: a bibliographical guide for local and regional historians, *The Local Historian*, November 1997, 201.
[53] Snell, 1991, 8; Paul Ell and T.R.Slater, 'The Religious Census of 1851: a computer-mapped survey of the Church of England', *Journal of Historical Geography* 20 (1994), 48.

Nevertheless, Snell also expresses misgivings that 'the registration district is slightly too large a unit', failing to do justice to small towns and the intricacy of local 'pays'.[54] At the same time the parish level is too small for rigorous analysis and, in any case, may not reflect the perceptual geography of dissenters, who looked beyond parish boundaries. This raises the possibility of analysis at an intermediate spatial level – at sub-registration district level but revising boundaries to distinguish market towns separately – which is the level of analysis adopted here. This produces a far more detailed geography than registration districts (76 units in Cornwall as opposed to 13 registration districts) and allows us better to understand intra-Cornish differences. It also requires building up the data from the original returns rather than relying on the published report.[55]

As Coleman has pointed out, religious practice in Cornwall was 'far from uniform'.[56] But a registration level perspective is too broad to identify the detail of this heterogeneity. For instance, Coleman also states that the 'six districts in which Primitive Methodism showed (in 1851) were all in the western half of the county, where they seem to have drawn support from mining communities'.[57] But a closer look at the ten sub-districts where Primitive Methodist attendances were significant suggests it was not just miners who provided support. Seven of these sub-districts were, indeed, dominated by mining. However, a relatively high attendance at Penryn would indicate that non-mining town dwellers were also attracted and the highest Primitive Methodist attendances of all – at St Ives and Paul – reveal that fishing, not mining, communities were in fact the most fertile ground for Primitive Methodists.

Turning to the broader picture of religious attendance in Cornwall revealed by the 1851 Census, Snell and Ell note that the Church of

---

[54] Snell, 1991, 52.

[55] In doing this, missing Anglican attendance returns were replaced by the average of the returns for the Church of England in the other parishes of the sub-district, if the latter amounted to more than half the population size of the district. This method results in just one sub-district in Cornwall, Tywardreath, with no COE data. In Devon three sub-districts, East Budleigh, Broadclyst and Christow, had insufficient data for inclusion and a further two, North Tawton and Holsworthy, insufficient COE data (The Devon data were extracted from Michael Wickes, *Devon in the Religious Census of 1851*, Appledore, 1990).

[56] Bruce Coleman, 'The nineteenth century: nonconformity', in Nicholas Orme (ed.), *Unity and Variety: A History of the Church in Devon and Cornwall*, Exeter, 1991, 147.

[57] Coleman, 1991, 147.

England was weak in 'most of Cornwall' as well as in Wales, south Lancashire, west Yorkshire, Durham and the Pennine uplands and urban industrial areas.[58] Cornwall was the 'exception' to the generally strong Anglican index of attendance in southern England. Figure 9.2 shows the detailed picture of Anglican attendances across Cornwall and Devon. While in Cornwall an Anglican IA (the total number of attendances as a proportion of total population) of higher than 30 was exceptional, in Devon districts with an Anglican IA lower than 30 were in a minority. The heartland of Anglican strength in east Devon near the cathedral city of Exeter is clearly shown in this map and this district has been described as one of the Church of England's 'core areas'.[59]

Figure 9.2. Anglican index of attendance, Cornwall and Devon, 1851

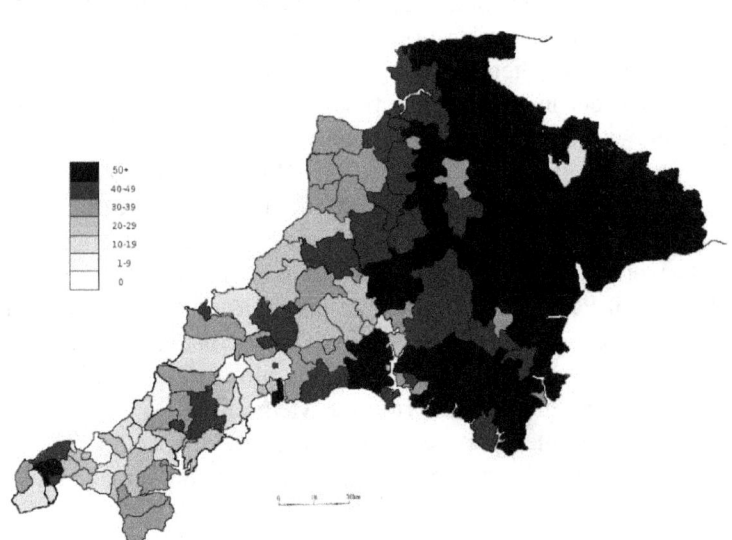

Explanations for local patterns of religious attendance have been sought either in terms of denominational reciprocities, the spatial relationship between the denominations, or in terms of socio-economic factors, relating patterns of attendance to non-religious variables. Our data allow us to investigate each aspect in turn. The dominant thesis, put forward originally by Tillyard and later restated by Robert Currie, is that there was an inverse relationship between old and new dissent. Methodism flourished in areas where Congregationalists, Baptists and Presbyterians were not strong.[60] Similarly, old dissent was correlated

---

[58] Snell and Ell, 2000, 58.
[59] Snell and Ell, 2000, 73.

positively with Church of England strength. Therefore, prior Anglican and old dissent strength would have been counter-productive for new Methodist expansion. Simply mapping the geography of Methodist and old dissent attendances in 1851 (see Figures 9.3 and 9.4) and comparing these with Figure 9.2 suggests that the situation in Cornwall bore out this simple relationship. Methodism in all but the far south east of Cornwall was strong; the Church of England and old dissent were both weak. In south and east Devon the opposite was the case.

Figure 9.3. Methodist index of attendance, Cornwall and Devon, 1851

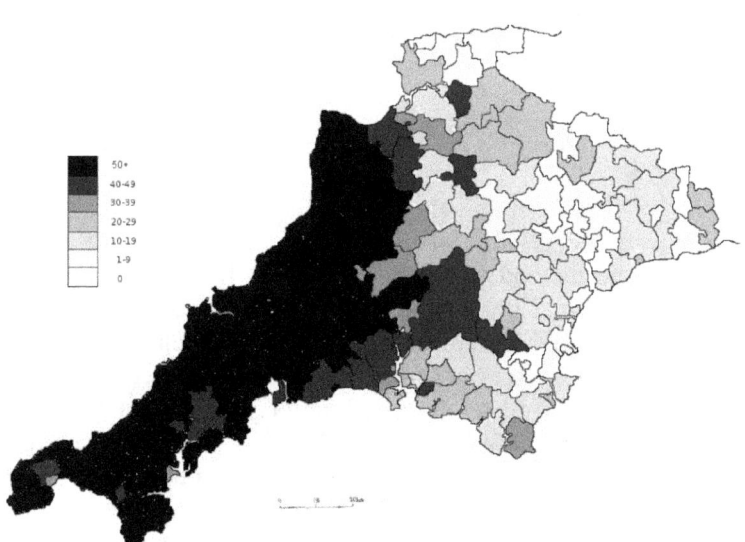

Snell goes further, using an explicit measure of correlation, Pearson's correlation coefficient, to test the relationship between two different denominations statistically. He finds that the negative correlation of old and new dissent and of the Church of England and new dissent is broadly true at registration district level in the north Midlands. However, when

---

[60] F.Tillyard, 'The distribution of the Free Churches in England', *Sociological Review* 27 (1935), 1-18; Robert Currie, 'A micro-theory of Methodist growth', *Proceedings of the Wesley Historical Society* 36 (1967), 65-73.

Figure 9.4. Old dissent index of attendance, Cornwall and Devon, 1851

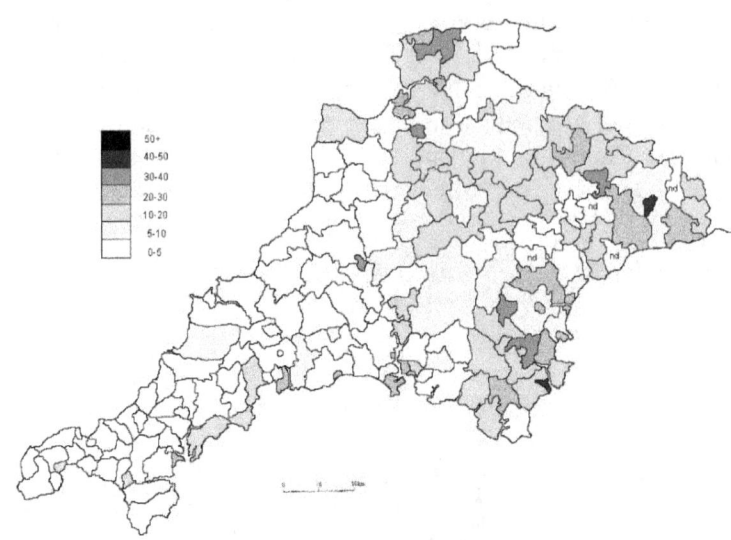

applying the same method to southern counties he finds 'considerable variations'. In particular there is a 'lack of any correlation between the Anglican Church and Methodism in Cornwall, which is contrary to expectation'.[61] If this were the case it would indeed require a major revision of the accepted picture. Thus, John Gay stated that 'over much of England the success of Wesleyanism varied in an inverse proportion to the strength and vitality of the Church of England in any particular locality. Nowhere was this truer than in Cornwall'.[62]

However, further examination of the Cornish data at sub-district level restores the Tillyard/Currie thesis as Table 9.2 on the next page indicates. The figures suggest the expected negative correlation between Anglican /old dissent attendances and Methodist, with a positive correlation between Anglicanism and old dissent. This in turn suggests that a relationship not apparent at registration district level re-appears at sub-district level.

In terms of the impact of external variables, the strength of the denominations has been related to urbanisation, with old dissent and Wesleyan Methodism supposedly appealing to lower middle-class support in the towns. Conversely, Anglicanism had failed to win the support of the growing urban populations and remained more rural-based. In testing this assumption in the north Midlands Snell found that old

---

[61] Snell, 1991, 49.
[62] Gay, 1971, 159.

dissent was, indeed, positively correlated with urbanisation (measured in terms of the number of persons per acre) whereas the Church of England and Wesleyan Methodism were negatively correlated, with the Wesleyans the most 'rural' denomination. The pattern in Cornwall was somewhat different as Table 9.3 shows.

Table 9.2: Correlation coefficients between denominations, using the total attendances for each denomination expressed as a percentage of the sub-district population, by county

	Cornwall	Devon	Cornwall and Devon combined
Anglican /Methodist	-0.202	-0.197	-0.571
Anglican/old dissent	+0.343	+0.113	+0.360
Methodist/old dissent	-0.196	-0.213	-0.400

Table 9.3: Correlation coefficients between index of attendance and urbanisation for selected denominations

	Cornwall	Devon
Church of England	+0.256	-0.166
all old dissent	+0.378	+0.049
all Methodist	-0.163	-0.032
Wesleyan Methodist	-0.073	-0.007
Bible Christian	-0.190	-0.180
Wesleyan Methodist Association	-0.017	insufficient data

As expected, old dissent showed an urban bias in Cornwall. However, Wesleyan Methodism was far less 'rural' in Cornwall (and even less so in Devon) than in the north Midlands, although there is still a weak inverse correlation. The Bible Christians show the anticipated bias towards the countryside, although not, perhaps, as marked as some commentators have implied. But the real contrast concerns the Anglican Church. When analysed at a sub-district level the Established Church in

Cornwall appears to have been associated with urban rather than rural districts. This may be a feature of Cornwall's settlement pattern, with its scatter of small market towns. In these latter, notably Penzance and Truro, the Anglican Index of Attendance held up well (see Figure 9.2). In addition, the lower IAs for the Church of England in nearby rural districts suggest that congregations were being pulled into the larger, more prestigious urban churches from surrounding rural areas. This was a pattern apparent, also, at Exeter, even though in Devon the relationship between the Church of England and urbanisation at this local spatial level conforms more closely to the expected pattern.

What makes Cornwall even more distinctive is that fact that in rural areas the Church of England had lost its dominance. The explanation for this can be found in the presence of mining across large swathes of rural Cornwall. In arguing for the 'indigenisation' of Methodism in Cornwall, Luker also suggests that it was in the mining and fishing communities that Methodism took on a popular functionality.[63] These claims for a relationship between Methodism and the socio-economic basis of the community can be tested more explicitly using the sub-district data of the 1851 Religious and Population Censuses.

Table 9.4: *Relationship between selected denominations and proportions of the adult male population engaged in selected occupations in Cornwall*

	mining/fishing	agriculture
Church of England	-0.622	+0.186
old dissent	-0.400	-0.397
all Methodist	+0.260	-0.059
Wesleyan Methodist	+0.309	-0.261
Bible Christian	+0.013	+0.155
Wesleyan Methodist Association	-0.353	+0.259

Much stronger correlations are obtained when relating denominational strength to these occupational variables than when studying interdenominational reciprocity. Wesleyan Methodism was positively correlated with mining and fishing communities in Cornwall, while the Wesleyan Methodist Association seems to have found its appeal more in

---

[63] Luker, 1987, 398.

agricultural communities. But even more strikingly, old dissent was negatively related to both mining and fishing and agricultural communities, reinforcing the point that its strength in Cornwall lay in urban, more middle-class communities. The strongest relationship of all, however, was the negative one between Anglicanism and mining/fishing communities. By the mid-nineteenth century, the people of these places clearly felt little attraction for the Established Church. To some extent, the religious vacuum had been filled by Methodism (although we might note that there is also a negative correlation of –0.322 between mining/fishing communities and total church attendances in 1851, suggesting a degree of working class secularisation, at least in terms of formal church attendance). We might conclude that socio-economic variables are more important in explaining the detailed spatial distribution of the denominations in 1851 than territorial differences *per se*. It was these variables that underlay and produced the differences perceived by contemporaries as regional.

These differences of context required an overarching narrative to be transformed into the distinctions that produced identity. In exploring further this notion of narrative it is time to move from the patterns of religious practice in 1851 to the more qualitative issue of the distinctiveness of the Methodist experience in Cornwall. In doing so we address the second of Hempton's key questions about Methodism, what he termed the 'nature of the Methodist experience'.[64]

From Methodism in Cornwall to Cornish Methodism

Cornish Methodists were quick to adopt the dominant narrative of a moral regeneration of West Barbary (cf. chapter 3 above), and to inject a critical strategic role for Methodism in this progress from darkness to civilisation. In 1820 the local Methodist Francis Truscott wrote that, in the 1740s, Cornwall 'needed to be humanized as well as evangelized; it was a dark place of the earth, filled with habitations of cruelty'.[65] Truscott had been influenced by Richard Warner's observations on the role of Methodism in Cornish society and happily accepted the responsibility of Wesleyan Methodists, who had 'completely reformed a large body of men, who, without their exertions, would probably still have been immersed in the deepest spiritual darkness, and grossest moral turpitude'.[66] Not only nineteenth-century Methodists concentrated on the

---

[64] Hempton, *Religion of the People*, 1996, 1.
[65] Francis Truscott, 'A letter to the Rev. Jabez Bunting', *Methodist Magazine* 43 (1820), 539.
[66] Richard Warner, *A Tour through Cornwall in the Autumn of 1808*, London,

role of Methodism in the moral regeneration of Cornish society. For Gay, 'Methodism completely transformed Cornwall'.[67] Yet this interpretation can be questioned.

While the role of Methodism was certainly important in preparing the ground for the remarkably widespread and rapid adoption of teetotalism in the later 1830s, its role as moral regenerator has been exaggerated. For example, Methodist critics failed to dislodge popular support for wrestling, often associated with excessive consumption of drink and with gambling. In the mid-1850s wrestling tournaments were reported (by a Methodist press moreover) as attracting 'at least 3,000' spectators, with prize winners coming from all parts of Cornwall.[68] Indeed, wrestling seems to reflect rises and falls in the mining economy, only itself finally declining as a major public spectacle after the traumatic years of the late 1860s. Other regularly condemned aspects of popular culture such as smuggling had remained important activities even as Methodism was establishing its cultural dominance at the end of the eighteenth century.[69] Luker, indeed, goes so far as to suggest that 'social-cultural custom and behaviour showed a remarkable degree of continuity' into the early 1800s. This qualifies the 'model of Methodism as an agent of social modernization'.[70]

As Hempton points out, as well as actively shaping society, Methodism was shaped by its 'local environment, context and locale'.[71] By the 1790s the Wesleyanism that had developed in Cornwall had taken on some specifically local attributes, attributes that began to distinguish it and allow it to be more easily imagined as 'Cornish' Methodism.

The first of the two ways in which Cornwall changed Methodism was by giving it a particularly revivalist aspect. During revivals, people became convinced of their sins, but were then 'saved', becoming regular chapel-goers and leading more godly lives (at least in theory). This process occurred in the public gaze, usually, although not always, on chapel premises. For Ward the distinctiveness of Cornish Methodism lay in the way extreme revivalism persisted within the Wesleyan connexion.[72]

1809, 299-302; Francis Truscott, 'The effects of religion on the miners in Cornwall, by the preaching of the Methodists', *Methodist Magazine* 33 (1810), 39-40.

[67] Gay, 1971, 161.
[68] *West Briton*, reports of wrestling in August 1855 and July 1856.
[69] See Harry Carter, *Harry Carter: The Autobiography of a Cornish Smuggler*, Truro, 1894.
[70] Luker, 1987, 380.
[71] Hempton, *Religion of the People*, 1996, 16.
[72] Ward, 1972, 245.

As we have seen, the two great surges of Methodist membership occurred around the revivals of 1799 and 1814. But such quantitative conclusions fail to do justice to the emotional turmoil surrounding and imbuing these and later years of revival. In 1832 at St Just, on a Saturday night in February 1832, a revival began at a meeting in the chapel:

> The report of what was going on soon spread through the town; and the people came out of the public houses, as well as their own, to see this strange sight. Though many came to look, none mocked, but rather stood amazed. The scene at this time was truly affecting. The loud and piercing cries of the broken-hearted penitents drowned the voice of prayer; and all that could be done at this stage of the meeting was to stand still, and see the salvation of God. At length, the penitents were conducted and upheld, each of them by two persons, into one part of the chapel. And now, when their cries and groans were concentrated, one of the most affecting scenes appeared before the people. Their humble wailings pierced the skies. Sometimes a burst of praise from the pardoned penitents mingled with the loud cries of the broken-hearted; and this greatly encouraged those that were in distress.[73]

Mass revivals of this kind reverberated across local communities and established the conversion processes of revivalist Methodism at the heart of local society. What made Cornwall, and especially west Cornwall, distinctive was the later survival of such mass revivalism to at least the early 1860s and the continuation of revivalism within the Wesleyan body after the 1820s. Unlike the north-east of England, where revivals were associated with the Primitive Methodists, revivalism 'was not the function of any particular segment'.[74]

In his account of Cornish revivalism Rule argued that its persistence is best explained by internal factors, rejecting earlier attempts to link revivals with exogenous economic and political events.[75] Revivalism 'operated in the space between the fully committed membership and those attached but not yet signed up for God, rather than in that between the membership and the more distanced community'.[76] In Cornwall there was a high overall ratio of adherents, occasional and regular chapel-goers, to members.[77] The number of such 'borderers', those interested in and

---

[73] John Trezise, *Memoirs of Mr John Edwards Trezise of St Just, Cornwall*, London, 1832, 84-85.

[74] Robert Colls, *The Pitmen of the Northern Coalfield: Work, Culture and Protest, 1790-1850*, Manchester, 1987, 118-189; Rule, 1998-9, 185.

[75] For an example of this see Eric Hobsbawm, *Labouring Men*, London, 1964, 32ff.

[76] Rule, 1998-99, 182.

[77] David Luker, 'Revivalism in theory and practice: the case of Cornish

affected by the language and practices of Methodism, had already reached numbers sufficient to support spontaneous community revivals in the west by the 1760s. The revivals of 1799 and 1814, by drawing ever-larger numbers into chapel-going, albeit sometimes temporarily, created the 'critical mass' on which future revivals could in turn flourish. In short, a popular culture of revivalism had been created. The Chartist missionary, Robert Lowery, in 1839 observed that 'the population possesses all the materials for such explosions, being full of warm religious feelings, which overrules knowledge. Their daily languages and religious services they attend are replete with rapturous exclamations'.[78] Lowery was describing a situation where, by the late 1830s, the discourse of Methodism had, perhaps, become the everyday 'structure of feeling', particularly among the mining population.[79] Mass revivalism was thus both cause and effect of a popular, folk religion. Once a certain threshold of adherents had been attained, a point reached early in Cornwall, a potential pool of converts was created. As successive generational cohorts came of age there were 'recurring generational pulses', as revivalism became a local tradition.[80] In support of the existence of a revivalist culture it is noticeable how many of the subjects of Methodist biographies report their own parents as 'sober' and 'honest', conscientious attenders of the parish church, or, more common later, of the Wesleyan chapel.[81]

By the 1810s the recurrent collective conversion of new generations of young people in a broadly Methodist-orientated chapel-going cultural stratum had become a 'local tradition'. As Wesleyan Methodists elsewhere turned their faces against revivalism in favour of steadier, sounder expansion based on systems of pastoral oversight and administrative efficiency, Cornish revivalism came to be seen, especially after the 1820s, as divergent. Revivalism, by this time, was confined to Cornwall, Wales, Scotland and Ulster and became prone to being attributed to Celtic excitability.[82] This interpretation was clearly established by 1841, when Charles Barham attributed the 'tendency to enthusiasm ... in part ... [to] ... their Celtic origin'.[83] But, whether

---

Methodism', *Journal of Ecclesiastical History* 37 (1986), 603-619.

[78] Cited in Rule, 1998-99, 176.

[79] Charles Barham, 'Report on the employment of children and young persons in the mines of Cornwall and Devonshire', *British Parliamentary Papers* 1842 (380) XV.1, 760.

[80] Hempton, *Religion and Political Culture*, 1996, 30.

[81] Kelk, 1804; R.P.Tabb, 'Memoir of Elizabeth Laurance Dunstan', *Bible Christian Magazine* 10 (1845), 320-324.

[82] Hempton, *Religion and Political Culture*, 1996, 30.

'Celtic' or not, revivalism has been viewed as the 'most explicit part of a popular indigenisation of Methodism'.[84] A revivalist culture, established by the 1780s in west Cornwall, then became an implicit 'critique of "foreigners" from up-country,' channelling local antagonisms into a continuing preference for revivalism.[85]

Associated with this, a second feature of local Methodism that later became synonymous with Cornish Methodism was the general lack of deference shown by lay members to the itinerant ministers and the desire of the former to govern their own societies. This was well established by the 1840s. In 1848 a minister arriving at Camborne was told 'uppish men are an abomination here and, not seldom, get awkward thumps and communications more frank than welcome'.[86] Another minister, superintendent at Helston, wrote in 1815 that the Cornish Methodists were 'less friendly and affectionate, than any I have met before. I am told this circuit is the worst in the district in respect of religion and attachment to Preachers'. Furthermore, 'not a few of the Cornish Methodists are filling their heads with foolish notions about Conference corruptions'.[87] Similar notions were later to fuel a series of vigorous secessions from the Wesleyan organisational framework.[88] By 1856, non-Wesleyans comprised over 40 per cent of all Methodist members in Cornwall, a proportion maintained throughout the remainder of the nineteenth-century.[89]

John Wesley himself had noted the long-standing independence of some Cornish Methodists. In 1788 he wrote to a minister that 'it has been observed of many years that some at Redruth were apt to despise and [be] very willing to govern their preachers'.[90] Indeed, it was to Redruth, in the heart of the mining district, that 51 leading Cornish lay members converged in June 1791 to discuss the administration of affairs after Wesley's death. They demanded a whole series of democratic reforms: for example, that 'the members constituting every class (or a majority of them) shall chose their Leader'; that 'the People in every Society ... shall choose the Society Stewards'; that the circuit stewards in turn possess a right of veto over the selection of travelling ministers.[91] The

---

[83] Barham, 1842, 760.
[84] Luker, 1987, 303.
[85] Luker, 1987, 123 and 49-50.
[86] Cited in Luker, 1987, 294.
[87] Thomas Shaw, 'A sidelight on the Great Revival of 1814', *Journal of the Cornish Methodist Historical Association* 1 (1963), 163-164 and 175.
[88] Rule, 1971, 264-282.
[89] From statistics in Hayden, 1982, 428-429.
[90] John Wesley, *The Works of the Rev. John Wesley*, London, 1841, 102.

language of the document is resonant of the opening sentence of the Constitution of the United States of 1787 – 'We, the People ... do ordain and establish this Constitution' – and should, perhaps, be viewed as a part of that 'transatlantic revolution' proposed many years ago by Palmer.[92] As John Probert observes, this document, had it been accepted, 'would have revolutionised Methodism'.[93]

The independent temper of this group of men, among whom can be identified merchants and mine captains,[94] was encouraged and fostered by their entrepreneurial role in the expansion of mining and trade. In a society of dispersed paternalism, where Methodist societies had, by the 1790s, produced an organisational structure paralleling, while still overlapping, the hierarchy of the Anglican church, 'traditional' pastoral responsibility was devolving to and was being appropriated by this class of newly financially secure and self-made men. Their legitimation flowed from the egalitarian and socially homogenous communities through which they moved, communities seemingly only intermittently responsive to the enfeebled ties of landlord paternalism. From the vantage point of traditional paternalism this was a vicious circle. Independent communities gave rise to Methodist societies possessed of their own self-importance. In turn, the plethora of self-governing Methodist communities fostered a sense of independence and self-confidence among their growing adherents. Observing the parish church attenders at Hayle in 1836 a regular visitor wrote:

> There is not so much deference paid to the higher ranks. At one time no person left the church after the service was over until the parson had walked out and he received the obeisances of the congregation as he went down the aisle. Now the congregation leave at once without waiting for the parson.[95]

The rise of Methodism reinforced a sense of self-confident independence and helped to break old patterns of deference. In doing this the foundations of a new public identity for Cornish Methodists, as part of a wider nonconformist identity, were laid.

---

[91] George Smith, *History of Wesleyan Methodism, Volume 2: The Middle Age*, London, 1862, 702.

[92] R.R.Palmer, *The Age of Democratic Revolution: The Challenge*, Princeton NJ, 1959.

[93] John Probert, *Dr Boase of Redruth*, Redruth, n.d., 2.

[94] See Rowe, 1993, 261.3.

[95] Cedric Appleby, 'Wesleyan Methodism in Hayle – 1826', *Journal of the Cornish Methodist Historical Association* 7 (1985), 15.

Narratives of identity: from the private to the public
The remaining task in this chapter is to reflect on Methodism's role in the formation of Cornish identity. Luker offers the most explicit claim that Methodism acted as a surrogate regional identity:

> the particular regional identity sensed by the Cornish became more clearly defined and expressed during the 19th century and as with nonconformity in Wales Methodism in Cornwall came to serve as a badge of regionalism, and as a buttress to Cornish "nationalism" in the face of encroaching forces and influences from "up-country" England.[96]

However, Luker goes on to suggest that the 1840s marked a watershed, as by then there had emerged an 'increased consciousness among the local middle class of a national [i.e. English/British] rather than a regional identity, and an intense desire to demonstrate their own credentials, both as middle-class citizens and as Methodists, on the national stage'.[97] Such a picture, of a turn away from regional consciousness and an attack on indigenous Methodism, appears at first sight to be at odds with the situation in Wales.[98]

In Wales there was a consensus that to be Welsh was to be nonconformist.[99] The Welsh turn to Methodism, perhaps because of a prior dissenting tradition, had, if anything, lagged behind the Cornish, despite the earlier evangelical awakening in the Wales of the 1730s.[100] It was only after the mid-1780s that Calvinist Methodism began to be widely embraced by the ordinary people of Wales.[101] The extremely rapid industrialisation of Wales in the early nineteenth century resulted in the multiplication of nonconformist chapels, which offered security and identity for those living through rapid social change. As a result, by the 1840s nonconformity was embedded in Welsh language and culture.[102] Moreover, this took a widespread political form after the 1860s, with the increased activity of the Liberation Society in Wales and with the Electoral Reform Act of 1867. It was the 1860s that produced that

---

[96] Luker, 1987, xi.
[97] Luker, 1987, 356.
[98] W.P.Griffith, '"Preaching second to no other under the sun": Edward Matthews, the nonconformist pulpit and Welsh identity during the mid-nineteenth century', in Pope (ed.), 2001, 61-83.
[99] Hempton, *Religion and Political Culture*, 1996, 51; Geraint Jenkins, *The Foundations of Modern Wales: Wales 1642-1780*, Oxford, 1987, 385.
[100] Philip Jenkins, *A History of Modern Wales 1536-1990*, London, 1992, 157-163.
[101] Jenkins, 1987, 347.
[102] Hempton, *Religion and Political Culture*, 1996, 54.

'confluence of nonconformist religion, Liberal politics and Welsh national identity' that many have noted.[103]

The distinction between a public and private identity is crucial here. In Cornwall the rise of Methodism had helped to construct, legitimate and reinforce a private identity in the eighteenth-century. This revolved around a desire for close fellowship and a valorisation of the family and the home, sentiments that were both cause and effect of the upsurge of cottage religion and of further Methodist growth in the later eighteenth-century. The private identities of individual Methodists focused on a loyalty to small-scale localised moral codes, looking to local dynasties for leadership. Such re-fashioned private identities fitted neatly into the small-scale, dispersed social geography of Cornwall. Then, revivalism transformed pockets of Methodism into a community religion, through the two great revivals of 1799 and 1814. These revivals 'indigenised' Methodism in Cornwall and made it into a folk religion that exercised a cultural hegemony within local communities. In doing so, Methodist allegiances began to take on a public identity, as the identity not just of God-fearing individuals but of whole communities. From the 1810s, the oft-repeated narrative of early persecution, a story of a time when Methodists suffered 'the most fierce and determined opposition throughout the county' added another dimension to Methodist self-identification.[104] Indeed, with the rise of Methodism to hegemonic status by the 1820s and 30s it was now easier to read this as the previous persecution of whole communities, who had re-discovered themselves in their passage through a baptism of fire. Yet in Cornwall revivalism was not explicitly associated with historical dreams of heroic ages, as happened in the Scottish Secession movement of the 1730s, with its explicit allusions to the Covenanting principles of the seventeenth century. Similarly, there is little evidence of that public articulation of the people in clearly nationalist terms that can be observed in Wales in the preaching of Edward Matthews or Ieuan Gwynedd.

Moreover, as in Wales, Methodism was not unambiguously welded to a Liberal political identity until the 1860s. Peter Hayden has pointed out that it was not until after 1867 that individual Methodists became much more directly engaged with formal Parliamentary politics.[105] In contrast, Ed Jaggard more recently re-affirmed a role for Methodism in reform politics in Cornwall from the 1820s onwards.[106] But Jaggard fails to capture the precise role of Methodism in Cornish political identity in that

---

[103] Hempton, *Religion and Political Culture*, 1996, 59; Bebbington, 1982, 495.
[104] Truscott, 1820.
[105] Hayden, 1982, 76.
[106] Edwin Jaggard, *Cornwall Politics in the Age of Reform*, Woodbridge, 1999.

critical period from the 1820s to the 1860s because of an over-readiness to conflate Methodism with dissent. Both Hayden and Jaggard agree that Wesleyan Methodists were involved in the anti-slavery campaigns of the 1820s, this involvement flowing easily from their religious commitment to the overseas missions movement. Yet, as Jaggard also notes, there was little contemporaneous support from Methodists for the repeal of the Test Act and even less for Roman Catholic emancipation in 1828-29. On these issues, significantly, Methodists in Cornwall stood apart from dissenters more generally and other reformers; they had 'chose to stand firm with the Established Church against any concessions to the Catholics'.[107] At public meetings at Truro, Helston and Callington in early 1829 prominent Methodists were vociferous in asserting their continued attachment to the Church of England and their loyalty to the Establishment.[108]

Methodists were thus still rejecting the label of 'dissenter' in the 1820s and early 1830s. This delayed their commitment to Liberal politics. Indeed, in the decades from the Reform Act of 1832 to the mid-1850s the evidence of electoral behaviour in Cornwall suggests that propertied Methodists could still vote Conservative in large numbers, this being a period when the Conservatives 'held their own' in the Cornish boroughs.[109] Because of the numerical dominance of new dissent and the relative weakness of old dissent, radical politics were slow to emerge in the second quarter of the nineteenth-century. It was only in the 1860s that the distinction between dissent and Methodism declined. When that happened Methodists more wholeheartedly embraced Liberal and reforming politics. In 1881, a letter from the Liberal solicitor, William Grylls, pointed out that Wesleyan Methodist 'preachers and people may now be depended on, much more than 25 years ago, as Liberals'.[110] The period from the 1820s to the 1850s had seen a growing coalescence of Methodists and reforming politics over specific issues such as church rates. But in the 1840s and early 50s, whilst the links between Methodists and the Church of England were still not entirely broken, those between Methodism and Liberalism had not yet been fully forged. By the 1880s Methodism and Liberalism had however become almost interchangeable.

Within the transition from a private to public identity the 1840s were, as Luker suggested, a significant decade. However, the effect of that decade was much more complex than he assumed. He was right to pinpoint an emerging, town-based middle-class respectability that

---

[107] Jaggard, 1999, 69.
[108] *West Briton*, 9 and 16 January 1829.
[109] Jaggard, 1999, 131.
[110] Cited in Jaggard, 1999, 203.

eschewed the popular revivalism of local Methodism. This, together with other factors such as mass emigration, began to undermine folk religion. But respectability was not merely associated with a simple replacement of regionalism by a sense of national identity. In fact, these small town middle classes were the same people who avidly consumed the burgeoning dialect literature of the 1840s and 1850s; who attended literary and antiquarian societies and began to cherish aspects of local heritage. Thus, Edward Boaden, who entered the Wesleyan Methodist Association ministry in 1849, had written a copy of the Apostles' Creed in Cornish as well as in English, while a solicitor's clerk in the early 1840s.[111] In a similar way, two of the mid-century leading Methodists of the central mining district, George Smith and Charles Thomas, also professed an interest in antiquities and the Cornish language respectively. 'Respectable' Methodists such as Boaden, Smith or Thomas are evidence not of a disappearing regional identity after the 1840s but of a re-made, much more public and more articulate regional identity. As part of this identity Methodism had begun to take on symbolic overtones as the allegiance of the mass of the Cornish people, at the very time that popular, revivalist fervour had begun to wane, sapped by emigration and by the diversion of energies into the need to maintain the institutional and administrative fabric of the various Methodist denominations. By the mid-1860s Methodism, along with mining and a Celtic heritage, were being cited as aspects that distinguished Cornwall from Devon.[112] Methodism was becoming an element in a symbolic repertoire of distinctiveness. Furthermore, this was, paradoxically, occurring at the very point that local Methodism was irrevocably mutating and losing its distinctiveness.

Growing 'respectability' among Cornish Methodists coincided with a gradual but unmistakable mid-century shift to an explicit non-conformity, which in turn fused with a wider nonconformist Protestant identity. In the emergence of a wider political identity for nonconformity after the 1840s the fear of Tractarianism has been cited as critical.[113] It is no coincidence that, in Cornwall, Tractarianism was an important element in the counter-offensive of a renewed Anglicanism after the 1840s.[114] For many Methodists the ritualist leanings of large numbers of Cornish clergy at

---

[111] Anon., 'Edward Boaden and the Apostles' Creed in Cornish', *Journal of the Cornish Methodist Historical Association* 4 (1973), 92-93.

[112] P.S.Morrish, 'History, Celticism and propaganda in the formation of the Diocese of Truro', *Southern History* 5 (1983), 247.

[113] Hempton, *Religion and Political Culture*, 1996, 149.

[114] H.Miles Brown, *The Catholic Revival in Cornish Anglicanism: A Study of the Tractarians of Cornwall 1833-1906*, St Winnow, 1978.

mid-century eased the transition from the borders of Establishment religion to explicit nonconformity. Anti-Catholicism, as well as reforming politics and an appeal to local patriotism, could all be seen, for instance, in the biography of the early nineteenth-century Methodist reformer and merchant, Thomas Pope Roseveare of Boscastle (1781-1853).[115] Roseveare prefigured the explicitly nonconformist Cornish Methodist who in the 1870s and 1880s provided the voting strength for Gladstonian Liberalism.

Yet, as later support for Liberal Unionism in Cornwall might indicate, nonconformists could also be pulled by anti-Catholicism into a wider British, and imperialist, Protestant nationalism. Indeed, mass emigration from Cornwall from the 1840s may have acted to make the Cornish Methodist and nonconformist identity more susceptible to imperialist tropes, especially after the 1860s, when population began to decline and economic stagnation in Cornwall undermined the self-confidence and dynamism of local Methodism. Religious nonconformity thus pulled in contradictory and complex directions after the 1840s, directions that were often in tension.

Conclusion
We can now clarify the role of Methodism in relation to Cornish identity formation and link it to the interpretation presented in the earlier chapters of this book. The economic and social changes of Cornwall's early mining-based industrialisation produced fertile ground in which Methodism rooted itself. By the 1810s it was established, particularly in the core western zone of Cornwall's industrialisation, as a cultural institution deeply embedded in the everyday life of local communities. It had become part of the institutionalization of the region, helping to reproduce the proto-industrial society that had grown out of Cornwall's social relations of dispersed paternalism. It was more than a surrogate in this period. It had become a part of the regional identity matrix, adding its quota to processes of distinction and integration and playing its part in the symbolic shaping of Cornwall.

In the generation from the 1810s to the 1840s Methodism in Cornwall became more clearly 'Cornish', clinging to revivalism when other parts of Methodism, especially the Wesleyan Connexion, rejected it and became hyper-sensitive to issues of local autonomy. Periodically, this sensitivity led to secessions from the Wesleyan parent body. This was a

---

[115] Thomas Shaw, 'Thomas Pope Rosevear 1781-1853: the Boscastle Methodist reformer', *Journal of the Cornish Methodist Historical Association* 7 (1986), 71-78; Luker, 1987, 232.

period of divergence, when the symbolic shape of Cornwall became more explicitly differentiated from other parts of the British Isles. Methodism became the most relevant institution for labouring and working-class communities, its world-view stitched onto older discourses of popular moral economy and custom. It thus helped to make Cornish proto-industrial society distinctive from both other urbanising industrial regions and from rural, agricultural regions. This period of 'divergence' in the early nineteenth century accompanied a parallel emergence of a more explicit consciousness of being 'Cornish'.

By the 1840s, the regional institutions produced by the local middle classes had given birth to a vigorous and more articulate sense of regional pride and 'difference', one underpinned by the continued role of the mining sector in Cornwall. However, by that decade, social change was beginning to undermine older proto-industrial social relations.

Some of the dynamics of this process, for example the growth of a respectable (often Methodist) middle class, can be viewed as factors leading to a convergence of Cornwall with other industrial regions. Conversely, the onset of mass emigration after the 1830s guaranteed that no dominant, urban settlement would emerge. This meant that local allegiances remained strong rivals to a Cornish territorial identity even as the final growth decades of mining spread the industry into parts of east Cornwall relatively untouched by earlier industrialisation. For a short, but important, period, the geography of Cornwall's historic identity based on the administrative territory and its re-formed industrial identity with its core in the west overlapped. During this phase, as the unique social relations of proto-industrial Cornwall were fading into history, a more confident and assertive territorial identity established itself, centred in the towns and the middle class and fed by the local press, dialect literature and literary institutions.

In this period, too, Methodism merged into a broader public and more political nonconformist identity. In practice less distinguishable from a general nonconformist identity, Methodism in Cornwall began to fill a role as a symbol of Cornish uniqueness. Perhaps the high point of the nineteenth century Cornish territorial identity was seen during the 1846 to 1876 campaign to achieve a separate Anglican diocese for Cornwall. In this long drawn out but ultimately successful struggle Anglicans somewhat paradoxically but consistently referred to Cornwall's Methodism as a unique factor, marking it off, along with its 'Celtic' history, from neighbouring Devon.[116]

---

[116] Deacon, 2017, 155-180.

But this territorial identity, the symbolic shape of which meshed tightly by the 1860s with nonconformity, was only briefly dominant in the public sphere. Just as the lived identity of Cornwall's proto-industrial communities was undermined by social change from the 1840s, so was Cornwall's re-forged territorial identity challenged by other narratives. In the final quarter of the century competing narratives jostled with those of mining-Methodist Cornwall, to expose the limits of the territorial identity that had emerged during Cornwall's industrial period.

Chapter Ten
From proto-region to proto-nation?

This final chapter draws together the themes of this research, reflecting on these in relation to the three conceptual tools introduced in chapter 1. These were my definition of identity; Anssi Paasi's model of regional formation; and the approach adopted by the new Cornish Studies. This is done by focusing on two territorially based campaigns for legislative and institutional change - one successful, one a failure. Both were influenced by religious feeling, this link re-emphasising the special role played by religion in the institutionalization of the Cornish identity in the nineteenth century.

The chapter proceeds by outlining the two campaigns before discussing the five elements of our definition of identity – context, difference, integration, narrative and process. To pursue the process of territorial identity reformulation, Paasi's model of regional formation will be revisited. I assess the Cornish identity via his concepts of territorial shape, symbolic shape, institutional shape and functional shape.[1] In doing this, certain parameters will become apparent for the regional identity as it had emerged by the early 1880s. More specifically, I will conclude that the functional shape achieved by Cornwall provided the territorial identity with a particular 'space of possibilities' that limited its role in the public sphere.[2] Cornwall's functional shape in the third quarter of the nineteenth century reinforces those who have criticised Paasi as under-theorizing the role of scale and of competition between identity formations at different scales. To insert a greater awareness of scalar inter-relations it will be suggested that more attention needs to be given to issues of power in identity formation.[3]

---

[1] Anssi Paasi, 'The institutionalization of regions: a theoretical framework for understanding the emergence of regions and the constitution of regional identity', *Fennia* 164 (1986), 105-146.

[2] For the concept of space of possibilities see chapter 8 above and Dror Wahrman, *Imagining the Middle Class; the Political Representation of Class in Britain, c.1780-1840*, Cambridge, 1995, 6.

[3] For a more recent re-assessment of these issues see Bernard Deacon, 'Regional identity in late nineteenth-century England: discursive terrains and rhetorical strategies', *International Journal of Regional and Local History*

Finally, the constraints of power structures are, perhaps, especially stark when viewed from an explicit Cornish location. In its academic guise of new Cornish Studies, such a perspective also reveals that identity change in the later nineteenth century was not the traumatic and sudden event implied by metropolitan writers. One type of identity did not rapidly and brutally displace another. Rather, there was a subtle adjustment in the balance of overlapping categories, a slower, though nonetheless real, shift in conceptualisations of place and people in Cornwall in the later nineteenth century. After the 1860s imaginations of Cornwall as an industrial region, as a centre of industrial civilisation and prowess, gradually gave way to imaginations of Cornwall as a Celtic periphery, primitive and marginal. But these categories to some extent always overlapped. The regional consciousness that had developed during Cornwall's industrial period persisted well into the twentieth century while the arguably more romantic Celtic representations had their roots in earlier periods. What did change was that, after the 1870s, there was no longer a hegemonic representation, at least not in Cornwall. The Cornish identity had entered a more hybrid phase, one more clearly marked by plural Cornwalls rather than a single Cornwall.

New diocese and Sunday closing
Two campaigns provide a context for reviewing the Cornish identity in the third quarter of the nineteenth century. During the 1840s demands surfaced for a separate Anglican diocese for Cornwall. This heralded a long campaign of 'public meetings and private lobbying, pamphlets, letters to editors, discussion in such assemblies as Convocation, Church Congress and diocesan conferences, and questions and debates in Parliament'.[4] Eventually, in 1876, the Conservative Government recommended a new bishopric for Cornwall, thus dividing the Diocese of Exeter, a territorial arrangement that had combined Cornwall with Devon for ecclesiastical purposes since the eleventh century. While led by clergymen and the gentry, the campaign, which saw its most intensive phase in the 1850s and 60s, eventually brought together Tories and Liberals, Churchmen and lay persons, Anglicans and nonconformists in a broad body of support.

The second campaign attracted even wider backing within Cornwall. This time, the origin of the campaign lay with nonconformists rather than the Anglicans. In the summer of 1881 a wave of petitions in favour of a

---

11 (2016), 59-74. and *From a Cornish Study*, Redruth, 2017, 155-180.

[4] P.S.Morrish, 'History, Celticism and propaganda in the formation of the Diocese of Truro', *Southern History* 5 (1983), 239.

Bill for the Sunday Closing of Public Houses flowed out of Cornwall. Nonconformist chapels of all denominations, particularly in mid and east Cornwall, were prominent in this petitioning. In November 1881 the agitation found its focus in a meeting at Truro to establish a Sunday Closing Association for Cornwall, which decided to sponsor a bill for Cornwall, on the lines of legislation already passed for Wales and Ireland. Over the ensuing year this association organised 170 public meetings and, within four months, in an impressive show of local canvassing, collected a petition of 121,000 names. This was equivalent to almost half the adult population of Cornwall.[5] 'Respectable opinion' was almost unanimously in favour. For example, at Newquay, all the clergy signed the petition, eight of the nine Poor Law Guardians, eight of the ten School Board members and seven of the eight Local Board members.[6] It was only in late 1882 that opposition surfaced. Predictably, this was organised by licensed victuallers, but their counter-petition, of a highly-disputed 20,000 signatures, remained a pigmy compared to the massive support for the Bill. However, virtual unanimity did not guarantee success. In July 1883 Earl Mount Edgcumbe moved the second reading of the Cornwall Sunday Closing Bill in the House of Lords but failed to convince sufficient numbers of his fellow peers.[7] The bill fell and did not re-surface in the pressure of parliamentary business caused by procedural wrangles as the Liberal Government struggled to deal with the obstruction of Irish Nationalist MPs.

Nevertheless, the debate around these campaigns, and the arguments adduced in their favour, open a window onto the ways that Cornwall was imagined at a point when its territorial identity was moving into another phase of change.

The elements of identity

We earlier identified five recurring elements in the literature on identity: context, distinction, integration, narrative and process. The Cornish identity in the 1870s and 1880s appears in hindsight to be on the point of change largely because its context, its specific historical site, was undergoing considerable change.

From 1866 the price of copper ore fell sharply. As a result, ore production collapsed. Figure 10.1 clearly indicates the effects of this in the shrinking income from copper mining in the 1860s. Tin mining

---

[5] *West Briton*, 3 November and 10 November 1881; 22 February 1883; 16 March 1882.
[6] *West Briton*, 23 February 1882.
[7] *West Briton*, 19 July 1883.

survived but was destined to suffer recurrent crises, noticeably in the mid-1870s and again in the 1890s, resulting from over-supply in the world market. While there was some diversification into arsenic and other minerals this had no significant impact on total production.[8] Meanwhile lead ore production in Cornwall had already tumbled to insignificant levels by 1880.

Figure 10.1. Real value of Cornish mines output, 1855-1920 (£thousands)

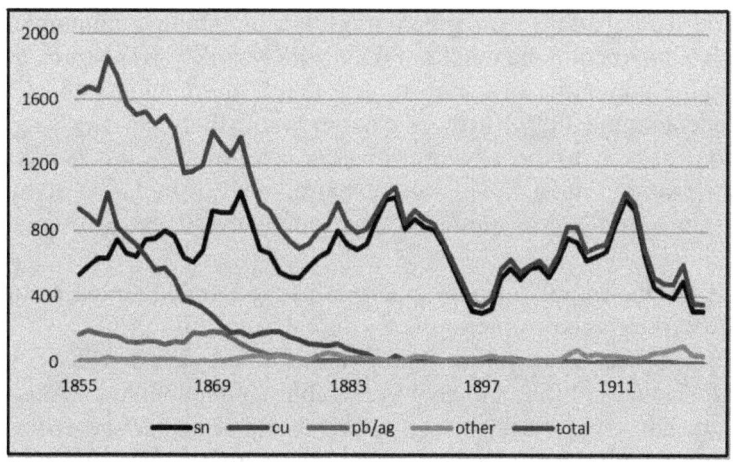

Source: Calculated from Burt et al., 2014, 56-73.

This picture of deteriorating income from mining in the final third of the nineteenth century has led some writers to claim there was an equally sudden transformation of Cornwall's cultural identity. Maxine Berg wrote that 'the region was rapidly transformed into a holiday resort', echoing Sidney Pollard's more cautious view that 'Cornwall began to convert from a leading industrial region into a holiday resort area'.[9] Social historians and anthropologists, over-influenced perhaps by Cornwall's late twentieth-century role as a leisure periphery, followed the economic historians' lead. Cornwall was opened up to new

---

[8] Roger Burt et al., *Mining in Cornwall and Devon: Miners and Men*, Exeter, 2014.

[9] Maxine Berg, *The Age of Manufactures, 1700-1820: Industry, Innovation and Work in Britain*, London, 1994, 112; Sidney Pollard, *Peaceful Conquest: The Industrialisation of Europe 1760-1970*, Oxford, 1981, 14.

representations, which, it is even suggested, 'helped to give Cornwall a visibility and representational identity ... creating its iconography'.[10]

It is certainly the case that new popularisations of broadly romantic representations began to appear around this time. For instance, the Newlyn school of painters in the 1880s brought to a wider, metropolitan audience an image of Cornwall as a place of harmonious folk communities, close to nature and engaged in heroic and tragic struggles with poverty and hardship. In their paintings Cornwall was re-presented as a part of rural (and maritime) England.[11] In place of the dominant representation of Cornwall as 'industrial civilisation' that we traced in chapter 3 this was a representation of Cornwall as primitive and liminal place. The focus had also shifted from mining to fishing communities, a switch also mirrored in the output of dialect literature.[12] At the same time, the emerging popularity of Cornwall as a tourist destination was, by the 1900s, encouraging the growth of a guide book literature stressing its picturesque aspects to the growing suburban and middle-class market of the south east of England. This was encapsulated in the Great Western Railway Company's re-invention of Cornwall as the 'Cornish Riviera' in 1904.[13]

The idea of the triumph of new, metropolitan-generated representations tends to be reinforced by notions of a 'great paralysis' in Cornish life. This proposes that Cornwall's society and politics were fossilised in a mid-Victorian mould for a hundred years, consequent upon the demise of its mining industry.[14] Nevertheless, although the rapid 'down-sizing' of the mining sector clearly led to major restructuring, a focus on the contraction of mining leads to an over-concentration on economic change in the late nineteenth century. This, then, under-estimates continuity and persistence in the cultural sphere.

Moreover, economic reality was not all depression after the 1860s. For instance, Cornish farmers survived the impact of falling prices and agricultural depression from 1873 comparatively well. By transferring resources from grain production to mixed farming and pastoral

---

[10] Philip Dodd, 'Gender and Cornwall: Chares Kingsley to Daphne du Maurier', in Keith Snell (ed.), *The Regional Novel in Britain and Ireland 1800-1990*, Cambridge, 1998, 124.

[11] Bernard Deacon, 'Imagining the fishing: artists and fishermen in late nineteenth century Cornwall', *Rural History* 12 (2001), 159-178.

[12] For example, Charles Lee, *The Widow Woman*, London, 1899.

[13] Philip Payton and Paul Thornton, 'The Great Western Railway and the Cornish-Celtic Revival', in Philip Payton (ed.), *Cornish Studies Three*, Exeter, 1995, 91.

[14] Philip Payton, *The Making of Modern Cornwall*, Redruth, 1992, 119ff.

husbandry and by making use of speedier rail connections to urban areas to market early vegetables and fruit, they survived the worst of these depressed years. Farm output at constant prices rose in Cornwall by five per cent between 1873 and 1894 and even faster thereafter. Over the whole period from 1873 to 1911, in England only Cheshire performed better. Land rents in Cornwall actually rose, by 4.6 per cent from 1872 to 1892, in contrast to a fall in England of almost 17 per cent.[15]

The strength of agricultural rents may have been boosted by demand from returning emigrants for small farms. This reminds us that even the mass emigration of the nineteenth century had some positive impact on Cornish society. Return migrants injected both economic and cultural capital into the Cornwall of the 1880s and 1890s.[16] Meanwhile, remittances from those who did not return enabled mining communities to survive the worst years of these decades.

Other industries expanded at the same time as mining shrank, and some diversification took place. Fishing communities enjoyed a brief railway-related prosperity in the 1870s and 1880s which only waned in the middle of the 1890s. Meanwhile, clay production steadily rose at about a million tons a decade from the 1860s onwards and diversification began to occur into industries such as ship repairing, food processing and explosives by the 1890s.[17] In that decade, too, a chain of hotels and seaside villas began to be built along the coast, marking the beginnings of the modern tourist industry. And yet, Cornwall's future, as a resort area dominated by tourism, was not by any means predestined. The same group of capitalists who were investing in hotels were also active in other sectors. Ronald Perry pointed to a Cornish 'modernizing bourgeoisie' active in the 1890s.[18] In 1898, in concluding a debate about Cornwall's future as a holiday resort in the pages of the short-lived *Cornish Magazine*, Arthur Quiller Couch stated, rather reluctantly, that if 'we must cater for the stranger, let us do it well and honestly. Let us respect him and our native land as well'.[19] By 1906, at a time when Cornish mining had recovered from the depths of the late 1890s depression, Quiller-Couch was feeling he had 'despaired too soon … our industries

---

[15] F.M.L.Thompson, 'An anatomy of English agriculture, 1870-1914' in B.A.Holderness and Michael Turner (eds), *Land, Labour and Agriculture, 1700-1920*, London, 1991, 226 and 232-233.

[16] Ronald Perry, 'The making of modern Cornwall, 1800-2000: a geo-economic perspective', in Philip Payton (ed.), *Cornish Studies Ten*, Exeter, 2002, 175.

[17] Perry, 2002, 171-175.

[18] Perry, 2002, 173-174.

[19] Arthur Quiller-Couch, 'How to develop Cornwall as a holiday resort', *Cornish Magazine* 1 (1898), 237.

seem in a fair way to revive'.²⁰ Even real income from mining almost attained the levels of the early 1870s in 1887-88 and again in 1912 (see Figure 10.1 above), although becoming more geographically confined..

What this suggests is that, a generation after the mining collapse of the 1860s, the image of the region in the eyes of the local elite was still related to industry as much as to tourism. Industry also remained central to the identity of the working class in the older industrial areas. Here, the role of the mining industry was buttressed in the later nineteenth century by the addition of several leisure pursuits familiar to industrial regions elsewhere, such as brass bands, male voice choirs, pigeon fancying and a mass spectator sport in (rugby) football.²¹

Continuity can also be discerned in other elements of the late nineteenth century identity. In chapters 3 and 4 we saw that, by the 1820s, there was a growing search for distinctiveness, as those elements that marked Cornwall off as different and unique were emphasised, or invented. This search for distinction underpinned many of the arguments put forward during the campaign for a separate diocese. At first, distinction was framed in social and economic terms. According to the *Royal Cornwall Gazette* in 1854 'the fact of there being a very large proportion of the Cornish people a great mining population, and some of them engaged in our fisheries, renders them an independent, and intelligent, and a self-relying people'.²² Distinction in occupations and attitudes between a Cornish (mining) population and a Devonian (farming) population were joined in the 1860s by 'racial' distinctiveness. Morrish cites Hobhouse as writing in 1860 that the Cornish were 'of a different race and of a different tone, habits and disposition, to those of Devonshire'.²³ During the 1860s this 'racial' distinction became described as the difference between 'Celt' and 'Saxon'. By 1869 it was being claimed that:

> no contiguous counties in England contain populations so entirely distinctive in race from one another as Devon and Cornwall ... The Cornish ... are mostly Celts, akin to the other Gaelic populations of these islands and Brittany ... The labouring classes of Cornwall, as a rule, are to this day decidedly distinct in habits, even in physical aspect, from their neighbours in Devon; and the

---

[20] Arthur Quiller-Couch, *From a Cornish Window*, Cambridge, 1906, 194.
[21] Bernard Deacon and Philip Payton, 'Re-inventing Cornwall: culture change on the European periphery', in Philip Payton (ed.), *Cornish Studies One*, Exeter, 1993, 62-79.
[22] *Royal Cornwall Gazette*, 29 September 1854.
[23] Morrish, 1981, 247.

differences of occupation (the Cornish being mostly miners or fishermen) widens the result of differences in race.[24]

In 1881 such reasoning re-surfaced. In the meeting establishing the Cornish Sunday Closing Association Canon Arthur Mason claimed that

> on the whole the Cornish people were different in birth (Laughter and applause). They were the relics of a grand old race which were in possession of the whole of England before the Saxons came over, and the Cornish people preserved characteristics which were recognised as distinct. (Hear, Hear.) [These were] reasons why Cornwall should be treated in the same way as Wales.[25]

In pursuing such distinctions contemporaries were also constructing integration and homogeneity. As we saw above, for Lach-Szyrma, the Cornish were 'mostly miners or fisherman', even though only around a quarter of men were directly employed in mining and fishing in 1871. Even this imagined homogeneity became increasingly difficult to construct after the 1870s, as the mining sector reverted to the original core copper mining (now tin mining) district of the west.

The limited but noticeable economic diversification after the 1880s also stimulated centrifugal pressures and, as we saw in chapter 7, in doing so, may have reinforced local territorial identities based on Cornwall's small towns. As economic fragmentation proceeded, however, it was overcome by an increasing appeal to a discourse of Cornishness. For example, at a meeting in support of the Sunday Closing Bill in January 1882 William Andrew of Truro who 'had come as a working man to represent the working class', told the (predominantly middle class) audience that 'there was a time when it was said in Cornwall "30,000 [sic] Cornishmen shall know the reason why" and they should now stand as honourable men, and show what Cornishmen can do today'.[26] Supporters and opponents of the campaign alike appealed to similar sentiment. A columnist in the *West Briton* was concerned 'that Cornishmen are being asked to march to certain defeat', while it was revealed by T.H.Lukes, a St Austell publican, that those promoting the bill were 'travelling preachers who were only in the county two or three years, and were not Cornishmen at all'.[27] Finally, when the bill was defeated in the Lords supporters were consoled by being told that 'all Cornishmen should be proud' of their efforts.[28]

---

[24] Wladislaw Lach-Szyrma, *The Bishopric of Cornwall: A Letter to W.E.Gladstone*, Truro, 1869, 8-11.
[25] *West Briton*, 10 November 1881.
[26] *West Briton*, 19 January 1882.
[27] *West Briton*, 26 January 1882 and 5 October 1882.
[28] *West Briton*, 22 February 1883.

The population of Cornwall was being appealed to recurrently, even monotonously by the 1880s, via this gender-blind language of shared Cornishness. But they were not just 'Cornishmen'; they were 'Cornishmen' with a shared history.

Shared historical narratives are crucial ways to promote integration and homogeneity. During the nineteenth century a more explicitly Celtic history gradually asserted itself. Morrish points out how the historical argument was crucial to the success of the campaign for a Cornish diocese.[29] An appeal was being made to redress the injustice of the loss of the Cornish bishopric in the eleventh century. By the 1860s the narrative of an independent British church in Cornwall, whose rights had been lost through the forced union with a Devon-based bishopric, was firmly established and merged into a wider narrative of Celticity. This more explicit (and romantic) Celtic imagination flowered in a speech in support of Sunday Closing by W.C.Borlase, MP for East Cornwall, at Penzance Wesleyan Chapel in 1882:

> It is a very remarkable thing that we in Cornwall should have taken up this movement next to Wales ... it seems to me as if it is the light of other days coming back to us. It seems to me as if we are part and parcel of that ancient people, that we have part of the Celtic blood in us, which makes us regard what is evil as a veritable reality ... which makes us feel that we must band together to extirpate it.[30]

The analogy with Wales and the other Celtic countries was one regularly made by supporters of Sunday Closing. Thus, the Reverend R. Sampson asked 'if such a bill could be carried for the sister kingdoms of Scotland and Ireland, and also for the Principality of Wales why should we not attempt similar legislation for the Duchy of Cornwall?'.[31]

However, side-by-side with the narrative of Cornish as Celt, there existed other narratives. At a public meeting in 1882 George Smith, prominent Methodist and magistrate, pointing to the Welsh precedent, argued that, like Cornwall, Wales was 'an integral part of the Empire ... if they lost the Bill he trusted that as Cornishmen and as Englishmen they were not ashamed if losing in a good cause'.[32] Twenty years earlier, in 1863, Hussey Vivian, MP for Swansea but of Cornish descent, had told the Welsh Eisteddfod to 'remember that you are all Englishmen, though you are Welsh'.[33] For the Cornish, a regional identity co-existed with a

---

[29] Morrish, 1983, 241.
[30] *West Briton*, 28 September 1882.
[31] *West Briton*, 10 November 1881.
[32] *West Briton*, 19 January 1882.
[33] Prys Morgan, 'Early Victorian Wales and its crisis of identity', in Laurence

narrative of Englishness. While this might be viewed as an example of nested territorial identities, this combination also provided constraining parameters, a certain 'space of possibilities' for the late nineteenth century Cornish identity that I shall return to later in this chapter.

The subtly changing elements of the local identity, from mining and industrial civilisation to Cornishness and Celtic history, together with the changing impact of broader identities (such as Englishness, imperialism, nonconformity and class), hint at the role of the final two elements in our definition of identity: process and scale. To demonstrate process we must turn for guidance to Paasi's model of regional formation.

Regional formation and the Cornish identity
Paasi proposed that regions are social constructions that appear and disappear in a process of institutionalisation. To aid understanding of this process, he distinguished four overlapping stages of institutionalisation, each producing a particular shape. These are territorial shape, when the boundaries of the region are established and awareness of territory distinct from others emerges; symbolic shape, when concepts and symbols associated with the region are created; institutional shape, when institutions based on the region appear and reproduce people's consciousness of inhabiting a particular region; and finally, functional shape, when the region is established in a wider territorial structure and in the spatial consciousness of society.[34]

The territorial shape of Cornwall was firmly established in the medieval period. Athelstan's settlement and the recognition of the Tamar as, with some exceptions, the eastern boundary of Cornwall endured to the nineteenth century. In the 1840s and 1850s the hazy outlines of an alternative territorial shape could be perceived as the mining industry spilled over the border into west Devon. Nevertheless, while west-east migration was temporarily significant at mid-century, the social relations of west Cornwall were not exported wholesale across the Tamar.

On the other hand, while Cornwall's territorial shape survived the process of industrialisation relatively unquestioned, it has been the argument here that a great number of the symbols of the nineteenth century territorial identity were either created or re-fashioned in those years. In the later eighteenth century new symbols of Cornish identity grew out of a set of shared activities and social relations, with their core

---

Brockliss and David Eastwood (eds), *A Union of Multiple Identities*, Manchester, 1997, 93.

[34] Anssi Paasi, 1986 and 'Deconstructing regions: notes on the scales of spatial life', *Environment and Planning A* 23 (1991), 239-256.

zone in the mining districts of west Cornwall. The dispersed, independent-minded communities, where life revolved around the fortunes of the local mines, provided the matrix of a unique set of social relations, described here as proto-industrial. Mining, together with a folk-religion of revivalist Methodism, gave this society many of the symbols – the chapel, the engine house and the ideal of industrial prowess among others – through which Cornish people saw themselves.

I have also suggested that, in the 1840s, the social relations constructed in the course of industrialisation in the eighteenth century began to fragment and decompose. Mass emigration, better communications, the rise of respectability, the extension of market relations all played their part in undermining the social compromise of Cornish merchant capitalism. But at the same time, we can discern an emerging civic consciousness. A more literate and more articulate sense of regional pride was visible, this time centred on the towns and the small, but growing, professional and trading middle classes. The symbols of the territorial identity were, from this point on, likely to be located in narratives of imagined distinction as much as in the solidarities built on common material conditions and shared activities. Yet, most of the narratives of Cornishness that appeared to be stated more stridently as the century wore on remained firmly rooted in the symbols of proto-industrial society.

For example, during the Sunday Closing campaign the slogan 'One and All' was regularly invoked. The purported instigator of the movement, Edwin Tregelles of Falmouth, had written hoping that 'they would act upon the old Cornish motto "One and All".[35] And, on the defeat of the bill, it was stated that 'the promoters of the Bill were possibly animated by the same spirit as those hardy miners of two hundred years ago, who joined so lustily in the song "And Shall Trelawny die; full twenty thousand Cornishmen shall know the reason why"'.[36] Earlier events may have been invoked but the symbols were creations of the first half of the nineteenth century.

The transformation of the basis of the symbolic identity from the shared activities of the mining industry to imagined attributes of Cornishness also had the potential to transform the geography of the territorial identity. As long as mining was the mainstay of the identity the core zone would remain in the west. In contrast, as Cornishness became more of a civic identity the micro-geography of mining became less fundamental. People, or more accurately men, anywhere in Cornwall

---

[35] *West Briton*, 10 November 1881.
[36] *West Briton*, 22 February 1883.

could, after the mid-century, be hailed as, and view themselves as, 'Cornishmen', whether touched by mining or not. Mining retained its iconic status in such cultural productions as dialect stories and the mining landscape retains to this day a special place in the 'moral geography' of Cornishness.[37] But anyone anywhere in Cornwall could read stories or view landscapes and, as we have seen, by the end of the nineteenth century the preferred location of dialect tales had in any case moved from mine to coast and the mining landscape was fast becoming a relict rather than a living landscape.[38]

Turning to Cornwall's institutional space, I argued in chapter 5 that formal middle-class institutions such as literary societies and the press were playing a key role in reproducing the Cornish identity by the mid-nineteenth century. Such institutions were, of course, familiar elements in local and regional identities across England and Wales. For the working class, the less formal social institutions of work and religion were more important. However, the period of industrialisation had also seen the demise of other administrative institutions that had helped to construct a unique territorial shape for Cornwall in earlier times. Principal among these was the institution of the stannaries. According to Allen Buckley,

> the formation of the stannaries, followed by the creation of the Duchy, helped to give identity to the Cornish, and to mark them out as different, not just in character and background, but legally, through a recognised status enshrined in the laws and constitution of the English nation, of which the Cornish became, perhaps reluctantly, a part.[39]

But this special legal status within England began to decay after the Tudor period. By the nineteenth century the 'ancient stannary system [had been] allowed to gradually wither on the vine and pass out of use'.[40] Abolition of tin coinage in 1836/37 and the Stannary Act of 1896, which

---

[37] Philip Payton, *Cornwall*, Fowey, 1996.

[38] While the argument here is that the link between mining and the territorial identity loosens after the mid-nineteenth century, the evidence for the geography of the Cornish identity at the beginning of the new millennium suggests a clear west-east gradient remains in terms of strength of identification with Cornwall (see Brian Gosschalk et al. *Community identity in Cornwall*, London, 1994; Phillipa Aldous and Malcolm Williams, 'A question of ethnic identity', in Philip Payton (ed.), *Cornish Studies* Nine, Exeter, 2001, 213-226; 2011 Census national identity question).

[39] Allen Buckley, *Medieval Cornish Stannary Charters 1201-1507*, Camborne, 2001, 2.

[40] Buckley, 2001, 21.

effectively made Stannary Courts a division of the County Courts, were the final death-knell for this unique medieval institution. In its place was put a new administrative institution, but one hardly unique to Cornwall - the county council of 1889. While, together with the new Cornish diocese, this gave Cornwall a political and institutional shape, the consequences were profound.

Paasi's fourth and final 'shape', the establishment of a region in the wider regional structure and in the spatial consciousness of the extra-regional society, is a central part of the formation of regional identity. For Paasi, identity does not emerge in a simple fashion out of the 'shapes' we have been discussing. Figure 1.2 from chapter 1 is reproduced below.

Figure 10.2. Paasi's model of the formation of regional identity.

factual ideal	insiders outsiders
ideas of community	
structures of expectation	images of region
regional consciousness of inhabitants	identity of the region
regional identity	

Regional identity is partly the product of the regional consciousness of the inhabitants, itself formed by 'factual' (shared activities) and 'ideal' (imagined) elements. As suggested above, both kinds of element can be perceived at work in the reproduction of the consciousness of Cornish people by the later nineteenth century. I have also suggested that the 'factual' part of this equation had given way to the 'ideal' after the 1840s. However, regional identity is also produced by the images of the region. Here, we might note the image of Cornwall as a mining region, held by both insiders and outsiders before the 1840s. We might also note a dissolution of this image and the appearance and re-appearance of other images: of Cornwall as a 'Celtic' place, of Cornwall as a primitive margin, of Cornwall as part of a harmonious rural England, of Cornwall as a place for leisure and relaxation, in the years after the 1870s. The changing kaleidoscope of popular images of Cornwall in the later nineteenth century implies a growing divergence. In addition, this divergence can, to some extent, be mapped onto the insider/outsider distinction. Insiders were more likely to cling to the 'classic' image of Cornwall as a centre of industrialisation (albeit a now failed industrialisation rather than 'industrial civilisation'). Outsiders were, on the other hand, quicker to adopt various romantic tropes of Cornwall.[41]

Nevertheless, there was one image that, in the late nineteenth century, both insiders and outsiders shared. This was the image of Cornwall as an English county. By the 1880s, Cornwall could be regarded as both socio-economically 'different' and culturally and historically 'distinct'. But, politically, 'Cornwall was in a different position to what Ireland and Wales was, being an integral part of England'.[42] Accepting this status, and few if any voices were being raised in the 1880s to deny it, meant that the proposers of the Cornish Sunday Closing Bill were forced to make a case for 'exceptional legislation' for Cornwall. The campaign was, from the start, bedevilled by the question posed by the Reverend D.T. Harrison at Penzance: 'why should a special act be required for it more than other parts of England?'.[43] As a *West Briton* editorial argued, this was 'piecemeal legislation brought to an absurdity. However remote Cornwall may be from London, and whatever may be said in joke about it being out of England, it is still one of England's counties'.[44] R.G. Brett, Liberal MP for Truro, argued that, while the Welsh Sunday Closing Act could be passed on 'special and exceptional grounds', these 'cannot be said to apply to so small an area as an English county – a principle of partial legislation which I cannot think is for the public advantage'.[45] Even worse, opponents claimed this was 'parochial' legislation, leading to 'Cornwall being isolated, as it were, from the rest of England'.[46] Accepting the same image, of Cornwall as an English county, meant that proponents of the Sunday Closing Bill found it difficult to follow the logic of their claims for parity with the 'sister kingdoms' of Scotland, Ireland and Wales. Indeed, at the same time as arguing for Cornish difference, Canon Mason, a leader of the campaign, accepted at the inaugural meeting of the Sunday Closing Association, that 'Cornish people were very happy to be united to England, and they did not wish for Home Rule. (Laughter)'.[47] The Cornish were, as the title of their most widely read newspaper reminded them every week, content to view themselves as 'West Britons' at this time.

---

[41] For examples see W.H.Hudson, *The Land's End: A Naturalist's Impressions in West Cornwall*, London, 1908; S.P.B.Mais, *The Cornish Riviera*, London, 1928.
[42] *West Briton*, 10 November 1881.
[43] *West Briton*, 5 January 1882.
[44] *West Briton*, 19 January 1882.
[45] *West Briton*, 16 February 1882.
[46] *West Briton*, 17 August and 5 October 1882.
[47] *West Briton*, 10 November 1881.

Thus, by the 1880s, Cornish men at least were uniting around a narrative of shared origins, contemporary economic distinctiveness and Celtic imaginings. A distinct regional consciousness had been re-forged over the years of industrialisation. Yet, ethnic consciousness was rendered opaque and hesitant by a parallel narrative of Englishness. The regional identity did not, at this time, produce a national identity. The latter was made difficult by the 'space of possibilities' that surrounded the Cornish identity. The absence of a distinct cultural institution such as, in Wales, the Welsh language, or formal institutions as, in Scotland, separate ecclesiastical or legal structures, meant that there was relatively little around which national imaginings could cohere. In contrast, the consensus was that Cornwall was an English county, albeit a distinct one, and this was to remain a dominant image right through the twentieth century.

The closest comparison is, perhaps, the Isle of Man. Here also, a campaign around a bishopric, this time to defend the independent Bishopric of Sodor and Man, introduced the language of modern nationalism into the island. This was buttressed by the late nineteenth-century Celtic renaissance and antiquarian enquiries into the dying Manx language and its associated folklore. In Man too, the local territorial identity was heavily influenced by wider tropes of Britishness, a 'relational' nationalism that was 'constructed and defined through complex interaction within wider cultural and political contexts'.[48]

Nevertheless, as Paasi notes, ideas can change generationally.[49] The Cornish generation that had been socialized in the 1840s and 1850s had adopted a narrative of cultural distinctiveness within a wider frame of a nonconformist English identity. But, by the 1900s, a small minority of a later generation were beginning to make more explicit analogies with other 'Celtic' countries and beginning to question the status of Cornwall as an English county.[50] Ideas of a non-English and Celtic history, plus the symbolic role of the Cornish language, remained available for appropriation as the raw material for a more explicit 'Celtic' revival. And appropriated they were in the Cornish 'Revival' of the early twentieth century. Nevertheless, this appropriation fundamentally rested on and

---

[48] John Belchem, 'The little Manx nation: antiquarianism, ethnic identity, and home rule politics in the Isle of Man, 1880-1918', *Journal of British Studies* 39 (2000), 220.

[49] Paasi, 1991.

[50] Amy Hale, 'Genesis of the Celto-Cornish Revival? L.C.Duncombe Jewell and the Cowethas Kelto-Kernuak', in Philip Payton (ed.), *Cornish Studies Five*, Exeter, 1997, 85-99.

ultimately blended with the sense of 'difference' that was created during the process of industrialisation.

Scale and Cornwall

The conceptual insights of Paasi's approach have been brought together here with an empirically informed study of one territory and its historical geography. This has allowed us to develop a comparative account of Cornwall and to comprehend aspects of the nineteenth century territorial identity. We have seen how a Cornish identity co-existed with spatial identities at different scales. On a larger scale, there was an identity of Englishness, one that merged with later nineteenth century British Imperialism. On a smaller scale, local and urban identities competed with a Cornish level of territorial allegiance. This looks like a classic example of the 'nesting' of identities within a hierarchy of geographical scales, as proposed by Guntram Herb and David Kaplan.[51] But the Cornish identity did not just 'nest' within other identities. Its setting also had politico-geographic implications. It was in competition with local identities and constrained by the wider identity of Englishness. It is here, as Gordon MacLeod points out, that Paasi's model is less helpful. There is 'little in the way of a theoretically guided discussion as to how competing narratives of place – national autarky, aspirant nationalism, unionism or regionalism – can often come to vie for hegemony within any given space, and thereby provide some capacity for a re-casting of its symbolic and institutional shape'.[52]

To pursue this issue further there needs to be more awareness of what Kees Terlouw has termed 'territories of control', the imposition of regulation via regional structures.[53] In this dimension of control the power to establish and to resist dominant territorial narratives becomes critical. To this extent, the construction of cultural spaces can be viewed as 'power geometries'.[54] In these power geometries, the role of the state is central, in delineating the possibilities of the 'regional' and in actively constructing an identity based on the territory of the state. In the 1800s the (English) national narrative was clearly 'hegemonic'. The Cornish

---

[51] Guntram Herb and David Kaplan (eds), *Nested Identities: Nationalism, Territory and Scale*, Lanham MD, 1999, 4.

[52] Gordon MacLeod, 'In what sense a region? Place, hybridity, symbolic shape, and institutional formation in (post-)modern Scotland', *Political Geography* 17 (1998), 839.

[53] Kees Terlouw, 'Regions in geography and the regional geography of semiperipheral development', *Tijdschrift voor Economische en Sociale Geografie* 92 (2001), 79.

[54] Don Mitchell, *Cultural Geography*, Oxford, 2000, xxi.

identity was subordinate to that broad spatial identity. Allowed some autonomy in the cultural sphere, it was severely circumscribed in the political. Attitudes that were to become common during the twentieth century, accepting Cornwall's cultural distinctiveness yet denying, belittling or ignoring any assertion of political distinctiveness, were already firmly in place by the 1880s.[55]

Adopting an explicit Cornish Studies perspective has thus alerted us to the constraints placed on the Cornish identity by wider territorial identities. Furthermore, it hints at the importance, if we wish to deconstruct 'Cornwall' as a concept, of moving from a focus on the distinctiveness of Cornwall towards an analysis of the power structures within which that distinctiveness has been reproduced.

Conclusion

What wider lessons does this study of Cornwall hold? The first lesson is methodological. Studying one territory reinforces the value of studying identity as a way to open up an interdisciplinary bridge across sometimes impassable boundaries. For instance, I have argued that local people exercised agency in the creation of their own regional identity. In this concluding chapter that agency has been traced even into Cornwall's 'post-industrial' period. But the study also reinforces the point that local agency always interacts with wider structures. This inter-relationship and the way it changes over time, plus the detailed configuration of the borders and overlaps between the local and the global, requires an openness to both representations and material structures.

Secondly, we might see this work as part of a project that revises the over-simplistic 'metropolitan' picture of Cornwall and its identity in the modern period. An approach sensitive to local agency and to the representations and discourses adopted by Cornish people in its industrial phase reminds us of the complexities of the period. It has been claimed that 'the historian's function is often that of restoring complexity to past reality which some bold and excessively binary conceptual scheme has made too simple'.[56] The same can be said of Cornish Studies. In examining the case of Cornwall from a Cornish Studies perspective, we see how, in contrast to claims made from a metropolitan perspective, ideas of Cornwall did not suddenly change somewhere around 1870. Continuity, rather than change, is restored to the post-1840 period. Local

---

[55] For a similar argument applied to Celtic Britain more generally see Murray Pittock, *Celtic Identity and the British Image*, Manchester, 1999.

[56] Cited in David Runciman, 'Conversation with the past requires an ironical twist', *Times Higher Education Supplement*, 13 July 2001, 28.

narratives of territorial identity that can be recognised in the later nineteenth century had their roots in the construction of difference that marked the first third of the century. Furthermore, the symbolic repertoire drawn on by these imaginings can be assigned to the experience of industrialisation that began in the early eighteenth century.

Cornwall's early industrialisation and the unique social relations accompanying it provided the context, the 'space of possibilities', for this identity. That industrialisation also generated a revised set of representations of Cornwall that came together in the early decades of the nineteenth century to produce an ideology of 'industrial civilisation'. In such ways Cornwall resembled industrial regions elsewhere in Britain. But this was an industrial region that, because of the constraints imposed by its resource and population base, could not move beyond a proto-regional phase. At the same time the clerical gentry and antiquarian classes in Cornwall reproduced a historical narrative that cemented older elements of ethnic distinction in Cornish memories. By the mid-nineteenth century, therefore, we can glimpse overlapping categories. A pride in dynamic industrialisation co-existed with a nostalgic county patriotism and a residual sense of ethnic distinctiveness.

Such overlapping categories continued into the later, post-industrial period. Cornwall's de-industrialisation did not destroy the symbols created during industrialisation. On the contrary, these clung on. Indeed, at times (for example when the Cornish rugby team won the county championships in 1908) they were revitalized. Mass emigration had also introduced an extra-territorial, overseas dimension into the reproduction of the Cornish identity. In the overseas diaspora, imaginations of 'industrial civilisation', in the form of what others have termed the myth of 'Cousin Jack', lived on into the twentieth century. This multi-focal international geography of Cornishness acted to replenish and reinforce more traditional representations of industrial Cornwall through the mechanisms of return migration and transcontinental communications.

But the images introduced in the course of Cornwall's industrialisation were joined by others. Most notably Cornwall was more likely to be explicitly imagined after the 1860s, by outsiders and insiders alike, as 'Celtic'. This imagination combined with other historical narratives, together with the considerable remnants of the Cornish language in the physical and literary landscape, to propel a Cornish cultural 'revival' in the twentieth century back more explicitly to its 'Celtic' roots. There had been a shift of balance, from proto-region to proto-nation, from homogenous mining and industrial region to hybrid, post-industrial and tourist region. However, to explain these post-industrial imaginings of Cornwall it is essential for us to understand the complexities of

INDUSTRIAL CELTS

Cornwall's industrial period. Those years of industrial Celts, with the emphasis on 'industrial', ought no longer to be viewed as an embarrassing void between the Cornish identity of the late medieval period and the re-discovered Celtic Cornish identity of the twentieth century. In contrast, while the roots of the industrial society that emerged in the eighteenth century can be traced back to that medieval period, the identity of the twentieth and twenty-first centuries can only be fully grasped in the light of the ambiguities of its industrial period.

Index

Aberystwyth school 17
Agar, Charles 177
Allen, John 152
Altarnun 158
Andrew, William 235
Anglesey – see Ynys Môn
anthropologists 32
archaism 181
Arthur 84-85
Associated Tinners 99, 130
associationalism 18
Athelstan 237
Australia 109, 156, 158-160, 165, 171

Baines, Dudley 27, 142, 156, 159
bal maidens 186-187
Balleswidden 183
bankers 95-96, 100, 134
banking 115, 127, 134
bankruptcy 99-100, 109
Barham, Charles 178, 182, 184-185, 219
Barry, Jonathan 145
Bartlett, Stephen 132
Barton, Denys 135
Basset, Sir Francis 55, 91, 98
Basset family 131, 177
Bath 65, 74
Beckett, John 99-100
Benson, Bishop 50
Berg, Maxine 108-111, 114, 125, 231
Berkeley school 17
Bible Christians 206, 213
Billig, Michael 8
Billinge, Mark 91
Birmingham 92, 95, 129, 142
Boaden, Edward 224
Bochym 98
Bodmin 46, 85, 90, 178
Bodmin Moor 158
Bohstedt, Jon 174

Bolitho family 100
Bolitho, Thomas 95, 97
Bolitho, Thomas Robins 97
Bolitho, Thomas Simon 97
Borlase, W.C. 236
Borlase, William 61-62, 81-83, 94, 116
Boscastle 225
boundaries 24
Boulogne 99
Bourdieu, Pierre 8, 11, 24
bourgeoisie, gentlemanly 21-22
bourgeoisie, grand 91
bourgeoisie, merchant 94-103, 106, 127-128
bourgeoisie, modernizing 223
Bradford 187
Brass industry 112, 116, 130
Breage 65, 99, 152
Brett, R.G. 241
Bristol 130
Brittany 11, 33, 81, 83
Brixham 98
Brunn, Gerhard 80
Buckley, Allen 95, 132, 239
Bull, Edward 126
Burke, Gill 130, 161
Burra Burra 171
Burt, Roger 101-102, 112-114, 116, 125, 127, 129, 135, 137, 154, 163, 175

Cabrera, Miguel 188
Caerhayes 98
Caernarfon 100
Calcutta 74
Callington 223
Calstock 152
Calvinist Methodism 221
Camborne 67, 77, 95, 119, 139-142, 144, 149, 153, 157, 177, 183-184, 186-187, 193, 219
Canada 164
capital market 127-136
Caradon 132, 139
Cardo, William 189
Carew, Richard 61-62, 73, 81
Carlyon family 98
Carlyon, Thomas 180-181

Carn Brea 6, 47, 119
Carne, Joseph 100
Carnmenellis 149, 184, 191
Carter, Erica 5
Carthew, Edward 183
Catholic emancipation 223
Celts 82-84, 219, 227, 229, 234, 240, 242, 245
Central mining district 123
Chacewater 158
chain migration 160
Chapman, Malcolm 32, 70
charity 177-178
Charlestown 139
Charlestown United 174
Charlesworth, Andrew 180
Chartism 75, 85, 168-171, 189-191, 193, 195
Chesher, Veronica 98
Cheshire 233
China 112
China clay 122, 134, 139, 194, 233
Church of England 199-200, 211-212, 214-215, 220, 223, 225-226, 229
Chyandour 95
class identities 168-170, 179-180, 188-189, 192
Clowance 45
Coleman, Bruce 198, 209
collateral aids 53, 185-187, 190
Colley, Linda 12
Collins, Wilkie 76, 168
combination 54, 172, 181
common land 186
cooperatives 175, 194
Conservatism 223
Consolidated Mines 48, 96, 132-133
context 4, 230-232
Coode, Edward 100
Cook's Kitchen 133
copper mining 115-122, 230-231
Cornish Assembly 11
Cornish Club 91
Cornish exceptionalism 170-172
Cornish historians 80-87, 236
Cornish identity, definitions 76-80

Cornish language 30, 51, 61-63, 69, 85, 224, 242
Cornish Metal Company 119, 128
Cornish nationalism 33, 76-77, 86-87, 221, 242
Cornish pride in lineage 71-76
Cornish Revival 77, 83, 245
Cornish Riviera 233
Cornish Studies 35-38, 244
Cornu-English 63-70
Cornwall Agricultural Society 90-91
Cornwall as Celtic space 29-31
Cornwall as local space 27-29
Cornwall, early modern 29
Cornwall Horticultural Society 90
Cornwall, integration into England 29-30
Cornwall Physical Institution 90
cost book financing 127-128, 143
cottage industry 109
cottage religion 204-207, 222
county consciousness 13, 90-91, 241, 245
County Library 90-91
Cousin Jack 74, 164-165, 245
craft regions 13
Crick, Bernard 28
critical mass 140, 142
Cromwell 78
Crook, Denise 92, 94
Cullum, David 109, 113-114
cultural provinces 13, 35
cultural studies 37
culture regions 17
Cumbria 14, 46, 99-100
Cummins, Thomas 178
Currie, Robert 210
Cury 98

Danes 84
Daniell, Ralph Allen 96, 100
Daniell, Thomas jr 99
Daniell, Thomas sr 96, 103
Darby, H.C. 19
Darby, Wendy 44
Dartmouth 98
Davey, Richard 96, 100

Davey, Stephen 96, 98, 100, 182
Davey, William 86
Davy, Humphrey 71
debt 177
de-industrialization 140-143, 156, 166, 245
De la Beche, Henry 37
Dellheim, Charles 59
denominational reciprocity 210-212
Derbyshire 100, 108
Devine, Tom 163
Devon 46, 51, 73, 77-78, 83, 98, 105, 118, 133, 139-140, 142, 145, 153-154, 166, 173-174, 180, 189, 210-211, 213-214, 224, 227, 229, 234, 237
Devon Great Consols 118, 132
dialect 63-64, 68-69, 152, 201, 224, 226, 239
Ding Dong 133
diocese for Cornwall campaign 86, 229-230, 236
discourse 37, 39, 50-57, 188-190, 192-195, 218, 226, 240-242
dispersed paternalism 180-182, 190, 192, 195, 199, 204, 220, 225
distinction 2, 36, 50-58, 85, 153, 166, 207-215, 226, 234, 238, 243-244
diversification 139, 142-143, 235
Dodd, Philip 31
Dolcoath 96, 133, 137, 183
Drew, Samuel 54, 57-58, 75-76, 79, 81-82, 101
dual occupations 113-115, 183, 190
Duchy of Cornwall 52, 86, 114
Duncan, Abraham 85, 189
Durham 210

East Cornwall Bank 96
East Crofty 133
East Midlands 121
East Wheal Rose 133, 137
economic historians and regions 20, 42
economy of makeshifts 182, 187
Ell, Paul 197, 208, 210
Ellis, Steven 28
emigration 54-55, 68, 79, 87, 142-143, 154-165, 193-194, 224, 226, 245

emigration culture 165
empirical tinkering 125-126
English/British nationalism 225, 236, 242-244
enterprise 54-55
Enys, Samuel 98
Erikson, Charlotte 162
ethnies and ethnic identity 4-5, 8-9, 34-35, 40, 77-80, 242, 245
Everitt, Alan 13, 72, 196, 199
Exeter 92, 142, 180, 210, 214

Falmouth 50, 65, 90, 96-97, 141-142, 149, 151-152, 201, 238
Farington, Joseph 55
farming 232-233
Feock 100
feudalism 113-114
Field, Clive 208
Finberg, Herbert 12
fishing communities 170, 180-181, 209, 214-215, 232-233
Forfar, William Bentinck 65-66
Foster, Richard 100
Foster family 97, 100
foundries 139
Fowey 48, 96
Fox, Charles 65-66
Fox, Robert Were 105
Fox family 92, 96-97, 131, 134
Fraser, Robert 48, 55
friendly societies 172-173, 175

Galmpton 98
Gay, John 212, 216
gender relations 153, 186, 205
generation 24, 242
gentrification 96-98
gentry 92-93, 97-101, 106, 175, 178
geographers and place identity 16-20
geography of Cornish identity 72
Giddens, Anthony 18
Gilbert, Ann 205
Gilbert, Anne 18
Gilbert, Davies 62
Gilpin, William 46
Glendurgan 98

Gloucestershire 100, 124, 133
Godolphin 65
golden ages 80, 84-87, 222
Goldsithney 99
Gooch, Thomas 46
Goodridge, J.C. 138
Gorsky, Martin 173
Grampound 98
Grand Union Canal 134
Great County Adit 95, 124
Great paralysis 232
Great Towan mine 96
Gregor family 98
Green, Adrian 15
Greenaway 98
Griffiths, Ralph 27
Grylls, William 223
Guiberneau, Montserrat 11
Gundry family 99
Gwennap 47, 48, 95-98, 132, 144, 152, 158, 187, 200, 202
Gwinear 47, 130, 205
Gwynedd, Ieuan 222

habitus 24
Hale, Amy iv
Hall, Stuart 4
Harris, John 72
Harris, William Arundell 74
Harrison, Reverend D.T. 241
Harvey, Collan 96, 98
Harvey, Francis 57, 72, 77-78, 83-84
Harvey, Richard 98
Hastings, Adrian 29
Hatcher, John 52, 127
Hawker, Robert Stephen 84
Hayden, Peter 222-223
Hayle 47, 57, 72, 136, 147, 189, 220
Heard, Thomas 57
Hebrides 109
Hechter, Michael 30
Helford estuary 97
Helston 50, 151, 158, 219, 223
Hempton, David 196, 199, 216
Henwood, George 55, 72, 74
Herb, Guntram 243
Hertfordshire 100

Hewitt, Martin 21
Hingston Down, Battle of 84
historians and place identity 12-16, 21-22
historical geography 19, 42
Hockin, William 206
Hoppit, Julian 109
Hornblower, Jonathan 126
Hornsby, Stephen 164
Hoskins, W.G. 12
housing 182-183, 185, 194
Hudson, Pat 20, 111, 129, 136, 143
Hunt, E.H. 145
Hunt, Robert 60, 105
hurling 51

identity, core elements of 2-4, 15, 38-39, 198, 228, 230-237
Illogan 130, 133, 139, 149, 151, 173, 182, 187
images of Cornwall 41-70, 232, 234, 240, 245
independence 22, 52-54, 67, 102, 175-181, 186-187, 190, 193-195, 219-220, 234
index of dissimilarity 123-124
industrial civilisation 52-58, 69-70, 79, 102, 153, 165, 229, 232, 241, 245
industrial regions 13, 19-21, 39, 42, 106, 111, 129, 136, 140, 143, 234, 245
industrial revolution 115-116
industrialization 108-120
institutionalization of regions 23, 88-89, 236-243
institutions 89-94, 239-240
integration 2, 166
interactionism 18
Ireland 109, 156, 162-163, 197, 230, 236, 241
Irish 85
Italy 156

Jaggard, Edwin 97, 223
Jago 83
Jamaica 97
Jenkin, A.K.Hamilton 50
Jenkin, Alf 181

Jenkin, William 177, 189
Jenkins, Richard 8-9, 12
Jones, Gareth Stedman 169
Jones, Rhys 4
Joyce, Patrick 12, 15, 63-65, 68, 169-170
Justices of the Peace 100

Kaplan, David 6, 243
Kearney, Hugh 28
Keating, Michael 10-11
Kelynack, Mary 74
Kennedy, Neil 34
Kenwyn 158
Key, Robert 10
Kidd, Colin 5
Kingcome, Nigel 34
Kirk, Neville 15, 21, 175, 188
Kitchen, Thomas 47, 51, 61
kitting 172
Koditschek, Theodore 187
Kynance Cove 45

labour force 122-123
labour markets 145-146, 152, 154, 161-162, 166
Lach-Szyrma, Wladislaw 83-84, 235
Lancashire 59, 65-66, 68, 78, 100, 121, 163, 194, 210
Land's End 45
Lanhydrock 177
landscape 17-19, 43-50, 239
landscape of Cornishness 49
landscape of industry 47-49
landscape of nature 45-47
landscape of power 45
language and social context 42-43, 189-190
Langton, John 20-21, 42, 70
Launceston 46, 74, 158
lay Methodism 219-220
Le Coadic, Ronan 33
lead mining 132-133, 137
Lean's Engine Reporter 126
leases, three life 53
Leeds 142
Leifchild, J.R. 56, 94

Lelant 99
Lemon, Charles 104, 122
Lemon, William 91, 93, 96, 98
Levant mine 133
Lewis, G.R. 109
Lewis, Jim 132
Lhuyd, Edward 82
Liberalism 139, 222-223, 225
Lincolnshire 201
linguistic turn 169-170, 188
Linkinhorne 158
Lipscomb, George 48, 51
Liskeard 96, 110, 139, 145, 152
literary institutions 91-92, 226
Liverpool 75-76, 95
Lizard 61, 158, 162
local history 12-13, 15, 34-45
locale 15
London 65, 74-75, 77-78, 91, 95, 111, 114, 129-130, 132-133, 135-136, 174
London Corresponding Society 189
Looe 48
Lostwithiel 97, 100
Lovett, William 75-76
Lowenthal, David 44
Lowery, Robert 189, 218
Luker, David 199, 205-207, 214, 216, 221, 224
Lukes, T.H. 235
Luxulyan 191
Lysons 86

McArthur, Mary 33
McDonald, Maryon 32
Macleod, Gordon 25, 243
Macclesfield 205
Macedonia 85
macro-inventions 125
Madron 95, 97
Magor, John 100
Manchester 95, 132, 142
Manchester Lit and Phil 91-92
manganese 137
Mann 242
manorialism 113
Marazion 83
marriages 73

Marshall, John 14, 19, 21
Mason, Canon Arthur 235, 241
Martin, Zacky 66-67
marxism 161-162, 169
Maton, William 47, 48
Matthews, Edward 222
May, Jon 7
memories 7
Meneage 149, 151
Mendels, Franklin 113
Menheniot 132-133, 137, 149, 152
merchant adventurers 94-95, 101, 128, 135
merchant capitalism 175-178, 195, 238
Merivale, Herman 50, 54, 58-59, 72, 82
Methodism 54, 58, 68, 85, 92, 106, 139, 165, 172, 191, 194, 196-227
Mevagissey 147
Mexico 160
Michaelstow 110
migration models 159
migration within Cornwall 144-154
middle class 92-93, 139, 215, 221, 224, 226, 238
mine captains 91, 101-106, 115, 181, 220
mining 48-49, 68-70, 93-94, 102, 110-143, 167-168, 170-171, 178-180, 189, 2909, 214-215, 230-235 and passim
Mining Association of Cornwall and Devonshire 105
mining interest 94, 101
mining school 104-105
modernisation 136-139
Mokyr, Joel 125
moral economy 174, 177, 192-194
Morcom, Captain 103
More, Charles 114
Morrill, John 28
Morrish, P.S. 81, 85-86, 234, 236
Morrison, T.A. 137
Morwenstow 84
Mount Edgcumbe, Earl of 230
Mount's Bay 180
Mount's Bay Commercial Bank 96
Mousehole 180
mules 139

Muller, Max 60
Murdoch, Brian 62
Murdoch, William 126
Murphy, Alexander 16

Nance, Robert Morton 62
narrative 3, 15-16, 166, 187-192, 215, 221-225, 227, 238, 242, 245
Natal 57
nationalism 5-9, 11, 76-80
Netherton, Edwin and James 65
new British history 28, 35-36
New South Wales 158
Newell, Edmund 128, 159
Newfoundland 176
Newlyn 75, 180
Newquay 230
Normans 82
North America 156, 159, 162, 165, 199, 202, 220
North Midlands 208, 211-213
Northern England 10, 15, 116, 123-124, 140, 145, 163, 173-174, 210, 217
Norwich 132
Nottinghamshire 178

O'Donoghue, Francis 65
Obelkevich, James 201
occupational structure 123-124, 140
old dissent 92, 200, 211-212, 215
one and all 54, 191-192, 238
Opie, John 103
Orientalism 2
Orkney 113
Other 77-78
Oxford 97-98
Oxnam, Richard 100

Paasi, Anssi 1, 22-26, 39, 43, 71, 88-89, 106, 166, 228, 236, 240, 242-243
Padstow 100
Parochialism 93, 142, 154, 235
Parys mountain 117
Pascoe 83
pastoralized margin 108-110
pasty 193
paternalism 172, 177, 181

patriarchal sexual cooperation 186
patriarchy 205
Paul 209
Paul, Rozzy 66-67
Pays 13, 16
Payton, Philip 30, 33, 35, 38, 55, 159, 161, 163-164
Pearson, Alan 90
Pembroke mine 133
Pendeen 184
Pengreep 98
Penjerrick 97
Penrhyn, Lord 181
Penryn 48, 95, 97, 139, 158, 209
Penzance 50, 90, 95, 97, 100, 109, 133, 141-142, 149, 151-152, 193, 214, 241
Perranarworthal 96
Perranzabuloe 158
Perry, Ronald 233
Petherick, William 183
Pezron, Paul-Yves 82
Philip, Alan 34
Phillack 206
Phoenicians 83
Phoenix mine 132
Phythian-Adams, Charles 13
picturesque 46-47
place 5-7, 14-15, 179-180
Plymouth 83-84, 92, 142, 147, 153, 180
poetic spaces 6, 80
Poldice 95
Polgooth 48
Pollard, Sidney 19, 231
Polwhele, Richard 59-60, 73-74, 78, 81-82
Pool 187
Poole, Robert 21
population 113, 139-141, 145, 154-155, 163
populism 169
Portreath 96-97
potato allotments 185-186
potato blight 192-193
Potteries 92
Pounds, Norman 145
power geometries 243-244

Praed, William 134
Preston, Thomas 46, 51-52
Price, L.L. 154
Price, Sir Rose 97
price changes 137-138
Primitive Methodism 206, 209, 217
Probert, John 220
process 3, 18, 236
professions 91, 93
proletarianization 113-114, 181-187, 195
proto-industrialization 112-114, 163, 166, 187, 225-226
Pryce, W.T.R. 148
Pryce, William 51, 61, 76, 94, 116

quarrying 122, 139, 194
Quebec 160
quietism 169, 171-175
Quiller-Couch, Arthur 233

race 234-235
Radcliffe, Sarah 12
railway 139, 232-233
Rawlings, Thomas 100
Redding, Cyrus 45
Redruth 47, 51-52, 77, 95-97, 100, 119, 123, 139-142, 151, 157-158, 160, 177, 182-184, 219
Reed, John 200
reformers 189, 223
regional geography 18
regional history 14-15, 21
regions and regionalism 9-12, 24, 87, 240
Registration districts 148
religion 196-227
Religious census 197, 207-215
Relph, Edward 6
respectability 223-224
return migration 157, 165, 233
revivalism 199, 203-205, 216-219, 222, 224, 226
Richards, Eric 109-110
Richmond, Anthony 7
riots 56, 173-174, 178, 180, 187, 190-193

risings, early modern 86
Robbins, Keith 28-30, 196
romanticism 31, 60, 79, 87, 154
Rose, Damaris 183-184
Rosevear, Thomas Pope 225
Rowe, John 47, 96, 115, 119, 138, 207
Rowse, A.L. 156
Royal Cornwall Gazette 90
Royal Cornwall Geological Society 90-94, 103
Royal Cornwall Polytechnic Society 90, 92-93, 105
Royal Institution of Cornwall 90, 92, 105
Rule, John 128, 145, 171-172, 174, 177, 183-184, 187, 189, 191, 193-194, 201, 207, 217

safety fuse 139
Said, Edward 2
Sampson, Reverend R. 236
Sandys, William 65-66
Sandys, Carne and Vivian 136
Savage, Michael 179-180
Saxons 81-83
scale 7, 39, 198, 209, 228, 243-244
Schrank, Gilbert 113
Scilly 151
Scotland 10, 25, 39, 46, 108, 156, 163-165, 197, 199, 218, 222, 236, 241
sectoral specialization 120
Sewell, William 188
Shaw, Ken 32
Shaw, Tom 198
sheriff, county 99-100
Shields, Rob 6
Shropshire 99
Sider, Gerald 176
Sithney 197, 201
Slater, T.R. 208
smallholdings 183-186, 193
smelters 95, 97, 99, 101, 103, 130, 133-135
Smith, Anthony 5-6, 8, 12, 80
Smith, George 224, 236
smuggling 216
Snell, Keith 197, 208-212

social mobility 102
social scientists and Cornwall 32-35
Somerset 100
South America 156, 160
space of possibilities 108, 143, 167, 228, 242, 245
Spain 12
spatial socialization 23, 178-180
Spender, Edward 83
Spurr, John 191
St Agnes 65, 96, 182, 184
St Austell 48, 75, 133, 139, 142, 147, 149, 151-153, 158, 174, 183, 235
St Blazey 149, 151, 158, 183
St Buryan 147, 149, 158
St Cleer 149, 152
St Columb 98, 151
St Day 96
St Ives 72, 193, 209
St Just in Penwith 147, 179, 185-186, 189, 191, 217
St Keverne 151, 158
St Stephen in Brannel 149
Stannaries 86, 239-240
Stanyer, Jeffrey 33
steam engine 124-127, 143
Stevens, Captain 74
Stevenson, Robert Louis 154
Stithians 95, 149, 200
Stokeclimsland 158
Stoyle, Mark 29-30
strikes 56, 168, 171, 174-175, 193-194
structuration theory 18
structure of expectation 24
structure of feeling 24
subsist 177
Sunday closing campaign 229-230, 235, 238, 241
superstitions 59-60, 79
suturing 4
Swansea 95
Sweet, Rosemary 22
symbolic shape 23, 41, 71, 106, 143, 166, 225, 238

Tavistock 118, 139, 153
Taylor, C.C. 39

Taylor, John 104, 128, 132, 168
Taylor, Peter 10
teetotalism 216
Tehidy 45, 91, 98, 177, 182
Trelouw, Karl 243
territorial shape 23, 88, 105-106, 166, 237
territory – see place
textile industry 109-110
Thomas, Charles 224
Thompson, D.M. 208
Thompson, E.P. 168-170, 174, 190, 193
ticketing 135
Tillyard, F. 210
Timbrell, Martin 137
tin mining 112-115, 120-124, 130, 133, 136-139, 231
Tincroft 177
Tintagel 6
Tiverton 142
Torquay 142
tourism 233
Towednack 147, 149
Townsend, A.R. 39
Tractarianism 224
trade unionism 169, 171, 175, 180, 194
tradition 57-60, 176, 187, 192, 194, 218
Trebah 97
Trebilocock, Jimmy 67
Tregellas, John Tabois 65-68
Tregelles, Edwin 238
Trelawny 84, 238
Trelissick 100, 103
Tremenheere, Hugh Seymour 74, 173, 183, 185, 192
Trengwainton 97
Trenoodle, Jan – see William Sandys
Tresavean 133
Trevithick, Richard 126, 160
tributing 172, 176, 178, 185
Truro 45-47, 52, 65, 79, 89-90, 96-97, 103, 105, 134, 141-142, 149, 151-152, 158, 189, 191, 193, 214, 223, 230, 235, 241
Truscott, Francis 215

Tuckett, J.D. 56, 167-168
Tyacke, Richard 197, 201
Tywardreath 149, 178

Ulster 218
United States – see North America
urbanisation 141-142, 165, 184, 187, 194, 212

Valenze, Deborah 204
value of mining output 137-138, 231
Vernon, James 31, 41, 64-65, 67
Vivian, Hussey 236
Vivian, John 94, 130-131
Von Tunzelmann, G.N. 124-125

Wadebridge 98, 193
Wagstaffe, Peter 9-10, 12
Wahrman, Dror 21, 108
Wales, 17, 27, 39, 46, 76, 82-84, 92, 100, 108, 121, 123-124, 133-134, 136, 140, 148-149, 157, 163-164, 173, 181, 197, 199, 201, 204, 206, 208, 210, 218, 221-222, 230, 236-237, 239, 241
Wallis, John 85
Walsh, John 199, 201
Ward, W.R. 216
Warner, Richard 46-48, 51, 55, 59, 215
Watt, James 116, 130
Webb, Daniel Carless 59
Wendron 147, 149, 202
Wesley, Charles 199
Wesley, John 46, 199-201, 219
Wessex 82
West Barbary 50, 56-57, 69, 77, 79, 215
West Briton 90
West Penwith 61, 109, 113, 178
Wheal Vor 99, 133
Whetter, James 116, 130
Williams, Colin 11
Williams, Gwyn Alf 38
Williams, John (1684-1761) 95
Williams, John (1753-1841) 95, 131
Williams, John Michael 95, 98
Williams, Michael 98
Williams, Raymond 24
Williams, Thomas 117

Williams family 100
Williams, Foster and Co. 95, 97-98, 134
Willyams, Humphrey 100
Woolf, Arthur 126
wrestling 51, 78, 216
Wrexham 149
Wyn Jones, E. 197

Ynys Môn 117
Yorkshire 59, 65, 78, 92, 108, 154, 163, 210

www.ingramcontent.com/pod-product-compliance
Lightning Source LLC
LaVergne TN
LVHW051623080426
835511LV00016B/2151